THE PHILOSOPHY OF MULLĀ ṢADRĀ

STUDIES IN ISLAMIC PHILOSOPHY AND SCIENCE

Published under the auspices of
the Society for the Study of Islamic Philosophy and Science

The Philosophy of Mullā Ṣadrā

(Ṣadr al-Dīn al-Shirāzī)

FAZLUR RAHMAN

State University of New York Press
Albany, 1975

The Philosophy of Mullā Ṣadrā

First Edition

Published by State University of New York Press
99 Washington Avenue, Albany, New York 12210

Printed in the United States of America

Library of Congress Cataloging in Publication Data
Rahman, Fazlur, 1919–
The philosophy of Mullā Ṣadrā (Ṣadr al-Dīn al-Shirāzī)
(Studies in Islamic philosophy and science)
Includes bibliographical references.
1. Mullā Ṣadrā, Muḥammad ibn Ibrāhīm, d. 1641.
I. Title. II. Series.
B753.M84R3 181'.07 75-31693
ISBN 0-87395-300-2
ISBN 0-87395-301-0 (microfiche)

CONTENTS

PART III. PSYCHOLOGY: MAN AND HIS DESTINY

PREFACE

The present work aims at a critical and analytical statement of the Philosophy of Ṣadr al-Dīn al-Shīrāzī known as Multā Ṣadrā (d. 1641), primarily contained in his monumental work *al-Asfār al-Arbaʿa*. As the following pages show, Ṣadrā's system, despite certain inner difficulties, is a highly original one revealing the extraordinary intellectual calibre of its author. Besides introducing Ṣadrā's thought to the modern reader, the work, it is hoped, will fully expose the mythical character of the belief, generally prevalent in Western Islamic scholarship, that Islamic Philosophy "died" after al-Ghazālī's attack upon it in the eleventh century.

Indeed, considerable valuable work has been done during the past two and a half decades in the field of post-Ghazālī Islamic thought, notably on al-Suhrawardī (d. 1191), the founder of the Illuminationist School. But most leading scholars in this activity, have, through their own spiritual proclivities, been led to emphasize the Sufi and esoteric side of this literature at the cost, as I believe, of its purely intellectual and philosophical hard core, which is of immense value and interest to the modern student of philosophy. I have tried to clarify this in the Introduction to the present work with reference to Ṣadrā who is hardly esoteric or Sufi, although he does emphasize intellectual intuition *vis-à-vis* purely logical reasoning. It is hoped, therefore, that the present work will further stimulate sorely needed *philosophic* research into this hitherto little explored but rich field of Islamic thought.

I warmly thank the officers of the Society for the Study of Islamic Philosophy and Science (SSIPS) for having this book published and the State University of New York Press, particularly its director, Norman Mangouni, for publishing it. My grateful thanks are also due to Professor Alford Welch of the Department of Religion, of Michigan State University, who kindly devoted his valuable time not only to reading the proofs but to preparing indices of this work.

FAZLUR RAHMAN

Chicago

INTRODUCTION

A. *Mullā Ṣadrā and the Character of His Philosophy*

Factual information about the life of Mullā Ṣadrā is extremely scarce. He was born in Shīrāz to a certain Ibrāhīm ibn Yaḥyā at an unnamed date, came to Isfahan at a young age, and studied with the theologian Bahā' al-Dīn al-'Āmili (d. 1031 A.H./1622 A.C.) and to an extent with the Peripatetic philosopher Mīr Fendereskī (d. 1050 A.H./1641 A.C.), but his principal teacher was the philosopher-theologian Muḥammad known as Mīr Dāmād (d. 1041 A.H./1631 A.C.). Mīr Dāmād appears certainly to have been a thinker of eminence and originality, but there is no modern scholarly study of him as yet. It seems that when our philosopher (named Muḥammad, titled Ṣadr al-Dīn, and generally known as Mullā Ṣadrā or simply Ṣadrā) appeared, philosophy, as it was generally taught, was the Peripatetic-neo-Platonic tradition of Ibn Sīnā and his followers. During the 6th/12th century, al-Suhrawardī had criticized some of the basic doctrines of Peripatetism and laid the foundations of the mystic Philosophy of Illumination (*Ḥikmat al-Ishrāq*) which subsequently found several followers. In the Peripatetic tradition itself, the important thirteenth century philosopher, scientist, and Shī'īte theologian Naṣīr al-Dīn al-Ṭūsī was influenced by certain views of the Illuminationist philosopher, although the exact extent and nature of this influence still needs to be closely determined. These Illuminationist injections into the Peripatetic tradition chiefly concern the Ishrāqī attack on Ibn Sīnā's conception of God's knowledge as forms or accidents inhering in God's mind but later grew in other directions as well—the most important being the view that existence is an unreal mental concept to which nothing corresponds in external reality. Mīr Dāmād himself, for example, held the latter doctrine. For the rest, however, there is little evidence of the existence of any important Ishrāqī school of thought at the time of the appearance of Mullā Ṣadrā. Nor is there any palpable evidence for the existence of a scholarly Sufi tradition immediately before Mullā Ṣadrā, although certain Sufi claims and clichés had become common due to the infusion of Sufi ideas into philosophy and, even more importantly, due to the permeation of Sufi terminology into poetry; the Shī'ī orthodoxy had shown itself to be unsympathetic to Sufism, an attitude which, by and large, has continued to modern times.[1]

In this background grew Mullā Ṣadrā's peculiar system of thought which he seems to have evolved as something quite distinct from the intellectual and spiritual situation of his times. His devotion to religion is partly brought out (apart from his numerous works on religion, of which we shall speak briefly below) by the fact that he is said to have died in 1050 A.H./1641 A.C. (the year of Mīr Fendereskī's death) at Baṣra, while going to the pilgrimage to Mecca or returning therefrom for the seventh time. His life-span is estimated at being seventy or seventy-one lunar years.[2]

While little is known about his external biography, we know something more about his intellectual and spiritual life thanks, mainly, to his autobiographical note prefaced to his *magnum opus, al-Asfār al-Arba'a*. Ṣadrā tells us that from the beginning of his career as a student, he was deeply interested in theosophy or philosophical theology and that he applied himself keenly to a study of the basic problems and fundamental issues in the field as expounded by the masters of the past, unlike most other students who, in order to gain vainglorious fame, devoted themselves to the hairsplitting details found in later learned books which offered little insight into real problems.[3] Our philosopher, having learned the wisdom of past philosophical traditions—the Peripatetic and the Illuminationist—wished to write a comprehensive work combining the wisdom of earlier masters with his own intellectual insights.[4] But this noble objective was thwarted by an intense opposition—indeed, persecution—by those religious men who showed the characteristic stolidity of traditionalism and unmitigated externalism in religion and who regarded any deviation from popular religious beliefs as pure heresy and dangerous innovation.[5]

Ṣadrā gives us no information as to what precisely the questions were on which opposition to his views centered, but the short biographical note in the new edition of *al-Asfār* by Muḥammad Riḍā al-Muẓaffar (dated 1387 A.H./1958 A.C.), states that Ṣadrā had expressed himself in a treatise, *Ṭarḥ al-Kaunain,* in support of a pantheistic doctrine of existence (*waḥdat al-wujūd*) which led to a severe criticism of him by the orthodox Shī'a 'ulamā'.[6] Ṣadrā himself tells us both in *al-Asfār* and *al-Mashā'ir* that in his early philosophical career he had held that essence was the primary reality, while existence was a merely derivative or "mental" phenomenon—like al-Suhrawardī and his followers including Ṣadrā's teacher Mīr Dāmād—and that it was later on that the primacy of existence dawned upon him.[7] But probably there was more to this opposition than the doctrine of the unity or pantheism of existence. The fact that many orthodox still frown upon Ṣadrā's philosophy is shown by the apology offered by the publisher of the recent edition of *al-Asfār,* Riḍā Luṭfī. After stating that works like Mullā Ṣadrā's are not free from controversy and that the efforts of all great Muslim philosophers to harmonize religion with philosophy "are mere intellectual attempts and personal views, *having nothing to do with the essence of religion,*" [8] Luṭfī goes on to say that the present edition of *al-Asfār* is therefore being offered *not* "as a religious or Islamic source" but represents an effort to preserve an encyclopaediac philosophical work.[9]

Be that as it may, Ṣadrā says that having been left with two alternatives—either to wage an offensive or to retire from the scene—he, following Imām 'Alī, chose the second path [10] and resorted to seclusion in "a certain place in the land." [11] Some say that he went to an isolated place in a mountain, possibly near Qum, where he is said to have stayed for as long as fifteen years.[12] Our philosopher began his seclusion with an acute sense of disillusionment with the world, its wayward behavior, and particularly with the extrinsic motivations of worldly glory and power common to scholars; and an awareness that he himself had gravely erred in having practically followed the same path and having relied on his own intellectual powers rather than submitting himself humbly to God's will and power with a sincere and pure heart.[13] His new posture was, therefore, one of prayer and utter resignation to God, with all his being.[14] Rather than operate by the superficialities and artfulness of logical reasoning, he contemplated deeply and sincerely the fundamental problems of God, being, and the universe and "gave himself up" to an intuitive invasion "from without." [15] This intense contemplation was accompanied by strenuous religious exercises.[16] As a result, his mind was indeed flooded with insights: not only did he rediscover what he had previously learned through rational proofs in a new, direct, intuitive way, but many fresh truths dawned upon him, which he had not even dreamed of before.[17] This experience infused an altogether new life into him. If he had gone into retirement totally disillusioned and broken-hearted, he now obtained renewed courage and vigor which drove him out of that seclusion and compelled him to write the work, *al-Asfār al-Arba'a.*

This account, given by Ṣadrā himself, requires interpretative elucidation of the exact nature of what transpired in his seclusion and the transformation he experienced. As we have seen, the training of Ṣadrā had been that of a philosopher (this does not deny that he had also learnt orthodox disciplines like *Ḥadīth, Tafsīr,* and *Kalām*) before he went into seclusion, partly because of persecution but largely because he was *unsure* of the philosophical truths whose purely rational method he regarded as superficial and extrinsic. He was, therefore, in search of a method that would give him certainty and would transform merely rational propositions into *experienced* truths. In his "confession" stated above, he makes precisely this point. This situation closely parallels that of al-Ghazālī, except that in al-Ghazālī's case, what was primarily to be transformed into living truth was orthodox Sunni Kalām-propositions, whereas for our philosopher it was the rational philosophic propositions that needed to be so transformed and "lived through." Neither in the first case nor in the latter is Sufism a source of *a new genre of knowledge,* but an *experience* or intuitive certainty: the cognitive *content* of this philosophy and this Sufism is identical, but the *quality* is different. This difference in quality is not a small matter, since, as Ṣadrā repeatedly tells us, the nature of existence and its uniqueness, for example, can be only experienced; the moment you conceptualize it, it ceases to be existence and becomes an essence. Yet, Ṣadrā has employed numerous and extensive *rational* arguments to *prove* this. This shows that for him, mystic truth is essentially intellectual truth and mystic experience is a cognitive experience, but this intellectual truth and this cognitive content have to be "lived through" to be fully realized; if they are only intellectually entertained as rational propositions, they lose their essential character—not as cognitions but as verities. There is an obvious and close analogy between this position and that of Plotinus, whose pseudo-*Theologia Aristotelis* is regarded by Ṣadrā as the highest expression of gnostic or spiritual philosophy. But whereas Plotinus makes *specific* claims to visions of the Intelligible Realm "lifted out of my body," Ṣadrā makes these claims only in general terms. Again, Plotinus also provided extensive *philosophic* proofs for the existence of the Intelligible Realm, like Ṣadrā. In more recent times,[18] Bergson told us that "pure duration" is an experience and may not be merely rationally understood; yet Bergson provided extensive intellectual proofs for this, which constitutes his philosophy.

The point we wish to make here is that Ṣadrā is a *philosopher* of the genre, say, of Bergson, since the *content* of his experience as well as of his thought is the same and is cognitive in character. Experience or intuition is needed not to produce new thought-content but to bestow on this thought-content a quality of personal experience. This is very different from those Sufis who deny intellectual content to their experience, which they declare to be ineffable. These Sufis, rather than dealing with philosophic or intellectual propositions, devote themselves to a purely experiential spiritual itinerary, divided into a hierarchical chart of "stations" (*maqāmāt*) and their concomitant spiritual "states (*aḥwāl*)," ending up in an ethico-ecstatic ideal. There is no trace of this in Ṣadrā's thought and *there* he differs fundamentally from al-Ghazālī. Hence his model becomes—presumably since his experiences in his seclusion—Ibn 'Arabī who, although he often uses Sufi terminology, is a *theosoph* with a cognitive content through and through. Under the roof of this over-arching model which has profoundly influenced Ṣadrā's ontology, psychology, and eschatology, all the thought currents of Islam are brought and synthesized—Kalām, philosophy, Illuminationism.

We have somewhat dilated upon this point because several contemporary scholars of Ṣadrā seem to insist that, according to Ṣadrā or even for understanding his thoughts, Sufism is needed *besides* philosophy, as though Sufism was an independent cognitive avenue to truth, indeed, over and above philosophy. This is simply not true. What Ṣadrā claims to have performed and he also strongly advocates is sincerity of purpose (*khulūṣ*), single-minded devotion (*tawajjuh gharīzī*) and light of faith (*nūr al-īmān*) in philosophic activity, which alone will result in intuitive certainty and direct appropriation of objective philosophic truth. This is what is meant by wisdom (*ḥikma*). Extrinsically motivated thought will be sterile philosophy, since extrinsic considerations—of gaining worldly power and fame—will detract from true philosophic pursuit. He denounces Ibn Sīnā for pursuing medicine and a professional career while God had given him the capacity for the highest art—philosophy: the result was a truncated philosophy full of doubts and uncertainties.[19] But this is true of every pursuit: if a scientist spends time in horse-racing and other hobbies *at the expense* of his work, his scientific work will be truncated. For Ṣadrā, this is most true of philosophy, the crown of all knowledge, since it is knowledge of God and man's destiny. This, however, is a far cry from saying that one should be a Sufi in order to be a philosopher and Ṣadrā gives no hint anywhere of his Sufism, except in the sense of theosophy, which he calls *ma'rifa* or *'irfān*—after Ibn 'Arabī's model. But whereas Ibn 'Arabī's *method* of writing is not philosophical—he works by analogies and images rather than rational proofs, Ṣadrā's method is out-and-out rational and philosophical. Indeed, just as Ṣadrā condemns philosophy without intuitive experience, so he denounces pure Sufism without philosophic training and pursuit.[20]

When Ṣadrā talks about experience, he is not talking about what is generally called Sufi or mystic experience at all, but about an intuitive apprehension of truth or rational experience (*marṣad 'aqli* or *mushāhada 'aqliya*). This he opposes to pure ratiocination, and particularly to superficial logical reasoning and rational disputation (*baḥth naẓarī* or *jadal 'ilmī'*). He insists that when something has been known repeatedly by direct perception or intuitive experience, *it cannot be disputed by purely logical reasoning* and such superficial disputationism is, for him, no more than verbal quibbles and noise. Particularly on two issues are such statements made by Ṣadrā. The first is the question of the reality of Platonic Forms which, we are told, have been proved by repeated experiences of different men. There may be differences of opinion and interpretation about the nature of these Forms but there can be no doubt about their existence.[21] The second important occasion on which he explicitly states this principle is when he seeks to bring the Muslim Peripatetic doctrine of transcendental Intelligences under the impact of Ibn 'Arabī's ontology, transforms them into positive Attributes of God (which Muslim Peripatetics deny) and declares their content to be the Platonic Forms (see below Part I, Chapter IV). In effecting this radical change in the Peripatetic tradition, Ṣadrā says:

> Beware of imagining by your perverted intelligence that the objectives of these great gnostics (i.e., like Ibn 'Arabī)—are devoid of demonstrative force and are mere conjectural frivolities and poetic images. Far it be from this: The (apparent) non-conformity of their statements with correct demonstrative proofs and principles . . . is due to the shortsightedness of the philosophers who study them and their lack of proper awareness and comprehension of those demonstrative principles; otherwise the status of their experience is far greater than that of formal proofs in yielding certainty. Demonstration, indeed, is the way of direct access and perception in those things which have a cause, since . . . on the principles of these very philosophers things which have causes can be known with certainty only through their causes. This being the case, how can demonstration and direct perception contradict each other? Those Sufis who have uttered (in the defence of experiences of men like Ibn 'Arabī) words like 'If you disprove them by arguments, they have disproved you by their experience' are actually saying, 'if you disprove them by your *so-called* arguments . . .' Otherwise, correct rational proofs cannot contradict intuitive experience.[22]

This forceful statement is most explicit that the intuitive experience Ṣadrā has in mind, far from denying reason, is a higher form of reason, a more positive and constructive form, than formal reasoning. But Ṣadrā also fully confesses that even experiential or intuitive truth cannot claim to be "The Truth." All experiences of reality are partial and even though they are characterized by certainty, the search for truth is endless since reality is endless: "For Truth cannot be confined to any single (man's) intelligence and cannot be measured by any single mind." [23] Again, "Nor do I, indeed, claim that I have said the final word in what I have said—not at all! This is because the ways of understanding are not restricted to what I have understood . . . for truth is far too great for any single mind to comprehend." [24] It is in this connection that Ṣadrā avers that in the *Asfār* he has not been content to give his own philosophic views, but has stated in detail the views of earlier philosophers, has analyzed and criticized them and then reached his own conclusions. Indeed, what makes *Asfār* so highly interesting for a student is this procedure followed by Ṣadrā which has bestowed upon this work a richness rarely matched by any other work except the *Shifā'* of Ibn Sīnā. Now, Ṣadrā tells us that he has followed this procedure to "whet the appetite and sharpen the mind" of the student.[25] This in itself is proof enough that, by the same token, Mullā Ṣadrā could not have regarded his views, however original, to be the final and absolute truth. What his philosophic genius fundamentally sought was both truth *and originality* and this is what makes him a genuine philosopher.

B. *Ṣadrā's Sources and His Originality*

1. *General*

This brings us to the question of the source of Mullā Ṣadrā's doctrines and the assessment of his originality which, in various contexts, he proclaims loudly and unreservedly. He does it particularly and recurrently when he expounds his doctrine of the sole reality of existence (as opposed to essences), of motion-in-substance, and of the identity of the subject and object of knowledge on the basis of his doctrine of existence. Mullā Ṣadrā had his critics in his own time, but later he was charged by some critics with having "stolen" the views of others and given them out in his own name. Particularly since Mīrzā Abū'l-Ḥasan Jilwa (d. 1312 A.H./1894 A.C.), a series of "Ṣadrā debunkers" have tried to prove that all of Ṣadrā's ideas were either borrowed or stolen. It appears that this trend parallels the opposite and stronger trend—since 'Alī Nūrī (d. 1246 A.H./1831 A.C.)—of an ever increasing number of his students, commentators, and admirers. Some of these latter also hold extreme views, and think that Ṣadrā represents the "truest" of all philosophy and the apogee of all Islamic philosophic thought.[26] Indeed, lately Ṣadrā has come to occupy a focal point of interest for many intellectuals in Persia, for some of whom our philosopher has become the greatest symbol of Persian intellectual nationalism.[27] That this spirit is diametrically opposed to Ṣadrā's own teaching is manifest enough, but it is basically a kind of symptomatic protest at the relative neglect, on the part of modern Western scholarship, of post-al-Ghazālī Islamic philosophy in the East, which—whether Sunnī or Shī'ī—occurred mainly in Iran.

While—partisan controversialism apart—the question of Ṣadrā's originality can only be fully settled after a comprehensive history of post-al-Ghazālī Islamic philosophy is written, the claims that Ṣadrā took over earlier doctrines whose sources he did not disclose must be summarily dismissed. This is because in the pages of his vast work, the *Asfār,* he has named the sources from whom he has quoted and either rejected or supported them. It is unthinkable that he should have had access to sources whom he considered important and yet chose not to reveal them.[28] This attitude also goes against the very grain of stern demands for sincerity, discounting of worldly importance, and fame, etc. that he makes on all would-be genuine students of philosophy. More important is the following consideration. Although Ṣadrā claims absolute originality in some of his fundamental doctrines, as indicated here, he is at times acutely aware that these doctrines will be branded as "novel" and rejected by the followers of traditional philosophy. He, therefore, makes strenuous and, indeed, often fruitless efforts—as we have pointed out in the body of the book on the discussions of existence and substantive movement—to draw support from the authorities of Ibn Sīnā or the pseudo-*Theologia Aristotelis* or the "Pahlavi Sages" to justify his stance. In doing so, Ṣadrā is in line with those ancient and medieval writers who attributed their opinions to earlier and more accepted authorities. These two positions, claims to originality on the one hand (although he usually claims originality only *within Islamic times*) and attribution of his ideas to earlier authorities, are apparently contradictory. What is true—and also what probably Ṣadrā wants to say—is that the inspiration for his doctrines on which he claims originality came from certain passages in these earlier writers, which he alone has been able to see in this new light.

Anybody who peruses the *Afsār* is struck by the hypercritical spirit displayed therein. Not infrequently does Ṣadrā reject all the alternative solutions to a problem given by earlier thinkers and finally give his own solution which is identically, or almost, the same as one of those alternatives. This is the case, for example, when he rejects, in the discussion of eschatology, the solutions of al-Ghazālī; and yet his own solution is hardly distinguishable from the one offered by al-Ghazālī on physical resurrection being of the order of an image-body. Al-Ghazālī, indeed, is the first Muslim thinker, so far as I know, who pioneered this line of thought on bodily resurrection—influenced undoubtedly by certain remarks of Ibn Sīnā—out of which grew the idea of a World of Images (*'Alam al-Mithāl*) propounded by al-Suhrawardī. Although Ṣadrā has criticized pretty well all of his Muslim predecessors, he reserves unqualified praise for the author of the pseudo-*Theologia Aristotelis* (i.e., Plotinus) and the "Pahlavi Sages" about whose identities, however, we are given no clue. Among Muslim thinkers, Ibn 'Arabī is criticized only rarely (for example, *Safar,* IV, Part 2, pp. 253 ff.), while Ṣadrā's most persistent targets are Fakhr al-Dīn al-Rāzī and Jalāl al-Dīn al-Dawwānī, about whom he sometimes uses unusually harsh language. Both of these men wielded great influence on the subsequent philosophical tradition in Islam and both were Sunnis. (Al-Dawwānī has been more recently claimed by some to be a Shī'ī, but apparently without requisite evidence.) Yet it would be wrong to conclude that their Sunnism was a motivating factor in Ṣadrā's criticism, since on occasion he supports al-Rāzī (and al-Ghazālī) against al-Ṭūsī and his own teacher Mīr Dāmād (for example, *Asfār,* III, Part I, pp. 380–82). Al-Rāzī, although an extremely learned man in philosophy, is basically an Ash'arite theologian, while al-Dawwānī is a rationalist philosopher in the Peripatetic line; neither's attitude is in harmony with Ṣadrā's gnostic orientation.

Ṣadrā's critical spirit stops only at texts which tradition regards as sacred: the Qur'ān, the Prophetic Ḥadīth, and the dicta Shī'ī tradition has attributed to the infallible Imams. Here faith must guide and inspire reason even if this leads to an interpretation which apparently the words of a text do not bear. A striking illustration of this is afforded by Ṣadrā's quotation of an alleged *khuṭba* (sermon) of the Imām 'Ali during the discussion of God's Attributes (*Asfār,* III, Part I, p. 135 ff.). Ṣadrā inveighs against those who deny God's Attributes and affirm a pure Divine Existence, as well as against those who affirm God's Attributes as being additional to His Being; and he wants to prove the identity of Existence and Attributes in God on the basis of his doctrine of the primordiality of existence. The relevant words of this quote are: "The perfection of sincerity for God is to deny attributes of Him, since every attribute is evidence of its otherness from its subject and every subject is evidence of its being other than its attribute. Thus a person who assigns an attribute to God, is guilty of pairing Him and anyone who pairs Him, duplicates Him. . . ." (p. 135, line 10–p. 136, line 2). Now, these words absolutely and uncompromisingly deny attributes of God—quite in Muslim Mu'tazilite rationalist spirit, and to think the opposite would render all language meaningless; yet Ṣadrā gives us an extensive commentary on this text where the words "deny attributes of Him" are simply restated as "deny *additional* attributes of Him."

2. *Ṣadrā's Predecessors*

Ṣadrā studied the entire philosophical, religious, and spiritual heritage of Islam, the apparent notable exceptions being the Spanish philosophers Ibn Bājja, Ibn Ṭufail, and Ibn Rushd—from Spain and the Islamic West; and was particularly indebted to Ibn 'Arabī, who exerted, indeed, one of the foremost influences upon him. The Peripatetic philosophical tradition emanating from Ibn Sīnā, the tradition of the Kalām theology, both Shī'ī and Sunnī, the Illuminationist philosophy of al-Suhrawardī and his followers and commentators and, finally, the Sufi tradition culminating in the theosophy of Ibn 'Arabī and his disciples and commentators—all these went into the intellectual makeup of our philosopher. Both Sunnī and Shī'ī Kalām had become thoroughly penetrated by the rationalist philosophical ideas and themes, the former at the hands of Fakhr al-Dīn al-Rāzī in the twelfth century, the latter in the work of Naṣīr al-Dīn al-Ṭūsī in the thirteenth. The more mystical ideas of Ibn Sīnā's philosophy, which had already found a home in the esoteric writings of al-Ghazālī, also gradually fructified in Sufi circles until they were finally incorporated in a developed form in Ibn 'Arabī's system and the writings of his followers. The three main strands of thought, therefore, which were—although there had already been a good deal of interpenetration among them—consciously combined by Ṣadrā to yield a "grand synthesis" are: (1) the Peripatetic tradition of Ibn Sīnā, (2) the Illuminationist tradition of al-Suhrawardī, and (3) Ibn 'Arabī's theosophy.

Of these three masters, Ibn Sīnā is, in a sense, the most important. This is because Ibn Sīnā's doctrines constitute the "floor" or the "fundament" upon which all discussion takes place. This is so not only with Ṣadrā but equally with al-Suhrawardī, as, indeed, it has been the case also with al-Ghazālī. Ibn Sīnā was the philosopher who had constructed a full-fledged philosophical system—on an Aristotelian-neo-Platonic basis—with an inner cohesion, that sought to satisfy both the philosophic and religious demands. In all fields—metaphysics, theory of knowledge, and theology—discussion must start with what *al-Shaikh al-Ra'īs* said. Ṣadrā criticizes him, modifies him, supports him against later criticism by al-Suhrawardī, al-Ṭūsī and others, and even seeks support from some of his statements for his own peculiar doctrines, like the reality of existence and inanity of essences. He blames al-Ṭūsī for having departed from his master's view of Divine knowledge, even though he had promised in the earlier part of his commentary on the natural and metaphysical parts of Ibn Sīnā's *al-Ishārāt* that he would not contradict the latter.[29] Ṣadrā's most persistent criticism of Ibn Sīnā is on the question of the latter's denial of the absolute identity of subject and object in knowledge. As has been said earlier, Ṣadrā attributes the philosophic failures of Ibn Sīnā to the fact that the latter wasted valuable time in pursuit of worldly concerns and particularly in the art of medicine, even though God had given him ample gifts for the highest art—philosophy.[30]

The greatest immediate formative influence on Ṣadrā's unique doctrines, however, is that of al-Suhrawardī, the founder of the Illuminationist school of thought on whose *Ḥikmat al-Ishrāq* Ṣadrā wrote a commentary. This influence, which we have briefly outlined elsewhere,[31] takes concrete form partly by criticizing and rejecting al-Suhrawardī and partly by accepting him. The view of al-Suhrawardī positively accepted by Ṣadrā is that logical essences are unreal, that logical definitions do not create sharp distinctions in reality and that Reality is, therefore, one single continuum of light punctuated only by distinctions of "more and less" or "more perfect and less perfect." Darkness being purely negative, what is real is the "grades" of light arranged hierarchically from the Absolute Light (God) downward to what he calls "accidental lights." This notion of a continuum of reality was taken over by Ṣadrā. But al-Suhrawardī had, at the same time, declared existence to be a mere logical notion to which nothing corresponds in reality. The only reality is the Light with its various "grades" without differences in "essence" but only in terms of "more or less intense." Ṣadrā centrally attacked the view that existence is a mere "notion" or a "secondary intelligible" and declared, on the contrary, that *existence is the only reality* and only existence is capable of "more and less" or "stronger and weaker" and that essences are unreal, arising "only in the mind." If existence is unreal, what is there left except essences? he asks, and essences are not capable of "more and less" since every essence is "closed," static and fixed. Further, by substituting existence for al-Suhrawardī's light, Ṣadrā takes the whole range of being in his purview: whereas al-Suhrawardī has left bodies and their accidents out of his concept of light, Ṣadrā even includes Primary Matter in his notion of existence, since Prime Matter at least has the potentiality of existence.

More important: Ṣadrā puts the entire field of existence into perpetual motion by saying that movement does not occur only in the qualities of things but in their very substance. This doctrine of "substantive motion (*ḥaraka jauhariya*)"—which is Ṣadrā's original contribution to Islamic philosophy—transforms the fixed "grades" of al-Suhrawardī into a systematically ambiguous (*tashkīk*) idea of existence. The result is that (1) "grades" of being are no longer fixed and static but ceaselessly move and achieve higher forms of existence *in time;* (2) "existence" is applicable to all evolutionary stages *bi'l-tashkīk,* i.e., with systematic ambiguity, and no other concept has this character: only existence is that principle which *"by virtue of* being simple and unitary (*basīṭ*) creates differences"; (3) this movement of the universe (which is irreversible and unidirectional) ends in the "Perfect Man" who becomes a member of the Divine Realm and becomes unified with the Attributes of God; (4) each higher stage of existence includes all the lower ones and transcends them; this is expressed by the formula, "a simple reality *is* everything," i.e., the higher a reality is, the simpler and more inclusive it is; (5) the more something has or achieves of existence, the less it has of essence, since, while existence is real, concrete, determinate, individual, and luminous, essences are exactly the opposite and arise only in the mind by the impact of reality upon it. Hence, God being pure existence, has no essence at all. Essences are the bearers of contingency and also infect existence at the lower levels of being which, therefore, are not absolute existence like God but are only "modes of existence (*anḥā' al-wujūd*)." We have, indeed, travelled far from Ibn Sīnā and al-Suhrawardī.

The third very profound influence on Ṣadrā's thought is Ibn 'Arabī, whom he quotes in various contexts. But Ibn 'Arabī's influence is particularly visible on three important issues: the non-existence of essence, the reality of Divine Attributes, and the psychological-eschatological role of the "Realm of Images." On the first, Ibn 'Arabī's famous dictum "Essences do not smack of existence" is quoted by Ṣadrā several times in support of his doctrine that existence is the sole reality and not essences, and it is quite possible that the Spanish mystic had a role in inspiring Ṣadrā's doctrine itself. On the second issue, which is perhaps the most interesting in terms of historical influence, Ṣadrā, under the impact of Ibn 'Arabī's teaching, drastically modified the Peripatetic-neo-Platonic view of the Intelligences, made them part of the Godhead, and identified them with Divine Attributes and their intellective content with the Platonic Realm of Ideas. He then couches the entire Muslim Peripatetic-neo-Platonic account of emanation in the language of Ibn 'Arabī and his disciples, specifically in terms of the propulsion of the "Self-Unfolding Existence" or "the Breath of the Merciful" which, as a kind of "Intelligible Matter" spreads over everything—is eternal with the eternal, temporal with the temporal, necessary with the necessary, and contingent with the contingent, etc.

Indeed, in Ṣadrā's thought these two ideas, the unreality of essences and the unitary principle of the "Self-Unfolding Existence" became much more closely allied than in Ibn 'Arabī's system, where essences still keep a good deal of reality, and Ṣadrā criticizes Ibn 'Arabī on this score. Ṣadrā's master stroke lies in combining these two ideas closely by perceiving their fuller implications for each other and making them yield his unique doctrine of the motion-in-substance: existence moves continuously and successively through higher and higher forms or evolutionary "modes" of being, culminating in the Perfect Man. These considerations make it undeniable, I think, that al-Suhrawardī, in Ṣadrā's mind, had to pass through the channel of Ibn 'Arabī before the novel doctrine of the *tashkīk* of existence could be evolved. In sum, it is this doctrine of *tashkīk,* according to which existence continuously evolves, which constitutes the very pivot of Ṣadrā's philosophy, a pivot around which all problems revolve and are solved.

Of great importance also is Ibn 'Arabī's impact on Ṣadrā's doctrine of the "Realm of Images," which, as we have said, was originally inspired by al-Ghazālī and later formally announced by al-Suhrawardī. But it was Ibn 'Arabī who not only elaborated on the "Realm of Images" but assigned to the human soul itself, particularly in the hereafter, a central role of erecting, at will, image-perceptibles, i.e., images which are as real as perceptibles. This doctrine is used by Ṣadrā as well as by Ibn 'Arabī to prove a "physical" resurrection: although what we imagine in this world is weaker than perception—since we are engrossed in the material world—what the soul will imagine in the hereafter will be so strong and real that it will literally take the place of material bodies and events. This doctrine is traceable ultimately from Porphyry [32] but was developed and used by al-Ghazālī and later Islamic thinkers, particularly Ibn 'Arabī, to prove the possibility of physical resurrection and physical pleasures and pains experienced by the saved and the damned respectively in the hereafter. It is not without significance that the colossal *Asfār* finds its very end with a quotation from Ibn 'Arabī to the same effect.

3. *Evaluation*

The significance of Ṣadrā does not lie just in the fact that he studied the entire heritage of Islamic thought and brought together all its significant thought-currents; it lies in the fact that he produced a veritable synthesis of all these currents. This synthesis is not brought about by mere "reconciliation" and superficial "compromise," but on the basis of a philosophical principle which he both propounded and expounded for the first time in Islamic history. An unfailing hallmark of a great and original thinker is that he discovers a master-idea, a grand principle under which the entire range of reality falls, and he interprets it to make sense, a new sense, and a significant one. It changes our very perspective of looking at reality and offers a novel solution to the age-old problems that have vexed human minds. If we are right in laying down this criterion—as Ṣadrā himself also does—then Mullā Ṣadrā must be accepted as a great and original thinker. He discovered the principle of the primordiality (sole reality) of existence and its infinite systematic ambiguity—despite it or, rather, as Ṣadrā insists, *because* of it. He expounded it and applied it to the entire range of the problems of Islamic philosophy—the nature of God, the nature of the World, and the nature and destiny of man, as the following pages of the present book show. Max Horten rightly observed (despite the numerous and important failings of his work), "Auf diese Weise gewinnt Schirāzī einen Standpankt, von dem er die gesamte zu seiner Zeit geltende Philosophie umgestaltet." [33]

But equally interesting and important is his wielding of philosophy *as an art:* his claim in the *Introduction* that the *Asfār* is an exquisite and clear composition is almost fully justified.[34] Both his power and style of analysis are engrossing; the most tedious and abstruse subjects are examined and analyzed by a razor mind with perfect clarity. (It is only occasionally that certain terms are used loosely, but there usually the context clarifies the meaning; at certain points al-Sabzawārī, his great commentator, is of real help: indeed, this man has so imbibed the master's thought that, but for the language, it would be often difficult to distinguish between the two.) The presentation is, in fact, so engaging that very often it is the *argumentation* rather than the thesis itself, the *process* of philosophizing rather than philosophy itself, that becomes the object of the reader's interest. The work is written with a lively spirit behind it. Here again Horten's appreciation is justified: "Als Ganzes betrachtet is sein Werk eine Leistung allerersten Ranges und ein eigenartiges Kunstwerk der Begriffsbildung und Begriffsdichtung. Man wird es nicht ohne Bewunderung aus der Hand legen können." [35]

Nevertheless, this system has its inner weaknesses, some of which seem to be inherent in Ṣadrā's thought, some in his formulations, and others due to his combining of so many different currents in Islamic thought, and particularly his combination of certain religious demands with philosophic requirements. Although the basic aim of the present work has been to present Ṣadrā's doctrine systematically and positively to the modern reader, since his thought is not yet known to the modern Western world, I have not shied from pointing out its important weaknesses, in the course of my exposition. We may classify these into tensions, inconsistencies, and contradictions. Tensions may be said to characterize all thought-systems that aim to synthesize polarities and is in itself not a weakness—indeed, it is a strength, when kept under control. For example, determinism and freedom are polarities. When a system attempts to synthesize them by some more basic or transcendent principle, it may either seek to break and resolve this polarity altogether or it may simply subsume these two categories under a higher principle while they remain "real" at their own level. In the first case, there will be a synthesis, in the latter, the tension will remain. Contradiction will result where the principle of synthesis or subsumption is formulated in a manner that will not do justice to both sides but will rather accentuate one side, thus contradicting the very purpose of the synthesizing principle. This is as far as synthesizing activity is concerned. Contradiction can, of course, occur also in an ordinary way when two contradictory statements are made. Inconsistency occurs when the implications of two statements are contradictory or, even more acutely, when a principle is enunciated that is sufficient to explain a certain phenomenon but then another extrinsic principle is introduced that has the effect of nullifying the first. An inconsistency, therefore, is but a contradiction one or more steps removed.

All of these weaknesses are found to exist in Ṣadrā's philosophy, as we have indicated below without fitting them into the categories mentioned above. Here we will illustrate by giving examples. According to Ṣadrā, existence is at once both one and many and it is only the principle of existence which is such in objective reality. There is, therefore, a tension built into this principle because unity and diversity are polarities. This polarity is resolved for Ṣadrā by the further principle of movement or *tashkīk* of existence. This means that both unity and diversity are real at their respective planes. But, as we have shown by several quotations from Ṣadrā in the last section of Chapter I of Part I, he often completely denies any reality whatever to the multiplicity of existence and simply attributes all reality to the

One, God. While the principle of *tashkīk* is a philosophic one, its denial, which attributes *all* reality to God, is done under the impact of the mystical impulse. This is a contradiction because it contradicts the very purpose of the principle of *tashkīk,* viz., to synthesize the polarities. A good example of inconsistency is in Ṣadrā's explanation of the world-process as continuous substantive movement. There is no need to ask why there is substantive movement, Ṣadrā tells us (see Chapter V in Part I), since this is the very nature or constitution of the material world, just as it is senseless to ask why fire burns since it is the very nature of fire to burn. But then Ṣadrā, under religious demands, brings in God to explain the world-movement and the successive forms it assumes: it is God who bestows these successive forms upon it. It is clear, I think, that this second explanation nullifies the first in terms of an immanent force. But Ṣadrā insists that we still need God, who has created the world *with this nature.*

There are other problems of serious magnitude, some of which appear to arise from the tension between monism and pluralism noted above, while others are traceable to his conscious effort to combine Ibn Sīnā's and Ibn 'Arabī's ontologies, although difficulties arising out of the former again affect issues produced by the latter. The most serious issue arising from the first problem is the source of contingency. According to Ṣadrā's standard view, the source of contingency is the essences which are also the source of all evil and we are told that existence in itself is absolutely simple and good.[36] Contingency is of the essence of essences, although even to attribute contingency to them is to posit some sort of reality for them and he seeks to correct Ibn 'Arabī on the matter.[37] This would be all right if, in finite existence, contingency were said to be due solely to their essences, which Ṣadrā normally does. But then Ṣadrā also tells us that those existences, *qua existences,* also have a contingency: this is that they are nothing in themselves and are thinkable only when related to Absolute Existence. Indeed, they are not even *something* related to God; they are *mere relations* to the Absolute,[38] a concept which is hardly intelligible.

But this ambiguity about contingency does not stop in the realm of finite or created existence but is carried over into the Divine Realm when Ṣadrā, under the influence of Ibn 'Arabī, interprets Ibn Sīnā's doctrine of Intelligences as concrete existents, lifts these from the realm of contingency, and makes them parts of the Godhead as His Attributes. Following Ibn 'Arabī, he distinguishes two levels of the Godhead, one the level of the Absolute Existence where, although God has no explicit Names and Attributes, yet he possesses them as implicit in His existence, while the second is the level of Godhead (*'ālam al-ulūhiya*), where Attributes appear explicitly and are identical with Intelligences. Now, Attributes at this second level are sometimes said to be still absolutely simple and necessary and Ṣadrā strenuously denies that they can be termed "God's essence,"[39] while at the same time they are recurrently characterized as contingent and as "pure notions (*mafāhīm*)."[40] They seem to be, indeed, on the border of the Realm of Necessity and the Realm of Contingency and this obscurity seems to have become permanently settled in Ṣadrā's system, without any visible possibility of relief.

Despite these difficulties and others of relatively minor nature, however, the overall judgment on this system must be, as we have said earlier, that it is highly fresh, original, and captivating and, of course, one of the most sophisticated and, indeed, by far the most complex in the entire history of Islamic philosophy. The mere fact that it seeks to criticize, analyze, and integrate all significant ideational currents in Islam developed from the fourth century of Islam to Ṣadrā's own day is a truly gigantic affair in itself, let alone the fact that Ṣadrā formulated a new master-idea under which he carried out his synthesis and produced a new system.

C. *Ṣadrā's Works and His Influence*

According to the list of Ṣadrā's works given by the editor of *al-Asfār al-Arba'a* (Vol. I, Tehran, 1958), in his *Introduction*[41] to the work, Ṣadrā wrote 32 or 33 treatises altogether, depending on whether his alleged commentary on Sura 93 of the Qur'ān is found or not. The editor states that he has not been able to find any copy of the book entitled *Kasr al-Aṣnām al-Jāhiliya,* written against some Sufis; but it was subsequently published, on the occasion of the celebration of the four hundredth year of Ṣadrā's birth, in Iran in 1961 by M. T. Danish-Pazhūh. Most of Ṣadrā's works have been published since the last quarter of the nineteenth century, some more than once, while certain smaller treatises have not yet been published. In one sense, his works may be divided into the purely philosophical and the "religious." The latter particularly include his commentary on certain Suras and verses of the Qur'ān and on the *Uṣūl al-Kāfī.* But these latter also represent an application of his philosophical ideas to the Scripture and other religious texts; and the editor of the *Asfār* rightly says that they are "an extension of his philosophy"—closely following the model of Ibn Sīnā. In another way, his writings can be divided into original works and commentaries on earlier philosophical writings, the most important being his commentaries on the Metaphysics of Ibn Sīnā's *al-Shifā'* and al-Suhrawardī's *Ḥikmat al-Ishrāq.*

To attempt a chronology of all or even most of Ṣadrā's works is at present an almost impossible task and probably will remain so. Broadly speaking, one can probably safely say that his "religious" works like the commentary on the Qur'ān and that on the famous *Uṣūl al-Kāfī* (also incomplete) were written after his philosophic thought had matured and after the execution of his *magnum opus,* the *Asfār.* So far as his pure philosophic writings are concerned, *al-Shawāhid al-Rubūbīya* (edited by Professor Jalāl al-Dīn Āshtiyānī together with al-Sabzawārī's commentary, Meshed University Press, 1967), is generally believed to be his last work, and we shall briefly discuss it below. But both this work and other treatises, with the possible exception of a treatise called *Sarayān al-Wujūd,* are certainly based on and some almost verbally lifted from the *Asfār.* Indeed, these works do not contain anything which is not found in the *Asfār*—no matter whether the subject of a treatise is movement, the origination of the world, the relationship of essence and existence, or the life after death.

An interesting problem is set by a treatise called *Ṭarḥ al-Kaunain,* which Ṣadrā himself mentions in the *Asfār* (I, 1, p. 47) and about which he says that he proved therein the unity of all existence, i.e., that the only real existence is God's, while all else is mere appearance. The editor of the *Asfār* states that this was probably the only treatise written before the *Asfār* and that it contained the heretical doctrine of the simple identity of all existence for which Ṣadrā was persecuted and from which he later retracted; [42] he then identifies this treatise with *Ṣarayān al-Wujūd* mentioned in the preceding paragraph. That *Ṭarḥ al-Kaunain* may have been written before the *Asfār* is probable since it is mentioned quite early in the latter work, but its identification with the treatise *Sarayān al-Wujūd* cannot be accepted. For this treatise (published along with eight other treatises of the author in 1202 A.H.) contains, on closer examination, nothing of the doctrine of the Unity of Existence (*Waḥdat al-Wujūd*); on the contrary, the very thesis of this treatise is the reality of plural existence. What leads us to posit the composition of this work to be prior to the *Asfār* is the strong internal evidence. For, in this treatise, Ṣadrā clearly states that God's causal or creative activity is related to essences (p. 135, line 12; also p. 144, line 3 ff.), while throughout the *Asfār* and his other works he sternly rejects this and asserts that it is only the particular existences that are caused by God and essences cannot, in any sense, be said to be caused or created—they are mere nothing. Again, also in this treatise, while the doctrine of the ambiguity of existence is stated, it is stated in a materially different form from the *Asfār* and other works. While here we are told that the *notion* (*mafhūm*) of existence is ambiguous (p. 134, line 9 ff.), in the *Asfār* Ṣadrā insists that while the notion of existence is one and common (*mushtarak*), the reality of existents displays systematic ambiguity—indeed, this principle of ambiguity later comes to be formulated as "that which by virtue of being one is many." Again, and equally and relatedly important, while here the actual existences are called *ḥiṣaṣ,* or "cases" of existence, in his later works, including the *Asfār, ḥiṣaṣ* or "cases" are sharply distinguished from and opposed to *afrād* (individuals) of existence with which real existence is identified. This is because "cases" are said to be identical with each other in essence (and al-Suhrawardī and others are accused of having recognized only "cases" of existence and not its unique individuals) whereas all *afrād* or individuals are unique. We, therefore, conclude that *Sarayān al-Wujūd* was written in a transitional stage of Ṣadrā's doctrine of essence and existence. Finally, if, as seems clear from Ṣadrā's own assertion, *Ṭarḥ al-Kaunain* did purport to prove the Unity of Existence, Ṣadrā, while referring to it in the *Asfār,* is not repudiating it but recommending it to the reader. This is what underlines what we have said towards the end of the preceding section of this *Introduction* and in the first Chapter of Part I of the present work, viz., that Ṣadrā, while insisting on the doctrine of *tashkīk,* at the same time contradicts it by his equal insistence that God is the only Reality and the only Existence, while all else is nothing. The editor of the *Asfār* has rightly rejected another identification of *Ṭarḥ al-Kaunain,* this time with the treatise *On Resurrection* (*fī'l-Ḥashr*) published in the collection of Ṣadrā's nine treatises referred to above (but reprinted twice again), on the ground that *Ṭarḥ al-Kaunain*'s subject-matter deals with the Unity of Existence, while the treatise *On Resurrection* has a very different subject matter (which is, indeed, squarely based on the *Asfār*).

Ṣadrā rarely gives cross-references in his works. But the few references that he gives are also of a highly dubious value for us. The reason is that while, for example, in his treatise on the temporal origination of the Material World (*fī'l-Ḥudūth,* published in the aforementioned collection of his treatises), he refers (p. 32) to the *Asfār,* in the *Asfār* itself (I, 3, p. 112, line 11), he refers to this treatise. Again, on p. 32 of the same treatise, he also refers to his book *al-Shawāhid al-Rubūbīya,* which, as we indicated above, is generally held to be his last work. The evidence adduced for its being Ṣadrā's last philosophic work is that it simply states Ṣadrā's theses without discussing and criticizing earlier philosopher's views. This may well be correct and to this evidence may be added the fact that in this work the discussion of the *Categories*—substance and accidents (to which Vol. II of the *Asfār* is devoted), has been completely omitted. It should be noted, however, that whereas in the *Asfār* (Vol. IV, 2, p. 151, last line ff.; p. 207 ff.) he criticizes al-Ghazālī's view of the after-life; here (p. 286), he seeks support from al-Ghazālī and agrees with the latter's interpretation of physical resurrection (p. 266, lines 10–11). The reason most probably is Ṣadrā's hypercritical attitude in the *Asfār* to which we have referred above. Besides this work, it is safe to assert that Ṣadrā's *al-Mabda' wa'l-Ma'ād* (where, in the introduction, a reference to the completion of the *Asfār* is found)—which is also the title of one of Ibn Sīnā's works—is later than the *Asfār*. These two works viz., the *Shawāhid* and the *Mabda* are, indeed, in the nature of a summary of the *Asfār*'s essential doctrines. As for the rest of the philosophical treatises, it is possible that they may have been 'wayside' compositions, probably written for the most part during the composition of the *Asfār* itself.

The present exposition of Ṣadrā's philosophy is essentially based on the *Asfār*, the full title of which is *al-Ḥikmat al-Muta'āliya fi'l-Asfār al-Arba'a al-'Aqlīya* ("The Sublime Wisdom in Four Journeys of Reason"). It was first published in 1282 A.H. in four over-size volumes comprising a total of 926 pages in small print. The most recent edition by Muḥammad Riḍā al-Muẓaffar (Tehran, 1958–) is accompanied by the expositions of al-Sabzawārī and al-Ṭabāṭabā'ī (the most recent commentator of the text) and occasionally gives notes by some other commentators. This edition leaves out Vol. II dealing with the *Categories*, and covers Vol. I in three parts, Vol. III in two parts (of which only Part I has appeared; hence we relied for the second part on the 1282 A.H. edition), and Vol. IV in two parts. The *First Journey* deals with the doctrine of being or ontology; the *Second* (which we have more or less left out in our present study, which al-Sabzawārī, the greatest of the nine commentators of the work, also ignored, which is generally omitted in the present-day teaching of the work in Iran, and which does not seem to contain any important new ideas) deals with substance and accidents; the *Third Journey* deals with God and His Attributes; and the *Fourth Journey* deals with man and his destiny—the end of the entire philosophic itinerary. Our reason for basing our treatment of Mullā Ṣadrā's philosophy on the *Asfār* is, first, that it gives all of the philosopher's mature ideas and gives them in the greatest detail and, secondly, that it contains Ṣadrā's full-length arguments in criticism of earlier philosophers, i.e., it displays Ṣadrā's mind in its entire philosophical process. Indeed, as we remarked earlier on in this Introduction, sometimes the method and process of argumentation themselves become so interesting and absorbing that they even philosophically supercede the reader's interest in the thesis itself.

Ṣadrā's influence in his own time was strictly limited and his school had but few followers, the most significant of them being Mullā 'Abd al-Razzāq Lāhijī, who survived his master by about twenty-one years.[43] It appears, as Āshtiyānī states,[44] that Ṣadrā's teaching permeated gradually, thanks initially to the fact that his commentaries on Ibn Sīnā and al-Suhrawardī's works attracted the attention of the followers of the Peripatetic and the Illuminationist schools respectively. This process, by a slow intermingling of these two schools of thought and further combined with Ibn 'Arabī's theosophy, brought Ṣadrā's own personal thought into focus. The first really important personality of Mullā Ṣadrā's school and one who created a number of able and active disciples is Mullā 'Alī Nūrī (d. 1246 A.H.), who wrote the first systematic commentary on the *Asfār*. Āshtiyānī states that during the Qajar period, all important teachers of philosophy in Tehran came from Nūrī's school. But the most perceptive and sensitive commentator of the *Asfār,* in my view, is al-Sabzawārī (d. 1288); my acquaintance with the commentary of 'Alī al-Mudarris (d. 1310 A.H.) is limited to a few notes, but Āshtiyānī declares him to be "the greatest of the followers and the best among the recent commentators of Ṣadrā." [45] As we noted earlier, at present Ṣadrā stands at the center of the traditional philosophic studies in Iran; besides the traditional *madrasas,* he is keenly studied by intellectuals at several modern universities. Persian intellectuals' pride in Ṣadrā can be measured by the following declamation of Āshtiyānī: "It may be said that with the birth of Mullā Ṣadrā, Metaphysics came to maturity in the East in the same measure as [at the same point of time] natural sciences progressed in the West." [46] Ṣadrā's commentary on the Metaphysics of Ibn Sīnā's *al-Shifā'* was studied in the Indian subcontinent and constituted the highest philosophical text in certain seats of learning.

In the West, the first study of Ṣadrā was written by Max Horten with the title, "Das Philosophische System von Schīrāzī" (Strasbourg, 1913). This is a summary of the *Asfār* and although it contains some serious misunderstandings of Ṣadrā's ideas, which this is not the place to go into, it does deserve respect as a pioneering work. As we have noted earlier, his judgment of Ṣadrā's overall performance as something new in the history of Islamic Philosophy is certainly sound. The only other work on Ṣadrā by a Western scholar is Henri Corbin's translation with commentary of Ṣadrā's treatise "al-Mashā'ir," published under the title "La Livre des Pénétration Métaphysiques," Tehran, 1964

NOTES

1. While this seems to be a fact, it needs closer examination and explanation in view of its obvious importance. So far, there appears to have been no satisfactory treatment of the subject.

2. *Asfār* (ed. M. Riḍā al-Muẓaffar), Tehran, 1378 A.H. ff. Vol. I, Part I, *Introduction,* p. 3, line 6.

3. *Ibid.,* p. 4, lines 1–10.

4. *Ibid.,* p. 5, lines 2–11.

5. *Ibid.,* p. 5, line 11–p. 6, line 2 *et seq.*

6. *Ibid., Introduction,* p. 5, lines 6–12.

7. *Ibid.,* p. 49, line 1 ff.; *al-Mashā'ir* (Persian translation—the original Arabic is not available to this writer—by Ghulām Ḥusain Āhanī, Tehrān, 1340), p. 44, lines 13 ff.

8. *Asfār,* I, 1, *Publisher's Introduction,* p. 3, lines 9–12.

9. *Ibid.,* p. 3, lines 9–12.

10. *Ibid.,* p. 7, lines 14–20.

11. *Ibid.,* p. 6, line 21.

12. *Ibid., Introduction,* p. 5, lines 13–14.

13. *Ibid.,* p. 11, line 18–p. 12, line 3; p. 6, lines 21 ff.

14. *Ibid.,* p. 8, lines 1–2; cf. references in the preceding note.

15. *Ibid.,* p. 8, lines 3–8.

16. *Ibid.,* p. 6, last line; cf. *ibid.,* p. 3, lines 10–12; p. 9, lines 18–19.

17. Reference in note 15 above.

18. Bergson's influence on modern mysticism in the West has been important; this mysticism, however, is cognitive and its content intellectual. Bergson himself is under a strong neo-Platonic influence. A striking example in the new Islamic tradition is the Pakistani thinker Muḥammad Iqbāl, who, with Bergson, distinguished the external rational processes from an intuitive experience called "love (*'ishq*)" but for whom the two are not divorced from each other. Iqbāl's *'ishq* is a close parallel to Ṣadrā's *Ḥikmā,* or wisdom.

19. See Chapter V of Part III of the present work, note 44.

20. *Asfār,* I, 1, p. 12, line 7; *al-Mashā'ir, op. cit.,* p. 3, line 4. In this connection, Ṣadrā even criticizes Ibn 'Arabī, for whom he generally reserves the greatest respect among Muslims: "Some points [given in the preceding quo-

tation from Ibn 'Arabī] differ from [my views]. This is because Sufis are apt to restrict themselves to their pure intuition and experience in their judgments. But we do not rely so much on statements for which no decisive rational proof is forthcoming, nor do we mention them in our philosophic works." (*Asfār,* IV, 2, p. 234, lines 16–18).

21. *Asfār,* I, 1, p. 307, lines 15 ff.

22. *Ibid.,* I, 2, p. 315, lines 2–12.

23. *Ibid.,* I, 1, p. 10, lines 3–4.

24. *Ibid.,* p. 10, lines 8–10.

25. *Ibid.,* p. 10, last line.

26. *Ibid., Introduction,* p. 3, lines 1–2; here the editor states: "But for the fact that it might be called an exaggeration. I would have said that he (Ṣadrā) is greater in philosophic ranking [than al-Fārābī and Ibn Sīnā]." He quotes his teacher (*ibid.,* p. 2, lines 14 ff.) to the effect that if he knew of anyone anywhere who understood the meaning of the *Asfār,* he would gladly journey to that place, no matter how distant it be, and then concludes from this that the pride of his teacher lay in the fact that he failed to understand the secrets of Ṣadrā's philosophy. See also note 47 below.

27. See note 47, below, quotation from Jalāl al-Dīn Āshtiyānī. Āshtiyānī also states: "No nation in the world possesses as much capacity of philosophic—and particularly theosophic thought as do Persians. In the Muslim world, it is the Persians who laid the foundations of philosophic schools [methods?]." (*Introduction* to his edition of Ṣadrā's *al-Shawāhīd al-Rubūbīya,* Tehran, 1346/1967)—with an English *Introduction* by S. H. Naṣr—p. 75, note 2). The pages preceding and succeeding the page where this note occurs are full of sweeping statements (see p. 78, lines 2 ff., where Ibn Rushd, "although he had a philosophic capacity," is nevertheless dismissed as highly superficial and "pedestrian") and a certain anti-Arab sentiment. Cultivation and encouragement of this kind of attitude is unlikely to lead to either serious scholarship or creative thought. This *Introduction* is otherwise extremely useful for copious information on the development of the philosophic tradition in Iran after Mullā Ṣadrā.

28. Ashtiyānī, *op. cit.,* p. 64, lines 11–12; see the whole discussion, p. 61, lines 14 ff.

29. *Asfār,* III, 1, p. 209, lines 6 ff.

30. See note 19 above.

31. In my paper, "Heavenly Bodies, Movement, and the Eternity of the World," in *Essays in Islamic Philosophy and Science,* ed. Professor George Hourani, State University of New York Press, 1975.

32. Zeller, E., *Philosophie der Griechen,* III, 2 (1923), pp. 714–15.

33. *Das Philosophische System von Schirazi,* Strassburg, 1913, *Preface,* p. I, lines 26–27.

34. P. 9, lines 8–17.

35. Horten, *op. cit., Preface,* p. vi, last line–p. vii, line 3.

36. For example, *Asfār,* I, 2, p. 311, lines 7 ff.; *ibid.,* I, 1, p. 87, lines 1 ff.

37. *Ibid.,* I, 2, p. 288, lines 20-22. This is indeed one of the most persistent themes in Ṣadrā.

38. *Ibid.,* I, 1, p. 86, lines 5–6, lines 13–14 *et seq.,* where a distinction is made between contingency in essences and existences.

39. See Chapter II of Part II on God's Attributes in the present work.

40. See Chapter IV, Part I, section on God-World Relationship.

41. P. 16, last line–end of the *Introduction;* see also *al-Mashā'ir, op. cit., Introduction,* p. 9, last line–p. 16, line 12.

42. See note 6 above.

43. Āshtiyānī, *op. cit., Introduction,* p. 96, para. 1 and note 1 on the same page; also, *Ibid.,* p. 99, lines 4 ff.

44. *Ibid.,* p. 104, lines 8 ff.

45. *Ibid.,* p. 114, lines 1–3.

46. *Ibid.,* p. 77, last line.

PART I

Ontology

CHAPTER I

THE METAPHYSICS OF EXISTENCE

A. *Existence*

In the development of philosophy in the Islamic East after Ibn Sīnā's famous distinction between essence and existence, the question as to which of the two was the primary reality played a capital role. Most philosophers argued on behalf of "essentialism" on the ground that existence, being a common attribute of all beings, is a most general concept and hence has only the reality of a "secondary intelligible *(maʿqūl t̲h̲ānī)*" to which nothing in reality corresponds. The "Illuminationist" philosopher al-Suhrawardī, in particular, strongly argued against the reality of existence. He argued that if we regard existence as a *real* attribute of essence, as Ibn Sīnā appears to do, then essence, *in order to have this attribute,* must exist prior to existence.[1] We have pointed out elsewhere that, on this point, Ibn Sīnā has been largely misunderstood.[2] Indeed, far from saying that existence is a mere attribute, Ibn Sīnā declared existence to be the sole nature or reality of God, while in contingent beings he regarded existence to be derived or "borrowed" from God and hence "additional to" *their essence but not additional to particular things that exist.* Al-Suhrawardī further argued that if existence were a constituent of external reality, then existence will have to exist and this second existence will, in turn, have to exist, and so on *ad infinitum.* He then enunciated a general principle that every general concept (like existence, unity, necessity, contingency, etc.) whose nature is such that, if a corresponding factor or form is assumed to exist in external reality, this will lead to an infinite regress, must exist only in the mind and not in external reality.[3] What these arguments really prove is that existence is not an *extra* factor or attribute in external reality but merely denotes a *status of being* more or less in Kantian terms. But what al-Suhrawardī actually concluded from them was that only essences are real and that existence is only a general idea, a secondary intelligible to which nothing corresponds in reality. Ṣadrā points out that al-Suhrawardī himself contradicted this principle by describing God as pure and necessary Existence,[4] and also by characterizing the human self as pure existence—although of a weaker degree of intensity than God.[5]

Ṣadrā strongly rejects the view that nothing in reality corresponds to existence and asserts, on the contrary, that *nothing is real except existence.* But this existence, which is the sole reality, is never captured by the mind which can only capture essences and general notions. Hence, there is a fundamental difference between the general notion of being or existence and those of essences. Since essences do not exist *per se* but only arise in the mind from particular forms or modes of existence and hence are mental phenomena, they can, in principle, be fully known by the mind; but the general notion of existence that arises in the mind cannot know or capture the nature of existence, since existence is the objective reality and its transformation into an abstract mental concept necessarily falsifies it. In other words, what exists is the uniquely particular, hence it can never be known by the conceptual mind, whereas an essence is by itself a general notion—and does not exist *per se*—and hence can be known by the mind. No wonder, then, that al-Suhrawardī and others who operated by an abstract notion of existence, declared it to be an empty concept, a secondary intelligible, for it is true that *to this abstract concept as such there is nothing that strictly corresponds in reality*. But their capital mistake was to think that the reality of existence is just this abstract concept:

> All notions which arise from [our experience of] the external world and are fully grasped by the mind, their essences are preserved [in the mind] even though the mode of their existence changes [in the mind]. But since the very nature of eistence is that it is outside the mind and everything whose very nature it is to be outside the mind can never possibly come into the mind—or, else, its nature will be completely transformed—hence, existence can never be [conceptually] known by any mind.[6]

It is true, then, that there is an abstract notion of existence arising in the mind out of different existents, but it is equally true that that abstract notion, far from giving us the real nature of existence, falsifies that real nature. Al-Suhrawardī's objection that, if existence were real, it will exist, i.e., will be existent and thus will result in a vicious regress, has no force, since it is not proper to say that existence exists. Existence is that primordial reality thanks to which *things exist* but it itself cannot be said to exist, according to the common use of the language; just as whiteness is that thanks to which things are white, but whiteness itself cannot be described as white in the common use of the language. It may, of course, be possible to say, as a special usage of terms, that existence is existent *par excellence* and that whiteness is white *par excellence*.[7]

If existence were to be treated only as an abstract general notion, then it must be regarded as some sort of an essence, of the order of a genus. We have forbidden this earlier on the ground that existences are unique and no general notion can do justice to the uniqueness of real beings. Further, essences, being static, each instance of an essence is identically the same. No instance of an essence is a unique individual (*fard*) but only a case (*ḥiṣṣa*) and yields indifferently the same result as any other instance of the same essence: "manness" of A, B, and C is identically the same essence. Existence, on the other hand, has unique individuals (*afrād*), not just cases (*ḥiṣaṣ*) of existence.[8] Existence is dynamic, ever unfolding itself in new and higher forms (*wujūd munbasiṭ*), and we shall study this movement of existence in Chapters IV and V of this Part treating respectively of higher causation and movement. It is this dynamism of existence which creates those modes which result in essences in the mind: "Real existences have no names (i.e., properties and descriptions). . . . While essences have names (and describable properties)." [9] Reality, then, is the proper place for existence, while mind is the proper home of essences, concepts, and static notions.

Against the view that existence refers to a unique, unanalyzable factor in everything, the objection is urged that, in that case, when existence is asserted of essences as something over and above essences, essences will be invested with being *prior* to their existence. When faced with this objection, some philosophers assert that existence is a special kind of attribute in that it does not presuppose the existence of an essence, whereas other attributes presuppose it; others accept this absurd conclusion, viz., that essences do have a sort of existence prior to 'real' existence; while still others say that 'existence' really does not mean anything beyond the fact that essences become somehow conjoined with the general notion of "is-ness." The truth, however, is that existence is *existence* of an essence, not of something which is then *asserted* of an essence, as in the case of black, white, round, etc. Existence is simply the status of being real, not an attribute of something which is in its own right already something real.[10]

In view of the fact, however, that existence is claimed to be the sole reality, on the one hand, and essences are also said to exist "for the mind," the precise relationship between existence and essence is to be determined. Having done this, we can proceed to describe the nature of existence as a dynamic, systematically ambiguous process. According to Ṣadrā, God is Absolute Existence. What the philosophers call Separate Intelligences are, according to him, God's attributes and he identifies them with the Platonic Ideas and what Ibn Arabī calls the "Essences of Contingents" and the "Fixed Ideas (*a'yān thābita*)." These have no external existence for Ṣadrā (nor for

Ibn 'Arabī) but form the contents of God's mind as His Ideas. Externally, at God's level, therefore, there is nothing but pure existence. This pure existence, which is absolute, manifests itself in different forms, through a process of self-unfoldment, and the resultant beings, which are contingent, are *modes of existence* (*anḥā al-wujūd*). These modes, although in their basic nature they are only existence, yet are differentiated from absolute existence in that they—being *modes* or *kinds* of existence—exhibit *certain essential characteristics to the mind.* It is *in the mind,* then, *not* in external reality that essences arise as a kind of secondary nature of the primordial reality which is existence.[11] It is just as though the sun, the source of light, is, in a sense, identical with the rays emitted by it, but the rays can give rise to different characteristics, as, for instance, in a prism.[12]

This quality of yielding essences to the mind is a clear sign for Ṣadrā of the attenuation of existence. The more existence is complete, the less of essences it exhibits; hence God has no essence. Essences, therefore, constitute negation of and are dysfunctional to, existence. Existence is positive, definite, determinate, and real; essences are vague, dark, indeterminate, negative, and unreal.[13] This is why it is more proper to say that, for example, "this is man," than to say, "man exists." [14] Since essences are *nothing* in themselves, whatever being they possess is due to their being "conjoined" with existence while existences are self-real, thanks to their being manifestations of and relations to the absolute existence:

> They [i.e., essences], so long as they remain unilluminated by the light of existence, are not something to which the mind can point by saying whether they exist or not. . . . They eternally remain in their native concealment [of non-being] and their original state of non-existence. . . . They cannot be said to be or not to be—neither do they create, nor are they objects of creation [the objects of creation being the contingent existences, not essences] . . . [contingent] existences, on the other hand, are pure relations [to absolute existence]; the mind cannot point to them either when they are considered out of relation with their sustaining Creator, since these have no existence independently [of God]. However, in themselves [unlike essences], these [contingent] existences are concrete realities, uninfected by the indeterminacy [of essences], pure existences without [the admixture] of essences and simple lights without any darkness.[15]

When we say that essence and existence are "conjoined" or "united," this talk can be grossly misleading if we imagine that two *things* or *realities* come together and are united, since we have seen that essences possess no reality of their own. We should rather think of this "union" in the sense that when absolute existence ceases to be absolute and becomes "modes" of existence, these modes necessarily give rise to essences, wherein existence is the real, essence, the subjective element. Indeed, God Himself gives rise to essences when He "descends" from His absoluteness and generates attributes as contents of His mind.[16] His attributes, thus viewed as pure ideas or quasi-essences in His mind (e.g., power, will, knowledge, etc.), have no real existence at all but are purely subjective to Him, but when viewed as His names (e.g., Powerful, Willer, Knowing), become *modes* of existence which Ṣadrā identifies with the Ideas of Plato and separate Intelligences of the Muslim Peripatetics. Thus, in its downward movement, when existence becomes further and further diversified into modes, these modal existences generate diverse essences.

The view that existence itself creates essences sets Ṣadrā apart from Muslim Peripatetics who believe that a concrete existent is a *composite* of essence and existence, each of them having a separate reality in its own right, and from al-Suhrawardī and his followers, who believe that essence is the reality while existence is a mere abstraction. Ṣadrā's view further clarifies and corroborates the doctrine, held also by Aristotle and the Peripatetics, that existence is not a genus. Aristotle had argued that existence cannot be a genus since genus and differentia each can be described as something which "is," and that "is-ness" comprehends everything, whether conceptual or real.[17] It is obvious that this argument confuses between positive existence and the general "is-ness" which Ṣadrā and al-Suhrawardī would call an abstraction. For Ṣadrā, existence cannot be a genus or a differentia, since it is existence that *creates* all essence, and whatever abstract "is-ness" belongs to essences, it does not belong to them *per se*—since in themselves essences neither "are" nor "are not"—but because their being is derivative from real existence. In other words, they are invested with this "is-ness" when they become objects of a mind.[18]

B. *Controversy with the "Essentialists"*

Ibn Sīnā had distinguished between essence and existence *in reality* and had declared existence to be some sort of an accident of the essence, even though it is not an accident of a *thing*. In the controversy after him in the Islamic East, most philosophers thought essence to be the reality and existence a mere subjective abstraction. As we have said earlier, al-Suhrawardī is the most relentless critic of the doctrine of the reality of existence and the pioneer of the doctrine that essence is the sole reality and existence a mental abstraction.[19] It is al-Suhrawardī, therefore, whom Ṣadrā makes the primary target of his criticism on this point, and whose arguments for the reality of essence he seeks to refute, one by one.

Al-Suhrawardī had urged in his *K. al-Talwīḥāt* that if existence were to be regarded as a real attribute of essence, then, if essence were to exist *after* existence was united to it, existence would then have existed *per se* and independently of essence; or if essence were to exist *together with* existence, then essence would exist *together with* existence, and not *through* existence and, therefore, would acquire this second existence. It is not difficult for Ṣadrā to refute this argument. Far from essence being something positive which *acquires* existence, essence *per se* is nothing positive at all. Indeed, in external reality, essence is simply not there. What is there is a mode of existence. When this mode of existence is presented to the mind, it is the mind that abstracts an essence from it, while existence escapes it, unless it develops a proper intuition for it. It is the mind, then, which comes to regard essence to be the reality and existence as a mere accident. This is because the basis of all mental judgments is essence, not existence. In reality, however, it may be far nearer the truth to say that essence is an accident of existence, although even this is not proper to say, since in reality existence is the sole original reality while essence arises from it as something secondary *for the mind.* There are not *two things or factors* in reality co-ordinate with each other, viz., existence and essence, but only existence.[20] When, therefore, the mind (a) differentiates between essence and existence and (b) declares the former to be real, it necessarily falsifies reality.

Similarly, al-Suhrawardī's worry that existence cannot be related to a non-existent essence, nor to an essence which is neither existent nor non-existent since in the latter case both sides of the contradiction will be eliminated, is met by Ṣadrā's statement that elimination of opposites is not impossible at certain levels of reality. Essence *per se* is *neutral* both to existence and non-existence, since *per se* an essence is simply what it is—e.g., horse is horse, man is man—and to exist or not to exist is no part of it. But when we regard essence as not *per se* but in reality, then essence has no separate reality from existence, since its very being is the being of existence itself. Existence, therefore, cannot be regarded as a quality of essence in reality, since 'quality' presupposes already something existent.[21]

Thirdly, the illuminationist philosopher argues that since in no contingent being is existence part of its essence—for we can conceive an essence but we still do not know if it exists—existence is additional to its essence. But we can go on asking the same question about existence, i.e., even after *conceiving* its existence we still do not know if it *really* exists. Ṣadrā says that this objection is valid against those who regard existence as separate from essence, but not against his thesis which posits existence as the sole reality. This sole reality *cannot be conceived* but can only be intuited directly. Al-Suhrawardī's argument has, therefore, no force either *against* the Muslim Peripatetics—when their doctrine is re-stated as existence being the sole reality—or *for* al-Suhrawardī's contention that existence is unreal.[22]

Fourthly, again, al-Suhrawardī seeks to deduce a vicious regress from the distinction between essence and existence: essence and existence will then be related to each other. This relation will have an existence and this existence, in turn, will once again be related to the relation, and so on *ad infinitum*. Ṣadrā's answer is that since the distinction exists only in the mind, the relation and the infinite regress generated by it also exist only in the mind and this mental regress can be terminated by the mind by ceasing its higher-order operations, as is the case with all forms of mental regress.[23]

The whole misconception of al-Suhrawardī arises out of considering existence as a general concept *of the same nature as an essence.* When he considers the being of existence in external reality and rejects it, it is thanks to the same misconception. But "existence" as an abstract noun, i.e., as "being existent," is a mental abstraction and as such has no real existence, while existence as a unique, unanalyzable *fact* is the concrete reality which never comes into the mind, as we have recurrently said. It is the same as "light," which as a general abstraction—i.e., in meaning "being illumined"—has no share of existence in the external world, but "light" as a fact is what exists externally. Just as light—in the second sense—exists *per se* and makes other things visible by illuminating them, so does existence exist *per se* and makes all essences exist accidentally. Existence is, therefore, *per se* light; essences *per se* are darkness.[24] Existence, as an abstraction, is related to real existence in the same way as "humanity", as a general concept, is related to a real man, while existence, as an abstraction, is related to essence in the same way as "humanity" is related to "a being capable of laughter." [25]

"The cause of effects and effects of the cause are nothing but real existents." [26] Neither existence as a concept nor any other essence shares this reality. Existence is not *something which has* reality; existence is reality itself.[27] People think of existence as that which has priority over all concepts, and is the condition of all meaningful attribution, and cannot become nonexistent. How can they say, in the same breath, that existence is no more than an intellectual abstraction? Shall the line between being and nonbeing, between reality and unreality, disappear? [28]

Ṣadrā's attempts, however, to support his thesis—that existence is the sole reality and that existence-essence dualism arises only in the mind—with quotations from Ibn Sīnā are not at all successful. It was Ibn Sīnā, in fact, who created the theory of dualism between essence and existence in reality, a theory which was rejected by Ibn Rushd but adopted in the West by Aquinas and in the East by a host of philosophers and theologians. Quotations from Ibn Sīnā may, therefore, be brought against later Muslim essentialists who did not consider existence to be real, for example al-Suhrawardī and others, but they certainly cannot be adduced to prove Ṣadrā's thesis that there is no essence-existence dualism in reality. For Ibn Sīnā, essences are real, not just mental, and he regards everything else thenceforward to be *a real composite* of essence and existence. This is, indeed, so clear from any passage that Ṣadrā quotes that one is astonished why a man of Ṣadrā's intellectual caliber failed to see its meaning. If this shows anything, it shows Ṣadrā's preoccupation with his own view to a point where he could not read Ibn Sīnā with full objectivity. Here is an example of a quotation from Ibn Sīnā by Ṣadrā: "That whose existence becomes necessary through another," says Ibn Sīnā, "be it an eternal being, cannot have a simple nature (*ḥaqīqa*), for that which it possesses *per se* is different from that which it possesses through the other. *Its being, therefore, in real existence, is a composite of both factors.*" [29]

But Ṣadrā goes on to conclude from this evidence: "No one disputes at all that the distinction between existence and essence occurs only in the mind and not in actual reality!" [30] His commentator, al-Sabzawārī, naturally points out that this is not consistent with Ṣadrā's own criticism of Muslim Peripatetics, whom he accuses of holding the existence-essence dualism in reality.[31]

C. *Systematic Ambiguity (Tashkīk) of Existence*

The classical tradition of Aristotelian logic had distinguished between two types of universal, one univocally applicable (*kullī mutawāṭi'*) and the other equivocally or ambiguously applicable (*kullī mushakkak*). An example of the first type is "man," which is univocally applicable to all humans, while an example of the second type is "soul," which is applicable to earthly souls and heavenly souls, with essential differences. Later Muslim Peripatetics, however, believe that there are no differences within a single essence and the differences are only in particular existences of an essence. Thus, when black color intensifies in a body, for example, there is no difference in general "blackness (*al-sawād*)" but instances of blackness (*al-aswad*) differ from each other because, when black color intensifies, a new species of black arises and the previous black goes out of existence.

In his works, al-Suhrawardī had criticized this view at length and contended that a single specific essence may have a range of intensity and need not be replaced by another specific essence, while a qualitative intensification takes place. Thus, when black color intensifies, not only does "blackness" but also "black" remain the same, yet a qualitative increase has taken place. Similarly, "animal" remains the same yet animality can increase or decrease. In other words, all essences are capable of "more or less" or "increase and decrease": an animal can be more of an animal than another, and a man more of a man than another. Indeed, for al-Suhrawardī, the category of "more or less" is the most basic and ultimately the only category applicable to the range of reality:

> The animalness of man, for example, is more perfect than the animalness of a mosquito. One cannot deny that the one is more perfect than the other merely on the ground that in conventional language one cannot say, 'the animalness of this is greater than that of the other.' The opponents' statement that one cannot say 'This is more perfect in point of essence than the other' is based on imprecisions in the conventional language.[32]

Ṣadrā has taken over this doctrine of "more perfect and less perfect" as the basis of his philosophy of existence. But in Ṣadrā this principle undergoes two fundamental changes. The first is that this principle, called *tashkīk,* is applied not to essence but primarily to existence—since existence is the only original reality—and only derivatively to essences. We have seen that while all existence is unique, essences are characterized by universality in the mind. Hence, whereas essences are univocal, existence is equivocal or ambiguous (*mutashakkik*). When something is characterized by such ambiguity, *it, by virtue of being a principle of identity, acts as the principle of difference—not* that it is a principle of identity in one sense or respect and a principle of difference in another sense or respect (*mā bihi'l ittifāq huwa 'ain mā bihi'l ikhtilāf*).[33] Only existence is such a principle, for it is the nature of existence and existence alone to create identity-in-difference:

> Now that you are convinced that existence is one single reality which has no genus and no differentia and it is identically the same in all things and its self-manifesting instances do not differ in their very nature, nor do they differ through additional instantiating factors (*huwīyāt*)—rather, these instantiating factors are identical with their very nature . . . you must conclude, therefore, that these existential instances (which are identical in nature) are (at the same time and by virtue of the same nature) different from one another in terms of priority and posteriority, perfection and imperfection, strength and weakness.[34]

The second all-important point of difference with al-Suhrawardī is that existence is not only ambiguous, it is *systematically* ambiguous.[35] This is because existence is not static but in perpetual movement. This movement is from the more general (*'āmm*), the more indeterminate (*mubham*), and the more diffuse levels of being to the more concrete (*k͟hāṣṣ*), determinate, and integrated or "simple" forms of existence. Every prior form of existence behaves like genus or matter and is swallowed up into the concreteness of the posterior form which behaves like differentia or form. This movement from the less perfect to the more perfect is, further, uni-directional and irreversible, for existence never moves backwards. We shall see later in the discussion of eschatology in Part III that Ṣadrā also rejects the reincarnation of human souls in animals on the basis of this theory.

We have said above that essences are dysfunctionally related to existence: the more a thing exhibits by way of essence, the less of existence it has. At the lowest rung of the scale of existence is primary matter which, in fact, does not exist but is merely a concept, i.e., an essence, since it is defined as "potentiality of existence." The highest point in this scale is God, who is absolute existence and hence has no essence and is not amenable to conceptual thought at all. Existence is not structured within this scale like static grades or levels of being, as al-Suhrawardī believed, but is actually moving from the lowest point towards the highest. The driving force of this universal movement is *'ishq,* or cosmic love, which impels everything towards a more concrete form and, as we shall note in Ṣadrā's account of eschatology, the philosopher believes that each of the intellectually and spiritually perfected members of the human species will become a species unto himself in the hereafter. The affinity of this doctrine of movement to Muḥammad Iqbāl's view of the dynamic process of reality resulting in the evolution of a more concrete and spiritual self-hood for man is obvious enough.

Since existence is the object of universal desire, it follows that existence is good and absolute existence is absolute good. This also shows that existence is real and not a mere concept, since no one desires to be a mental concept or a secondary intelligible.[36] Also, absolute existence has no opposite, nor peer, because opposites and peers are subsumable under a genus, and existence has no genus. Evil, therefore, is never absolute, but only relative, partial, and negative, and arises out of partial existence, which is subject to essences which are the source of evil both because they are partial and because they are infected with absolute contingency and, as such, suffer from the darkness of negation.[37]

The proposition that existence is systematically ambiguous means: (1) that, in a sense, existence in all things is basically the same; otherwise, if there were utter difference between things in point of existence, the term "existence" would not have the same meaning at all and there would not be ambiguity or analogy but utter difference; (2) that existence, by being the same, yet creates fundamental differences which render every existent unique: existents are not like onions, which can be entirely peeled off without a residue, but rather like "family faces" which have something basic in common yet each is unique; and (3) that, thanks to substantive movement in existence (to be studied in Chapter V of this Part), all the lower forms of existence are contained in and transcended by higher forms. Ṣadrā also reiterates in his discussion of essence that the higher form of contingent existence contains all the lower forms in itself in a simple manner. The Perfect Man, therefore, both contains and sustains all the universe. But for him, the world would go to pieces.[38] This is Ṣadrā's formulation—under Ibn 'Arabī's influence—of the famous doctrine of the Sufis that the Perfect Man is the Pole (*quṭb*) of the universe and that, but for him, the universe would be destroyed. The higher, then, emerges from the lower but, in turn, sustains the latter and becomes the cause of its continual existence. At the point of the emergence of the Perfect Man, the contingent realm enters the divine. The Perfect Man becomes analogous to or part of the Transcendental Intelligences which are nothing else than parts of godhead. This brings us to the very difficult question of the relationship of the Necessary and the Contingent in Ṣadrā.

D. *Tension between Monism and Pluralism*

Ṣadrā tells us that he had not always held the view that existence is the primordial reality, that in his earlier philosophic career he had strongly advocated essentialism, and that it was only later that the truth of existentialism dawned upon him.[39] We also learn from his scanty biography that Ṣadrā had been an advocate of existential monism, for which he was persecuted by orthodox theologians, but that later he grew out of it.[40] It must be concluded, then, that the doctrine of the systematic ambiguity of existence was the result of Ṣadrā's mature thought, i.e., the view that although existence is, in a sense, one single reality, yet in each case it is basically different and *sui generis* as well.

Yet there is clearly discernible a real tension in Ṣadrā's thought between a monistic trend where contingents literally vanish into nothingness in the face of God,[41] who alone is identified with reality and existence, and between the doctrine of the systematic ambiguity of existence, where every contingent being has a unique reality of its own which cannot be reduced to anything else. An example of the first trend is in a verse he quotes: "Everything in the world (except God) is (of the order of) imagination or a fancy or a reflection in a mirror or a mere shadow." [42] An extreme and more explicit statement is the following: "It must be borne in mind that our affirmation of different levels of multiple existences and the *concessions we make—in the interests of pedagogy*—concerning the diversity and multiplicity of existence do not contravene what we really wish to prove, God willing, viz., that both existence and the existent are but one and unitary." [43]

Indeed, this strain of thought that God is the only Reality and all else is mere appearance is so superabundantly displayed in Ṣadrā's writings that it becomes difficult not to regard it as a most fundamental one, and we are constantly reminded that "in the Abode of Existence, there is no other inhabitant save God." [44] This line of thought strongly suggests that one can perfectly analyze any contingent being into essence and existence, shear it of all essence, and simply give the existence back to where it ideally belongs. Ṣadrā quotes two passages from Ibn Sīnā's *Ta'līqāt* where Ibn Sīnā insists that the necessity of the Necessary Existent (God) is constitutive of that existent, while the contingency of the contingent and its dependence upon the Necessary Being is equally constitutive of it, so that no interchange or mutation can occur between the two since the two have a separate, fixed, nature. Yet, in the teeth of these passages, our philosopher comments upon them, "Any intelligent person can intuitively perceive therefrom what we intend to prove . . . viz., that all contingent beings and relational entities are mere appearances and modes of the Necessary Existence. . . . They have no existence-in-themselves. . . . Not that these possess realities of their own which then come to be related to another [i.e., God] with a relationship of dependence, but in the sense that their beings consist in pure poverty and dependence; they have no reality of their own except their being relations (of dependence) to a single Reality. Reality, therefore, is only One, there is nothing else besides. . . ." [45] One will, indeed, need an intuition like Ṣadrā's to perceive in Ibn Sīnā's statements the view that contingents are not things related to God by a dependence relationship but are *mere relations!* Even a ray of light or a reflection or a shadow has a reality of its own. What Ṣadrā's dicta amount to, from this point of view, then, is that God alone is real as Reality, while the contingent is real only as appearance. The difficulty we confront then is: how to square this Reality-Appearance thesis with that of the systematic ambiguity of existence?

But that is not the whole story, for, indeed, the real story of existence is brought out only by Ṣadrā's doctrine of the systematic ambiguity of existence. According to this doctrine, existence itself is many, not one, and this multiplicity is a consequence of the very nature of the principle of existence, which, by its very virtue of being the principle of identity and sameness, is the principle of multiplicity and difference. Hence it is called the principle of *tashkīk* and it is the only ultimate principle of *tashkīk*, according to Ṣadrā. Existence, then, inherently manifests itself in existents ordered according to existential priority and posteriority and in terms of intensity and diminution of existence. Since these manifestations are a consequence of the very nature of existence itself and are not due to any extrinsic factor, each and every existent is unique and irreducible. It is, therefore, impossible that a contingent be analyzable into two constituents: an essence and an existence, and the latter be simply "given back" to God, the Primordial and Original Existence. Indeed, on this theory, all existents, whether Necessary or Contingent, are original and primordial, since each one of them is unique and irreducible. The fundamental difference between God and the contingent existents is that God is pure, undiluted Existence without any admixture of essence, while in contingents this existence is diluted and suffers diminution in a graded scale and, in proportion to the diminution of their existence, they display or manifest essences. This is the meaning of Ṣadrā's repeated statements that essences are inversely related and dysfunctional to existence. On the principle of *tashkīk,* therefore, there is no question of existence becoming shorn of essence and being regarded as God or part of God.

Indeed, on the basis of the principle of *tashkīk,* Ṣadrā explicitly rejects existential monism. He criticizes those Sufi thinkers who hold that "existence is represented in only one individual, God, and that existence of essences which are [according to them] positive realities, means their coming into a relationship with the Necessary Existence. . . . Thus, existence for them is one single individual entity, while 'existent' is a universal having multiple [relational] instances." [46] Ṣadrā rejects this view, saying that it is impossible that God's being itself should form the existence of contingents—substances or accidents. This is because, in the case of many existents, whose essence is identical (like man, for example), there will remain no distinction at all between them, should their existence also be identically the same, viz., the individual being of God. Indeed, this very difficulty proves that existence can never be identically the same in any two existents whether they stand under the same essence or not.[47]

The same rejection of monism results from Ṣadrā's famous principle, "That which is of simple nature is everything *(basīṭ al-ḥaqīqa kull al-ashyā')*," of which he deems himself to be the first formulator in Islam.[48] God, being absolutely simple, *is* all existence. Ṣadrā's commentator, al-Sabzawārī, rightly points out that this principle does not mean unity in diversity, as it has been generally misunderstood, but means diversity in unity. That is to say, this principle does not yield the possibility of predicating everything of God but, on the contrary, yields the denial of that possibility: the absoluteness of God means that nothing relative or conditioned can be attributed to Him. We shall now see what "absolute" and "conditioned" mean in this context. If we conceive a species in terms of its definitional notions alone, e.g., plant as a "growing body," then we can add more specific definitional notions or differentiae to it and obtain the definition of another species. For example, by adding "capable of perception and locomotion" to "growing body," we can get the definition of animal. In such cases, we can always predicate the more general definitional notions of the species resulting from the addition of these differentiae. Thus we can predicate "growing body" of animal. But if we regard "growing body" not just as a definitional notion but as a concrete, existential species, i.e., plant, then we cannot predicate "plant" of "animal." Now, whereas philosophers think of "absolute" and "conditioned" primarily in notional terms alone, Sufis mean by them concrete realities. When they say God is absolute, they mean He is the absolutely concrete reality in the sense that nothing else concrete, being partial, can be predicated of Him: one may not say, e.g., that God is man or angel or anything else. This is because the absolute is beyond all that is conditioned. What the Sufis call "absolute" is thus equivalent to what the philosophers term "simple." God, then, being absolutely simple, cannot be identical with anything that is composite. Since a composite is a composite because it tolerates the ascription both of affirmative and negative attributes, God only has positive attributes, i.e., only non-being is negated of Him.[49]

The relative contingent has thus a reality of its own, its proper being, however imperfect it be and however invisible it might become under the Titanic shadow of the Absolute. But this is a very different language from the one also often used by Ṣadrā to describe the contingent in its relation to the Absolute, viz., that it is a mere relation, not something related, a mere manifestation, not something manifested. The contingent is not related to God as an accident to a substance, nor yet as a conventional predicate to its subject, for each of them is supposed to possess a being of its own, however weak. The contingent has no being at all which could be related to God, and our philosopher severely takes Jalāl al-Dīn al-Dawwānī (whom he is ever prone to attack, even going out of his way!) to task for describing the God-world relationship in terms of the relationship of a body to black color or that of a piece of cotton to cloth, for black cannot exist without body and cloth is inconceivable without cotton. Ṣadrā's attack is launched on the ground that black and cloth have the status of at least accidental being, which the world does not possess.[50]

But when we say that it is impossible for the contingent to be analyzed artificially into essence and existence and the latter to be shorn of the former, we must not assume that contingent existence is fixed and static. For the principle of intrinsic movement of being upward (*ḥaraka fī'l-jawhar*) is the twin grand theme of Ṣadrā's thought besides *tashkīk*. Indeed, he often presents the principle of movement as a manifestation of *tashkīk,* since physical nature, by constantly moving towards higher forms of existence, gives rise to and assumes these higher forms. If the utter diminution of being into prime matter is a metaphysical mystery of pre-eternity, for whose solution we have little clue,[51] the upward surge of reality towards ever higher forms of being is an attestable phenomenon of temporal existence. Indeed, it is this perpetual transformation of the lower into higher modes of existence which, for Ṣadrā, validates the principle of *tashkīk*. This is what makes the field of existence a spatio-temporal continuum which is the subject of our discussion of Ṣadrā's concept of movement. As the ultimate consequence of this dynamic process, arises the Perfect Man (*al-insān al-kāmil*), where the Contingent and the Eternal meet, and although one may not say that the contingent sheds its contingency altogether and becomes God, one may say that it becomes identical with God's Attributes, the Transcendental Intelligences of the philosophers.

NOTES

1. *Opera Metaphysica,* Vol. I (ed. H. Corbin), Istanbul, 1945, p. 22, line 10 ff.

2. "Essence and Existence in Avicenna," in *Medieval and Renaissance Studies,* London, 1958, pp. 2–3.

3. *Opera Metaphysica,* Vol. II (ed. H. Corbin), Tehran, 1952, p. 64, line 10 ff.

4. Ṣadrā, *Al-Asfār al-Arba'a,* I, 1, Tehran, (1387 A.H.), p. 43, lines 1–3 (all subsequent entries are to this edition, referred to as *Asfār*).

5. *Loc. Cit.,* Ṣadrā regards the "essentialists' " description of God as "pure existence" as a mere convention; *Asfār,* III, 1, p. 54, lines 7 ff.

6. *Asfār,* I, 1, p. 37, lines 16–19.

7. *Ibid.,* p. 39, line 8 ff.

8. *Ibid.,* p. 43, line 4 ff.

9. *Ibid.,* p. 49, lines 13–16; *Asfār,* I, 2, p. 348, line 7: "That which is *experienced* is existence but that which is *understood* is essence."

10. *Ibid.,* p. 43, line 16 ff.; p. 47, line 17–p. 48, line 12, which includes quotations from Ibn Sīnā and Bahmanyār.

11. This is the standard teaching of Ṣadrā on essences, for example, *Ibid.,* pp. 86–87, *Asfār,* I, 2, p. 36, line 8 ff.

12. *Ibid.,* p. 70, line 18–p. 71, line 4.

13. *Loc. Cit.* in note 11 above.

14. *Asfār,* I, 2, p. 290, lines 2–5; indeed, it is instructive to read the entire text from p. 286 (Chapter 25) to p. 290 on the relationship between essence and existence.

15. *Asfār,* I, 1, p. 87, lines 1–11.

16. *Asfār,* I, 2, p. 308, line 8–p. 318, line 4.

17. E.g., *Metaphysics,* 988, l. 17.

18. Cf. references in notes 14 and 15 above.

19. In his doctrine of the essence-existence relationship, Ṣadrā has been profoundly influenced by Ibn 'Arabī, who also declares that essences (as contents of God's mind) have no share of existence. While essences or universals do not exist for Ibn 'Arabī, they nevertheless have certain consequences by way of judgments (*aḥkām*) for external existents.

20. *Asfār,* I, 1, p. 54, line 16 ff.
21. *Ibid.,* p. 58, lines 5 ff. (see also *Asfār,* I, 2, p. 4, lines 7 ff.) on the nature of the violation of the Law of Contradiction.
22. *Asfār,* I, 1, p. 60, line 16 ff.
23. *Ibid.,* p. 61, lines 12 ff.
24. *Ibid.,* p. 63, lines 15 ff.
25. *Ibid.,* p. 65, lines 12–14.
26. *Ibid.,* p. 65, lines 14–15.
27. *Ibid.,* p. 66, lines 9–10; see also references in note 10 above.
28. *Ibid.,* p. 99, especially lines 19–20 where the concept of existence is radically differentiated from other concepts; p. 66, lines 10–11; p. 68, lines 4 ff.; see also *al-Shawāhid,* p. 10, lines 2–3, where it is stated that the very denial of existence involves existence.
29. Quoted in Ṣadrā, *Asfār,* I, 1, p. 66, lines 18 ff.; also *ibid.,* p. 46, lines 5 ff.
30. *Ibid.,* p. 67, lines 3–4.
31. *Ibid.,* p. 61, note 1.
32. Quoted in Ṣadrā, *Asfār,* I, 1, p. 441, lines 8–10; also al-Suhrawardī, *op. cit,* I, p. 156, lines 17 ff.
33. *Asfār,* I, 1, p. 35, lines 10 ff.; p. 68, lines 4–7; p. 120, lines 14 ff., especially lines 19–22; *Asfār,* III, 1, p. 14, lines 14 ff.; *ibid.,* p. 17, especially lines 4–5; *ibid.,* p. 21, lines 7 ff., etc.
34. *Asfār,* I, 1, p. 433, line 13–p. 434, line 2.
35. This has been treated in my paper, "Ṣadrā's Doctrine of Being and God-World Relationship" in *Essays in Islamic Philosophy and Science* (ed. George Hourani), SUNY Press.
36. *Asfār,* I, 1, p. 340, lines 1 ff., especially lines 7 ff.
37. *Asfār,* I, 1, p. 340 ff.; I, 2, pp. 347–52 (Chapter 31); *ibid.,* p. 289, lines 7 ff.
38. In *Asfār,* I, 2, p. 35, lines 5 ff., Ṣadrā describes this final outcome of the world-process as the "Final Differentia," cf. al-Sabzawārī's comment No. 2, p. 98 of *Asfār,* III, 1.
39. *Asfār,* I, 1, p. 49, lines 1 ff.
40. *Ibid., Introduction,* p. 5, line 6 ff.
41. *Ibid.,* I, 1, p. 47, lines 1 ff.; p. 49, lines 5 ff.; *Asfār,* I, 2, p. 292, lines 7 ff., etc.
42. *Asfār,* I, 1, p. 47, line 8.
43. *Ibid.,* p. 71, line 7 ff.
44. *Asfār,* I, 2, p. 292, line 9.
45. *Asfār,* I, 1, p. 46, last line to p. 47, line 6.
46. *Ibid.,* I, 1, p. 71, last line to p. 73, line 3.
47. *Ibid.,* I, 1, p. 73, line 5 ff.

48. *Ibid.*, III, 1, p. 110, beginning of Chapter 12; *ibid.*, I, 3, p. 312, line 16 ff.

49. *Ibid.*, p. 115, line 1 ff.

50. *Asfār*, I, 1, p. 330, line 15–end of p. 331.

51. See below, Section B, Chapter IV of this Part, the discussion of the "self-unfolding being," where we are told that, when the "self-unfolding being", the supreme intelligible matter, casts its shadow on the spatio-temporal world, prime matter—the least intelligible entity—comes into existence, for, the "highest" in the realm manifests itself as the "lowest" here below.

CHAPTER II

ESSENCE

Although essence possesses no ultimate reality like existence, nevertheless it is real *in a sense,* because it occurs in the mind and, further because there *is* something in external reality which causes it to arise in the mind, even though it is secondary to existence. Now, essence is sometimes defined as that which is an answer to the question with reference to something, "What is it?" In this sense, essence is only a general notion existing in the mind and need not refer to something exisetnt which can be known only through sense-perception. When, however, essence is defined as that "which makes or renders a thing what it is," it covers both the mental and the existential. This distinction has an Aristotelian basis, but it seriously modifies Aristotle, since, according to the Stagirite, only existential objects possess an essence or a real definition, while in the case of fictional or imaginary objects, only the meaning of the term can be given, not a proper essence.[1] In Saḍrā, however, essence in any case has only a semi-reality; while according to Aristotle, an essence must exist in order to be a proper essence.

An essence, taken by itself, says Ṣadrā (following Ibn Sīnā), is neither one nor many, neither universal nor particular.[2] Neither is it existent nor non-existent by itself. This is because existence and non-existence are meaningful only within the context of real existence, where they assume a mutually exclusive character, not with reference to an essence by itself. If, therefore, the question is asked, "Does man [as an essence, i.e., manness] exist or not?", the proper reply would be, "neither the one, nor the other." [3] Since an essence is not by itself a universal, in one sense it is "a nature spread out among particulars" and, so long as one particular exists, this essence will exist for "its relation to different particulars is not like the relation of a single father to different children, but rather like the relation of different fathers to different children," i.e., a one-one relationship.[4] At this level it is called "a natural universal" (*Kullī ṭabī'ī*).

But essence at the second level where it comes to exist "in the mind" does *become* a universal. The exact nature of this universal, the mode of its existence "in the mind"—indeed, whether it does so at all (since Ṣadrā holds that rather than "existing in the mind" the universal is *perceived* by the mind)—will be more fully discussed later when we treat his theory of knowledge.[5] But its relationship to objects will be dealt with presently, when Ṣadrā affirms the existence of the Platonic Ideas. Ṣadrā defines the universal as "something representative and cognitive which does not exist independently in the world and is a kind of shadow." [6] The question, however, arises as to whether a mental image cannot fulfill these requirements. The answer is that a universal is shorn of all particularities; that is why it applies and is related to all objects of a class equally.[7] An image cannot do this (as al-Ghazālī and later Berkeley contended),[8] for images themselves have to be subsumed under a universal. Also, an image can have an original, independent existence in the mind, like the existence of external objects in the world, but the existence of the universal is derived from and secondary to the primary existents—be they external objects or mental images.[9]

What is the nature and constitution of the individual? In his answer to this question, Ṣadrā disapproves of the doctrine that matter or other differentiating factors can constitute an individual. The individual, for him, is nothing but the unique mode of existence which is the reality (*ḥaqīqa*) of every individual. Individuality is not the same as distinction. Even a thousand distinguishing factors taken together cannot constitute an individual, although it is possible that distinctions produce the capacity for individual existence in a thing [10] and, further, since existence itself cannot be captured by the mind, conglomerates of distinguishing conditions can serve to *locate* an individual. But *identification* is not the same thing as *identity*. In his doctrine of the identity of the individual as *existence*, Ṣadrā invokes the support of al-Fārābī,[11] but not of Ibn Sīnā, who is the first philosopher to have introduced the distinction between essence and existence and to have affirmed that the existence of a thing cannot be derived from matter and form. The reason is that Ibn Sīnā had characterized existence as an "accident" of the essence, while for Ṣadrā existence is the primary—indeed, the sole—reality and, if anything, essence may be an "accident" of existence. Indeed, as we have seen in the preceding chapter, essence is a *negation* of existence.

Ṣadrā then proceeds to criticize and interpret all previous doctrines of individuation so as to reduce them to his own way of thinking. First of all, he notices the failure of al-Suhrawardī to resolve the problem. The Master of Illumination rightly rejected the view that distinguishing factors can produce an individual for all distinguishing factors, taken severally, are universals, and conglomerates of universals can not result in an individual. But he equally rejected the reality of existence and upheld the reality of essence alone, which is not individual but universal.[12] Then there are those who say that the individuality of a thing depends on a mental analysis where existence becomes distinguished from essence, but this will not do because existence is the *given*.[13] Those phlisoophers who regard matter as the principle of individuation must be interpreted to mean existence rather than matter, since matter itself has to be particularized by something else. Indeed, matter as such can not only not individuate, it can not even produce distinctions.[14] When a piece of wood becomes a table, the matter is the same and yet the two things are different. Indeed, all philosophers—e.g., Ibn Sīnā's pupil Bahmanyār—who speak of individuation by factors like spatial position, time, etc., are not talking of individuation proper but of signs of identification,[15] just as are those who say that each one of any two things identifies the other.

While affirming the intelligible or mental character of essences, Ṣadrā also affirms the existence of Platonic Forms "in the Divine Realm," [16] i.e., as ramifications of Divine Attributes, and equates them, after Ibn 'Arabī, with what the latter calls "The Stable Essence (*al-a'yān al-thābita*)." Ibn Sīnā, however, says Ṣadrā, interpreted the Platonic Form as an "abstract essence," devoid of all particularity. But it is incredible that a philosopher of the sophistication of Plato would not distinguish between an *intellectually abstract* entity and a separate but concrete and existential order of existence which contains within it all particularities and determinations. It is clear that here Ṣadrā is projecting his own doctrine of the movement and continuous emergence of concrete being into the Platonic philosophy of Ideas. Indeed, Ṣadrā accuses Ibn Sīnā of confusing unity-by-abstraction with unity-by-integration and concretization, between which Plato must have distinguished.[17]

Ṣadrā then points to the view of al-Fārābī and his followers (including Ibn Sīnā)—which is based on neo-Platonism and particularly on the later Hellenic amalgamation of Aristotle and Plotinus—according to which Platonic Forms exist either in the mind of God or of separate Intelligences. This view is wrong since Plato's dicta (Ṣadrā actually quotes neo-Platonic texts and even Hermes on this point!) and those of his critics clearly point to the existence of Forms as *independent existents,* not as the content of a mind—God's or an Intelligence's.[18] Ṣadrā also quotes and rejects the interpretation of his teacher, Mīr Dāmād, of Platonic Forms. Mīr Dāmād distinguished two levels of existence, the temporal (*zamānī*) and the eternal (*dahrī*): in the temporal realm things exist at different places and times, but in the eternal realm where they become objects of God's knowledge, they exist without spatial and temporal differentiation even though they are not abstract from matter (but matter in that realm does not *precede* the existence of objects as it does in the temporal realm, rather it is simultaneous with them). Ṣadrā rejects this doctrine—which appears to follow the position held by Naṣīr al-Dīn Al-Ṭūsī on God's knowledge of particulars—on the ground that these objects of Mīr Dāmād are *individual* and do not represent *species* as do Platonic Forms.[19]

Our philosopher then details the arguments of al-Suhrawardī to prove that every species of existents must have a Lord of Species (*rabb al-naw'*), which is of the nature of Light and is the guardian and regulator of that species and its members; otherwise those species will not be continuous but discontinuous, for example, a non-horse could be generated by a horse and a non-human by man, etc.[20] Particularly in the case of plants, whose "souls" are held by philosophers to be "accidents," it is not possible to hold that organic life can be created by mere accidents. Hence, there must exist Lords of different Vegetative Species which organize them and ensure their continuance.[21] These luminous Lords (of the ancient Persian sages) are identical with Platonic Forms, according to al-Suhrawardī, who also insists on the Principle of Higher Contingency, which lays it down that if a lower order being is found to exist, then *a fortiori* that being exists in a prior higher order of reality.[22] Al-Suhrawardī also holds that these Lords of Species represent essences but not extrinsic properties; e.g., essence of man is represented by a Lord, but not man as possessing two legs, two hands, etc. According to al-Suhrawardī, finally, the universality of these essences does not mean that "they are shared in by all individuals," as is commonly held. Indeed, these essences exist in the higher realm as *independent, individual existents.* Their universality simply means that their relationship to all individuals of a species is the same.[23]

Ṣadrā accepts al-Suhrawardī's position but criticizes him on three counts. First, it is not clear from al-Suhrawardī's account whether these Lords are of the same nature as members of a species or not. I think Ṣadrā's commentator, al-Sabzawarī, rightly points out that the Principle of Higher Contingency argues for similarity in nature.[24] Secondly, if legs, hands, etc., are parts of man,why exclude them from the Lord? This, of course, does not mean that the essence of the Lord is material and has literally a body, yet Ṣadrā insists that body cannot be excluded from the essence or the Form since higher *includes and transcends* the lower, and this is why Ṣadrā criticizes the doctrine of abstraction whenever he sees an opportunity to do so.[25] Thirdly, and most importantly, Ṣadrā attacks the dualistic nature of al-Suhrawardī's account of reality. The realm of the Lords of Species—the realm of Light—is uniform, according to al-Suhrawardī, admitting only the distinctions of "more and less." How can this realm create in the material world stereotyped and static essential differences whereby every species is "clearly" marked off from others, according to him? The trouble lies, Ṣadrā believes, in al-Suhrawardī's regarding essences as primary beings and "existence" only as an accident. For Ṣadrā, on the other hand, there is no dualism: there is only one reality, viz., existence, which, by a progression from the lowest rung to the Highest Being—God—gives rise to an infinite multiplicity. But this multiplicity is not of stereotyped essences but of existence which, thanks to its ceaseless flow, gives rise to certain characteristics at each level, *which the mind comes to treat as static essences.*[26]

We now come to see more clearly Ṣadrā's view of essence and its relationship, on the one hand, with the transcendental reality and the reality of the material world, on the other. Ṣadrā agrees with al-Suhrawardī, then, that Platonic Forms are transcendental beings, each having an individual existence of its own. They are not universals but particular beings. Their universality means simply that, *to the mind,* they appear universal, i.e., applicable to members of a certain class. At the lower end, there are equally individual but material objects. When the mind looks at these objects, a power is generated in it whereby it is able to look at or contemplate the transcendental, *individual* Forms. But since the human mind, still engrossed in the material world, is weak, its vision of the Form is blurred, as is a weak-sighted person's vision of an object in a misty atmosphere; hence it is able to regard a truly concrete, particular, existent reality *as a universal essence applicable to a whole number of things.*[27] In reality, however, there is nothing but a continuous flow of existence, just as there is a continuous flow of numbers, say, from one to ten, where each number exhibits different properties to the mind.[28]

Whether the analogy of numbers is quite acurate or not, the sense of the argument is clear. It is clear that, on this view, the *epistemological* function of Platonic Forms is nullified, which is consistent with Ṣadrā's general doctrine that intellectual cognition cannot capture reality which is pure existence. However, Ṣadrā still wishes to retain the *metaphysical* function of Forms, which appears to me to be inconsistent with not only his doctrine of the flow of existence but his position on the present issue. If Forms-in-themselves (as opposed to their effect on the mind) are not universal and do not have the character of an essence, how is it that they are creatively (i.e., metaphysically) related to the objects *of a class* in the material world? Indeed, the whole notion of a pre-existent, superior order of the world contradicts the idea of continuous, evolutionary, emergent movement of existence. This is undoubtedly a case of contradiction between Ṣadrā's pure philosophy and his theological preoccupations, a contradiction which seems to run throughout his system as we shall see in the chapter on movement.

Let us revert to the story of essences. As Ṣadrā pursues his analysis of essence, it ends up in pure existence. The steps in this analysis are: (1) that genus is identical with or parallel to the potentiality of matter, while the differentia is identical with the actualized form; (2) that genus, because of its imperfection and indeterminacy, *requires* and is perfected by the differentia;

(3) that differentia is the only reality, since genus, as a pure potentiality in the nature of matter, cannot form part of *actual existence;* (4) that, hence differentia equals existence; and (5) that what is called "species" or "specific nature" is nothing but a *classification* of objects by the mind since actual existents exhibit certain characteristics whereby the mind is able to compare and contrast them and put them in different classes.

The idea that in composite things the genus represents matter, Ṣadrā borrows from Ibn Sīnā. Composite essences can, according to Ibn Sīnā, be considered at three levels. If we consider, e.g., "animal" as such and by itself, i.e., on the condition that nothing else, e.g., "rational," is made part of it (*bi-sharṭ lā-shai'*), then it will be matter relative to the whole, i.e., "rational animal" and a material constituent to the whole. In this sense, "animal" cannot be asserted or predicated of the whole. But when "animal" is taken not in this material sense, but without any condition (*lā bi-sharṭ shai'*) as to whether "rational" be part of it or not, then it ceases to be matter and becomes genus and can be predicated of the whole "rational animal." Thirdly, when "animal" is taken with the condition that "rational" can be part of it (*bi-sharṭ shai'*), then it gives rise to a species and it can be predicated of the whole, i.e., we can say "[man is] an animal." [29] This shows that genus can be treated as matter or as something potential whose actuality is the form or the differentia. Indeed, Ṣadrā says that just as matter offers the "contingency of potentiality (*al-imkān al-isti'dādī*)" i.e., an actual possibility to become a form, so does a genus offer the "inherent contingency (*al-imkān al-dhātī*)" to end up in a differentia.[30] The only difference between the two is that whereas matter refers to something in the real world (although only a potentiality), genus is in the realm of concepts.[31] But in either case, what *concretely* comes to exist both in the real world—proceeding from matter—and in the mind—proceeding from genus—is the differentia for both matter and genus "lose themselves" in its concreteness.[32]

If we consider more closely the relationship between genus and differentia, it appears that this distinction is purely mental, for in reality only the differentia exists. This is brought out clearly by a consideration of "simple" differentiae as opposed to composite ones. In the case of "black color," e.g., what exists is black and *apparently* there is nothing in reality corresponding to "color." In view of this, some philosophers have denied that, in the case of colors, there is either a real genus or a genuine differentia. This, however, is a capital mistake. For although the analysis into genuses and differentiae is only a mental operation, there is some warrant in reality to make these distinctions and classifications.[33] Nevertheless, what this shows is that existential reality is not composed of genuses and differentiae but of *modes of existence,* i.e., simple differentiae. For, in truth, there is no such thing as a composite differentia in reality; there are only successive modes of existence.

In this context, Ṣadrā asserts that the whole reality is nothing but a succession of differentiae which, in turn, are nothing but successive modes of existence (*anḥā' al-wujūd*).[34]

When an unorganized body becomes a plant, it does so through a simple, differentiating quality. So is the case when plant becomes animal or man. This view, of course, is also taken from Ibn Sīnā, who contended that real differentiae are not apparently knowable,[35] and although Ibn Sīnā did not say that genuses and species are unreal and that their reality is limited to the operations of the mind, nevertheless Ṣadrā's debt to him in developing his differentia-existence equation is immense. We have seen that Ibn Sīnā had distinguished between the species-aspect and genus-aspect of a thing. For example, plant, when viewed as a species, is a complete and finished product, but when viewed as a genus, remains incomplete and is perfected by the animal form. When genus "plant" is thus perfected, e.g., by the form of man, its characteristics which it had as a concrete species become transformed into a new nature. Thus, the vegetative functions in man are no longer the vegetative functions of a plant; the differentia that is man has entirely transformed their nature. So also do the animal functions—of perception and locomotion—become transformed in man and are no longer animal functions as such. Ibn Sīnā, therefore, affirmed that man cannot be regarded as a composite or aggregate of three types of functions—of plant, animal, and man—since the human soul or the differentia of man had bestowed upon them a new organic unity which is indivisible. Vegetative and animal functions in man are truly *human*.[36]

The doctrine is, of course, based on the Aristotelian matter-form formula; but, by transforming it into a genus-differentia formula, the status of the differentia has been assigned a far greater importance in the system of Ibn Sīnā, and particularly by declaring differentia to be simple and irreducible, it has become allied to the unique and unanalyzable *fact* of existence.

But differentia, for Ibn Sīnā, is certainly not *identical* with existence which in some sense stands outside the matter-form or genus-differentia formula even though the differentia helps bring the genus into an existential situation. Differentia, indeed, as part of the specific essence (composed of genus and differentia) is subsumable under a genus and is, therefore, part of what Aristotle called "secondary substance." For Ṣadrā, on the other hand, the differentia is neither a substance nor an accident, since it is identical with individual existence. To support this last proposition, Ṣadrā develops an argument which interprets the genus-differentia formula in accordance with his doctrine of emergent existence or "substantial change" and thus assimilates it to essence-existence principle.

In the progression of reality, we see that the movement is from the potential to the actual where every prior is matter or genus for every posterior: wood, e.g., is matter or genus for a chair.[37] Now, both matter and form are described as "secondary substances" (as opposed to "primary substance," which is the finished product of the two as an individual existent) by Aristotle and his followers. In the case of primary matter itself—which, however, does not exist—one can distinguish a quasi-genus and a quasi-form element. For, primary matter is characterized by pure potentiality; hence it is *something* that *has potentiality,* where *something* stands for the genus and *has potentiality* stands for the form, but of course the conjunction of the two is still a mere potential, without actual existence. Ṣadrā, therefore, insists recurrently that prime matter itself is not a pure genus but a species, since it does possess a differentia and it is thanks to this differentia that it has a positive tendency of potentiality which brings it out of pure nothingness and, further, that this species is restricted to one individual, i.e., that something which has the potentiality of existence.[38]

Just as prime matter has only a potentiality for existence, so is the case with every genus relative to its form or differentia, the only difference between prime matter and other genuses being that prime matter, even with its differentia, is only potential, whereas other genuses become actual when a differentia becomes available. Now, since a genus is only a potentiality relative to its differentia, and since genus at the same time is "secondary substance," it follows that a secondary substance does not exist. It is a mere "something," a mere logical subject, not a real subject.[39] Real subjects are only existential objects, which are the differentiae, not genuses. Further, since the potential is caused and actualized by something real, it follows that genus is brought into existence and actualized by the differentia.[40] The differentia is the final cause, the perfection of the genus. With the differentia, the genus as such evaporates and is taken up in it. It is not the case that the differentia is simply "added to" or exists alongside of the genus in a thing; it *is* the actualized genus; it is *the thing.* Hence Ṣadrā equates the differentia with existence and pronounces it to be a mode of existence.[41]

In the entire progression of existence, therefore, each preceding mode of reality becomes genus for and "loses itself" in the succeeding differentia: "It has become clear to you from what we have said . . . that that whereby a thing is constituted and exists . . . is nothing but the principle of the *last differentia* wherein all the preceding differentiae and forms which become united in it come to be nothing but potentialities, conditions and instruments for the reality that is the last differentia." [42] Thus, in the realm of nature, man is the final differentia. This movement represents a progressive diminution of essence and preponderance of existence until we reach God, who is pure existence without essence. It also lies within man's power to reach the realm of pure existence by contemplating the Intelligible

World and leaving the field behind where essences proponderate. To emphasize this point, Ṣadrā quotes a Persian verse: "It is a veritable village, not a mind which is pre-occupied by cows and donkeys, property and land"! [43]

From this account follows the unreality of species, or specific essences. A species is obtained by the mind by combining a genus with a differentia and subsuming the latter under the former. But existentially, the case is exactly the opposite: there the genuses lose themselves in the concrete reality of the differentiae and vanish without a trace; they become simple and unique modes of existence. How does the mind then carry out its analyses and produce definitions with their multiplicity of concepts? According to al-Sayyid al-Sharīf, three positions have been held concerning the relationship of this conceptual multiplicity with the external reality, viz., that these conceptual factors exist outside: (1) as both distinct in themselves and distinct existentially so that the external object is an aggregate of them; (2) as distinct in themselves but existentially united (which is the position held by those who believe that essence is constituted *prior to its* existence); and (3) as united both in themselves and existentially, a view on which it becomes difficult to explain their mental multiplicity, of course. Ṣadrā's reply [44] to this question is based on his view of the disparate nature of the realms of existence and the logical or conceptual mind, which we discussed in the previous chapter. In the existential world there is existence or modes of particular existence where every existent is basically unique. When, however, these existents are presented to the conceptual mind (as opposed to the true nature of the mind which is a member of the transcendental existential Intelligible realm), the latter extracts from them certain "essential" and "accidental" qualities whereby it classifies them. This classification, although it certainly does not exist in the external world, is, nevertheless, warranted by it *for the mind.* That is to say, it is only an operation of the mind although not a fictional one: "The reality and being of the differentiae consists only in particular and unique existences of the essences, which are true individuals. What exists externally is, therefore, only [modes of] existence but, thanks to sense-perception, they give rise in the conceptual mind to certain general or specific notions (i.e., genuses and differentiae), some of which are attributed to their essence and others to their accidental qualities. The mind then *attributes these existentially* to these objects." [45] We may note in passing that his words "of the essences" in "particular and unique existences of the essences" are not quite consistent with his view of the differentiae given above.

The differentia is thus not a secondary substance; it is a primary one in Aristotle's sense, for it is the differentia that *exists.* It is the mind that makes it a part of the secondary substance by combining it with an extracted genus, constructing a definition in terms of a species and by subsuming that species under that genus. But even then it is only "accidentially" a secondary substance which is really applicable only to the genus and the artifically constructed species. Ṣadrā also seeks to support this view on the basis of traditional Muslim Peripatetism (in essence Ibn Sīnā) according to which (a) a genus vis-à-vis its differentia is a necessary accident and a differentia vis-à-vis its genus is a property or particularizing quality (*khāṣṣa*) and (b) a genus equals matter and a differentia equals form. These two propositions taken together prove that differentiae, even when taken as external qualities, cannot be regarded as substances, i.e., they cannot be subsumed under a category of substance as species are subsumable under their genuses. He then declares absolutely that no existential form can be regarded either as a substance or accident, although it may be viewed as a substance only accidentally. These forms are, in fact, simple beings and are to be equated simply with existence.[46]

A question arises about the human soul: the human soul, according to traditional philosophy, is the form of the body, yet it has been established to be a substance. To this question, Ṣadrā gives two answers, one based on his own view, which he shares with that of al-Suhrawardī, viz., that a human soul is a transcendent spiritual reality of the nature of Light, i.e., pure existence, which is neither substance nor accident.[47] But he attempts first another answer, using concepts of traditional Aristotelian philosophy which has always confounded the two different meanings of substance, viz., a primary individual existent and a specific nature. The gist of his reply is that although the soul is in itself a "particular and unique being,"[48] yet in its relation to the body it behaves as a form or differentia. It is obvious that this line of thought gravely imperils his view of the differentia, which is for him anyway unique and, indeed, he regards the differentia "rational" as consummating all natural reality, as said before.[49] This failure arises from confusing two different issues: human soul as differentia in the realm of nature and as a transcendent reality. Another equal weakness in this reply of Ṣadrā is that here he treats of the soul as being something relational to the body in one respect and as being an absolute reality in another respect. This is a repetition of Ibn Sīnā's view of the soul, which Ṣadrā explicitly rejects in his discussion of the nature of the soul in Chapter I of Part III. Al-Sabzawārī is right in saying that this answer is not his own view but is based on traditional Peripatetic philosophy;[50] but the point is that Ṣadrā's answer is incorrect and appears to violate his own teaching on the differentia. Indeed, not infrequently does he lapse into the notions of traditional thinking, failing to make necessary adjustments that his revolutionary principles require. The correct reply to the question would be that the human soul, in the realm of nature, is the consummate differentia and hence cannot be strictly regarded either as substance or accident, but is treated by the mind as a specific nature. But, contrary to other natural differentiae which are destructible, being material, the human soul has also a unique and transcendental existence.

NOTES

1. For Aristotle's various statements on essence and existence see my article "Essence and Existence in Avicenna" in *Medieval and Renaissance Studies,* IV (1958), Oxford, p. 1.

2. *Asfār,* I, 2, p. 3, line 2–p. 6, line 1; see particularly p. 4; also *ibid.,* p. 288, lines 12 ff.

3. *Ibid.,* p. 5, lines 3–5; p. 6, lines 5–8.

4. *Ibid.,* p. 8, lines 3–5.

5. See below, Part III, Chapter II, Section B, first three paragraphs.

6. *Asfār,* I, 2, p. 9, lines 2 ff.

7. *Ibid.,* p. 9, note 1 by al-Sabzawārī.

8. Van den Bergh: Averroes' *Tahāfut al-Tahāfut,* Oxford, 1954, Vol. I, *Introduction,* p. xxxiii, last para.

9. See above notes 6 and 7.

10. See the entire discussion in *Asfār,* I, 2, p. 10, line 5–p. 13, end, particularly p. 10, lines 12–16, and note 2 of al-Sabzawārī on the same page.

11. *Ibid.,* p. 10, lines 6–8.

12. *Ibid.,* p. 11, line 1–p. 12, line 2.

13. *Ibid.,* p. 12, line 3 ff.

14. *Ibid.,* p. 12, line 16 ff.

15. *Ibid.,* p. 13, line 4 ff.

16. *Ibid.,* p. 4b, line 10 ff.; also Part I, Chapter IV, Section B, the discussion of the "Breath of the Merciful" and its contents; also reference given in note 5 above; also Part II, Chapter II on God's knowledge and Platonic Forms.

17. *Ibid.,* I, 2, p. 47, lines 10–13.

18. *Ibid.,* p. 48, line 9 ff.

19. *Ibid.,* p. 50, line 12 ff.; on al-Ṭusī's view of God's knowledge, see Part II, Chapter II, Section B, p. 35 ff.; Part III, Chapter IV, p. 17.

20. *Ibid.,* pp. 53–59, particularly p. 56, line 2 ff.

21. *Ibid.,* p. 53, line 9 ff.

22. *Ibid.,* p. 58, lines 1 ff.

23. *Ibid.,* p. 57, lines 2–12.

24. *Ibid.*, p. 59, note 2.
25. See Part III, Chapters II, III, and particularly IV, p. 2 ff.
26. See this discussion in Chapter I of this Part; Chapter V of this Part, and *passim* throughout the book.
27. See reference under note 5 above.
28. *Ibid.*, p. 61, last line–p. 62, line 5.
29. *Ibid.*, p. 16, line 9–p. 17, end.
30. *Ibid.*, p. 38, lines 4–8.
31. Self-same reference as in the preceding note, particularly lines 5–7, where matter is related to existence, while genus is a "notion"; also p. 34, lines 7–8.
32. Self-same reference as in the preceding note; also p. 35, line 5–p. 36, line 10.
33. *Ibid.*, p. 26, line 4.
34. *Ibid.*, p. 36, line 10 ff.; also p. 28, line 3–p. 29, line 3, and particularly the two notes by al-Sabzawārī on p. 28.
35. *Ibid.*, p. 35, line 5 ff.; *Avicenna's De Anima* (ed. F. Rahman), Oxford, 1959, p. 6, line 9; p. 39, lines 9 ff.; p. 56, lines 15 ff.
36. References to *Avicenna's De Anima* in the preceding note.
37. *Asfār*, I, 2, p. 33, line 3 ff.
38. *Ibid.*, p. 33, line 14 ff.; p. 18, lines 5–7; p. 45, lines 12 ff.; I, 3, p. 136, lines 1 ff.
39. *Ibid.*, p. 21, lines 11 ff.; p. 22, lines 8 ff.; p. 23, lines 3 ff.
40. *Ibid.*, p. 30, line 2–p. 31, line 5.
41. *Ibid.*, p. 36, lines 9–10.
42. *Ibid.*, p. 35, lines 5–9.
43. *Ibid.*, p. 35, line 1.
44. *Ibid.*, p. 28, lines 11 ff.
45. *Ibid.*, p. 36, lines 10–12 (cf. reference in note 34 above).
46. *Ibid.*, p. 39, lines 1 ff. and the two important notes on the same page by 'Alī Nūrī and al-Sabzawārī, especially that of the latter; see also note 3 on the same page by al-Ṭabāṭabā'ī in criticism of Ṣadrā's argument. This commentator's statement, however, that genus being an accident of the differentia is only in the mind and cannot affect the relationship of their objective counterpart, i.e., the matter-form complex, seems to me dubious. For Ṣadrā's point is that, *on this issue*, there is no difference between the mental phenomenon, i.e., the genus-differentia relationship, and its external counterpart, i.e., the matter-form relationship, since just as in the one case genus loses itself in the differentia entirely, so in the other case matter is "absorbed" in the form completely. Thus, both cases are equivalent (see Ṣadrā's discussion on p. 38). Al-Ṭabāṭabā'ī's many criticisms of Ṣadrā are centered around the relationship of the mental to the real; sometimes he has

a real point but often, as in the present case, the criticism seems to miss the point. In his comment, referred to herein, 'Alī Nūrī clearly points out tha by "differentia" Ṣadrā does not mean the nominal differentia but the "rea differentia (*al-faṣl al-ḥaqīqīy*)" which gives rise to the nominal differentia which is part of a definition, as Ṣadrā recurrently points out. See also, *ibid.* p. 44, line 10 ff.

47. *Ibid.,* p. 44, lines 1–7.

48. *Ibid.,* p. 41, lines 11–13; see the whole discussion to the end of p. 43

49. See reference under note 35 above.

50. *Ibid.,* note 1 on p. 44.

CHAPTER III

CAUSE I: NATURE OF CAUSATION

A. *Cause-Effect Relationship*

All contingents require a cause which tips their inherent balance between existence and non-existence in favor of the former; no contingent, therefore, can come into existence without a cause. Conversely, when the proper cause obtains, the contingent effect must come into existence and cannot be delayed; it thus becomes necessary. Now since the world is contingent, God must be its cause or the cause of the first of the series of its effects. Since God is eternal, the world must, therefore, be eternal. Or, if God alone is not its cause but is dependent for His causality on something else which must first come into existence so that God brings the world into existence, then this something becomes God's first effect, which must come into existence from God without delay, since God is its necessary cause. But then the world must also come into existence forthwith and hence must be eternal. Ṣadrā says that it makes no difference whether this something-other-than-God upon which the world's existence is supposed to depend is a particular time or a purpose, a motive or a will (of God), since all of these are supposed to be God's effects and thus cannot be delayed.[1] That is to say, if God says, "I shall create the world at such-and-such time or when I will to create," this time or this will must nevertheless immediately follow since these become His first effects as their necessary and eternal cause.

There are those, however, who deny this account and say that God is a voluntary being who may choose in eternity that He will create the world at a certain time, so that while His choice is in eternity, His actual act of creation is temporal. This view, which is held by al-Ghazālī and Thomas Aquinas and seeks to avoid both eternity and necessity of the world's existence, without attributing any "newness" to God, is criticized by Ṣadrā. The first question is whether this will is free or necessary, i.e., whether God could equally choose another time for the world's creation or not. If it is necessary, then God is not free. Also, on this supposition, God's act of creation must be eternal since the arrival of that particular time of creation cannot be delayed after the necessary will and hence the postulation of a time-lag between the will and the act of creation is untenable. Thirdly, this will or choice turns out to be contingent, not necessary, for it terminates with the act. Hence, like every contingent, it must have a cause other than God's being, for if it were caused only by God's being, it would be necessary and eternal, not contingent. But the assumption of another cause besides God results in a vicious circle, for while everything is supposed to depend on God's will, God's will is now made dependent on something else.[2] This criticism has a certain validity because in this case God's will is constructed on a wrong analogy as, for example, a man may say in winter that he would build a house in summer. The point of the criticism is that if this will is unconditional and absolute as God's, i.e., if it is will proper, then summer must arrive *now,* otherwise the will must become dependent on a condition, viz., the arrival of the summer, and ceases to be necessary and absolute. It is not, therefore, properly speaking a will but only a preliminary decision (*al-ʿazm*), as Ṣadrā's commentator Al-Sabzawārī says, and the will proper will come at the time of the actual act as its necessary cause.

If, however, God's choice is held to be free in the sense that He could equally choose another time for the world's creation, then neither of the two, or indeed an infinite number of, alternatives has any priority over the others. At this point, Muslim voluntarist thinkers have propounded different views. Some say that it is possible for a voluntary being to choose among equal alternatives as a man fleeing in fear may choose one of two paths open to him without any preponderating reason (*murajjiḥ*). A slightly different and more elaborate but obviously allied view (taken by al-Ghazālī) is that it is an inherent quality of the will to choose between equal alternatives without any other reason that might confer priority on one of them, i.e., the will itself creates distinction and priority. Since this function is an inherent prerogative of the will, the question "why *this* choice?" cannot be asked. A third position taken in this regard subjugates God's will to His knowledge, for it states that God knows what is possible and what is not possible and hence His will attaches itself to those things which are possible. Further, things are possible only at *their* proper times, not before or after; hence God's will carries them out at the proper times. A fourth view (attributed to the Muʿtazilī al-Kaʿbī), which is an elaborated version of the preceding one, attaches importance to purpose and says that every act of God has a purpose and hence comes at its proper time, whether or not we are aware of God's purposes. Fifthly, it has been held that God's non-creation of the world in eternity is not due to Him but due to the inherent nature of action for all action requires a beginning and is, therefore, opposed to eternity. Creation, therefore, can take place only in time, not in eternity. Lastly, there is the view of Abū'l-Barakāt who attributed an infinite series of successive wills and actions to God.[3]

In his criticism of these views, Ṣadrā appears to ignore the last one, which he undoubtedly cannot accept (and which al-Suhrawardī before him had denounced in most slanderous terms[4]) because this would clearly bring God into the realm of time and change. In rejecting the first position, the philosopher denies that choice can take place without a preponderating reason or cause, conscious or unconscious, and avers that whenever a man in fright chooses one of two roads or a man dying of hunger chooses one of two equal pieces of bread, etc., the choice takes place because of reasons which are not known to us. Further, he says the view that an open possibility can be realized without a preponderating factor does away with the notion of a cause and hence with that of the ultimate Cause, thus blocking the way to prove God's existence.[5] It should be pointed out that Ṣadrā himself, in his proof of God's existence, regards the causal argument as a good one but of secondary importance (see below, Part II, Chapter I); he is, therefore, following here the general Peripatetic line.

Ṣadrā equally rejects as spurious the idea that will itself can create distinctions and hence can act as a preponderating cause in favor of one alternative. Would this will not have the same alleged characteristic, i.e., of creating distinctions if, rather than the alternative actually realized, the other possibility had been chosen? Therefore, the attribution of such a characteristic to the will does not answer the real question: Why one alternative rather than another? For, the alleged characteristic remains unchanged in both cases. Indeed, there is no such thing as an empty will, a will-in-general which then attaches itself to an act (except as an abstract notion); for all will is a will-to-do-*this* and is thus particular. The question then is: how does this particular will arise?, and this is not answered by this voluntarist view.[6] As we shall see in the following chapter and more elaborately in Chapter III of Part II, Ṣadrā does not believe in an absolute act of will which he reduces to "knowing and doing what one likes." This process of knowing-and-liking or desiring can be weak or can become intense enough so that the effect follows. When the effect actually follows, it is, at that stage, as determined as any other physical effect of a physical cause. The question at issue here, however, is whether will is a *sui generis* original and uncaused act which by itself can create such a distinction as to tip the balance among alternatives.

As for the third position, viz., that God knows which things can happen and at which time and thus His will follows His knowledge, Ṣadrā criticizes it on two grounds. First, he seeks to accuse it of a vicious circularity, since God's knowledge is made to follow things as and when they happen and

His will—through which things happen—is made to follow His knowledge. The truth, however, is that God's omniscience, if taken seriously, renders His will impotent and superfluous. But on this view—which al-Sabzawārī attributes to the Ash'arites—even God's knowledge becomes redundant because, if things *will* happen as a matter of course at their appointed time, then there is no God but only Fate. Secondly, God's knowledge is creative, not receptive, and therefore does not follow but precedes the existence of things.[7]

On the question of purpose and interests of creatures (*maṣlaḥa*) tied to a particular time, Ṣadrā contends that these cannot depend on any particular time but must be eternal since God, being eternal, cannot be assumed to be void of them at any time. It is also impossible to conceive how the interests of creatures could have been adversely affected if the world had been created much earlier than the alleged point of time of its creation, or if its size had been much greater than it is supposed to be. It would also follow that God's absolute and primordial act—as opposed to specific temporal actions—is conditioned by something other than Himself, viz., an extraneous interest.[8] The same consideration is urged against the fifth view which says that every action takes place in time and therefore cannot take place in eternity. This is true for particular and specific actions, but not for the absolute primordial act of God, since the world's need for a cause is due to its contingency and not for its temporal origination. Hence the world, which is eternally contingent, is eternally caused and thus eternal causation is God's absolute act.[9]

God's act of creation, which is among His attributes, is, therefore, eternal and the world as a whole is also eternal. The individual contents of the world—the *ḥawādith*—are temporal but also have an eternal cause—God's primordial act. Some people, arguing on behalf of the temporal origination of the world, say that just as an individual temporal event is both temporally originated and yet attributable to God's causation, so can the world as a whole be regarded as temporally created and also attributed to God's causation. Ṣadrā replies that, in the case of a temporal emergent, its temporal antecedents are not its cause (*'illa*), but only its preparatory conditions (*mu'iddāt*), its cause being the eternal creative act of God (*amr*). That which receives the impact of this creative act (*khalq*) is the temporal flow of matter which prepares the ground for God's creative act. This is why the temporal flow of matter has no beginning, for whatever is supposed to be the beginning point must itself have its preparatory antecedents. But the creative act of God is unique and eternal as being beyond time, whereas the world-process is temporally eternal (i.e., beginningless). This is because the stuff of which the world process is made—matter—is inherently incapable of receiving the impact of God's act timelessly and all at once and can only receive it in terms of newness and emergence. This also demonstrates, for Ṣadrā, that the world-process is not made of discrete events but is a continuous process, thanks to substantive change (*ḥaraka jauharīya*).[10]

The contingent, which in itself is in a state of abeyance between existence and non-existence, becomes necessary when accompanied by its perfect cause and impossible in the absence of such cause. Although Ṣadrā holds after Ibn Sīnā that separate Intelligences are contingent (since everything except God is infected with contingency), nevertheless, they are, according to him, only theoretically contingent and in actual fact are necessary. This is because they are, in a sense, part of God and flow from His pure being directly. They exist not because God *causes them to exist* (*bi-ibqā' Allāhi iyyāhā*) but because He exists (*bi-baqā' Allāhi*), as Ṣadrā often puts it. It is only temporal emergents, therefore, which are authentic contingents and whose existence is necessarily preceded by time and non-being. Muslim theologians generally hold that the basis of need for a cause in the case of a contingent emergent is its temporal emergence (*ḥudūth*): since it was non-existent before, it needs a cause in order to *come into existence from non-existence*. The philosophers hold, on the other hand, that the basis of need for a cause is contingency, not temporal emergence. Ṣadrā supports the philosophers in this respect and insists that "coming into existence from non-existence" or "being preceded by non-existence" is the very nature of the emergent and hence does not require a cause, just as it is the very nature of fire to be hot and fire does not require a cause to be hot. The cause, therefore, is solely concerned with the bestowal of existence on the contingent emergent, and is not concerned with its having been preceded by non-existence.[11]

From this point on, however, Ṣadrā parts company with the philosophers. For the latter, the bearer of contingency in a contingent is the essence. The cause, therefore, causes the essence to exist, i.e., relates the essence to existence. This is called "compound production (*ja'l murakkab*)," since a relation is created between two terms—essence and existence. Ṣadrā, however, denies all reality to essences: in themselves they are *nothing*, i.e., even "something" cannot be predicated of them except when they are conceived by the mind; otherwise, they are absolutely indiscernible in their native darkness. The locus of contingency is, therefore, the contingent existent itself insofar as it has the possibility of existence. The action of the cause is, therefore, a "simple production (*ja'l basīṭ*)," i.e., the contingent being is made to exist. The cause, therefore, authors only existence, not an essence. When the contingent comes to exist, it then manifests its proper essence, which had been previously locked in the limbo of pure non-being. Insofar, therefore, as one can speak of the contingency of the essence, this is indirect and derivative from the contingency of the concrete existent.[12]

Every temporal existent is composite and has a composite cause. Several prominent latter-day philosophers, like al-Suhrawardī, have maintained, however, that a compound cause may have a simple effect. Al-Suhrawardī's argument is that if, for example, a number of men try severally to move a heavy stone, they will fail, but if these men exert themselves together, they can move it. This shows that none of these men, as a single factor, can produce the effect or even a part of the effect, but as a collectivity they can produce it. Thus, a single man is absolutely without effect whatsoever, while the totality of them can produce the totality of the effect. Ṣadrā's reply is that a composite or a compound is of two kinds: one is a mere aggregate which has no reality or character over and above that of the individuals which it comprises, while the second is a specific form of a material composite. In the second case, it is the specific form—which is unitary—that produces the effect—which is also unitary—as, for example, magnet attracts iron, although even in this case both the cause and the effect are not absolutely simple. In the case of a number of men moving a stone, there is nothing but an aggregate. It is not true to say that individuals in this case have severally no effect at all; on the contrary, every individual has an effect. The reason why the effect of a single person does not appear, when he handles the stone separately, is that when he leaves, his effect is destroyed and is not conserved by the stone. If there were a way to conserve the effects of the efforts of several separate individuals, the last man alone would be seen to move the stone just as well as the collectivity of them together. In any case, every individual in a collective effort has a direct contribution and the effect is no more than an aggregate of these contributions.[13]

A being which is authentically a unity (*al-wāḥid al-ḥaqīqīy*) and simple (*basīṭ*) cannot directly give rise to more than one effect.[14] This is because in such a being its essence and its being a cause are indistinguishable and identical, since its causality is not something additional to its essence. If, therefore, such a being were to produce more than one effect or a single composite effect (which will be the same as producing multiple effects), its being will cease to be unitary. In order to avoid any suggestion of multiplicity, Ṣadrā points out that terms like causation and even emanation must not be understood as implying any notion of relation which necessarily involves two terms but because of the difficulty of language such terms have to be used as suggest some sort of multiplicity. Indeed, the effect in this case has no being except that it is an effect, i.e., its entire being lies in the cause.

The full impact of this doctrine, based on Ṣadrā's doctrine of existence, will be seen in the next chapter, which will deal with his notion of God-world relationship. But here it is only a statement of the famous philosophic principle, viz., "from the one only one can proceed." Ibn Sīnā, in a letter to his pupil, Bahmanyār, had said on the subject that if the authentically one were to be the source for two entities, A and B. then it would be the source for what is A and what is not A, viz. B, and this would be contradictory. Al-Rāzī tried to refute this by saying that the contradictory of "emanation of A" is "non-emanation of A," not "emanation of not-A"; hence, there is no contradiction in a multiple emanation from the One, i.e., God. Al-Rāzī here represents the general orthodox stand against the philosophers since al-Ghazālī; the orthodox, who believe that God directly created the multiplicity of the world, severely reject the philosophers' God who can only create one entity. Al-Dawwānī, seeking to defend Ibn Sīnā, says that, in the case of a simple being like God, "emanation of not-A" is reducible to "non-emanation of A" because the former would introduce multiplicity in God.[15]

B. *Impossibility of Causal Regress*

Ṣadrā gives ten arguments, traditionally held, for the impossibility of an infinite causal chain, some of which he criticizes and rejects. Some of these arguments, again, are not specifically concerned with causality, as we shall see, but attempt to show the impossibility of any actual infinite. The first of these arguments, which Ṣadrā calls "the soundest of all arguments" is stated by Ibn Sīnā. The gist of this argument is that a genuine causal chain must realize three conditions: (1) a pure cause at the beginning, (2) a pure effect at the end, and (3) a nexus of cause and effect—i.e., a nexus each part of which is both a cause and an effect—in the middle. This is because being a cause and being an effect are two different things. Thus, in a genuine and complete causal chain, we have:

C ------ CE --- CE --- CE --- etc. E

Now, if we suppose an infinity of causal nexus, what we have is only a middle and an end, no beginning, i.e., we have CE --- CE --- CE --- etc. E, but no C. It is, therefore, impossible to posit a causal chain which does not have a C or a pure cause at the beginning.[16]

This argument appears to me sound and proves the impossibility of an infinite causal chain. For, a beginningless causal chain is truly inconceivable, since a series that does not begin cannot exist. Indeed, a causal chain that does not begin is self-contradictory, for it means a causal chain without a cause. The difficulty (or prejudice?) that is felt in the concept of an initiated causal chain, in the idea of a beginning for the world, does not on balance seem as weighty as that involved in the idea of a beginningless chain, and the answer to the question, "What was there before the beginning?" is "Nothing." Kant, while criticizing the idea of the impossibility of an infinity in the past, held that there was no difficulty in conceiving such an infinity since it is possible to hold that, no matter how far back one traveled in the past, one would not find the beginning or the first cause. It is obvious enough that Kant was conceiving the past on the model of the future, since it is possible to conceive that, no matter how much one travels into the future, one will not come to an end. But there is an intrinsic difference between the past and the future, between the actual beginning and the potential end. The past is actual and no actual can be infinite.

It is important, however, to understand precisely the sense in which the Muslim philosophers after Ibn Sīnā take this and other similar arguments. Al-Ghazālī, in his attack on Ibn Sīnā's doctrine of the eternity of the world, had argued that the philosophers were thereby committed to an actual infinite. Ibn Rushd, in his reply, said that there was no contradiction in the eternity of movement since parts of movement were successive, not together. Later Muslim philosophers, particularly al-Suhrawardī, therefore, hold that eternity of the world in terms of an eternal or infinite *succession* (*'alā sabīl al-ta'āqub*)—as opposed to a structured infinite or *infinite-together* (*'alā sabīl al-ijtimā'wa'l—tarattub*)—is harmless: what is impossible is the latter. Then they distinguish between real cause (*'illa*) and its preparatory conditions (*al-mu'iddāt*): an infinity of serial preparatory conditions (called the "horizontal" series) in time is not impossible while an infinity of a causal nexus (called the "vertical" or causal series) is impossible, since cause is present in the effect and an infinity of causes would, therefore, result in a structured, actual infinite presence. This distinction has been indicated above in the first section of the present chapter, but is fundamental to this doctrine of causation. This is, in fact, a result of superimposing Plotinus upon Aristotle: God (or the Active Intelligence) is the only real cause, all temporal antecedents are only preparatory conditions. But it is obvious that the difficulty is still there, for the cause has been present with all the antecedents which thus become part of the cause in order for it to produce a later effect:

Cause
↙ ↓ ↘
Effect 1 ⟶ Effect 2 ⟶ Effect 3
Antecedent 1 ⟶ Antecedent 2 ⟶ Antecedent 3

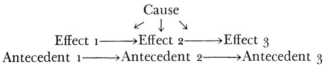

Thus, an infinity of antecedents becomes an infinity of causes. This confusion pervades their discussion of causation.

The second argument to disprove infinity of a causal chain is the argument from correspondence (*burhān al-taṭbīq*) much discussed and elaborated by later Muslim philosophers. The argument says that if we have a supposed infinite series, we can get another series by taking away one term from it from its finite (i.e., present) side so that this second series is shorter by one term on the side of the finitude. Now if we compare the two series, term by term, we find that they are unequal since one series is shorter by one term and is therefore finite. The supposedly infinite series is, therefore, greater than it by only one term, and hence is also finite, for a finite added to another finite results only in a finite. The opponent contends that this is not true since both series are infinite on the infinite side and are hence equal, the difference being confined to the finite side alone, just as an infinite multiple of tens is as infinite as an infinite multiple of ones, even though a finite series of tens is ten times shorter than a numerically equal and finite series of ones.

To this objection Ṣadrā replies that one-one correspondence cannot be done in series of numbers because, so far as theologians are concerned, they do not believe in their reality and, as for philosophers, correspondence can be effective only in the series whose terms are not only existential, but are together and are also structured (as in a cause-effect series), whereas numbers are out of consideration since they do not exist together but *seriatim* as are the motions of the heavens while in the case of disembodied souls, a structure does not exist. The reason why correspondence is not effective in things that do not exist or in things which are not structured by an intrinsic relationship between them is because these correspondences become a purely mental operation and each term in one of the two conceived series has to be explicitly related to one in the other series; but it is obvious that the mind cannot conceive an infinite series in this way. In an existential series, like the motions of the heavens and a causally structured series, as theologians hold, or only in the latter as philosophers hold (Ṣadrā here agrees with philosophers, not with theologians),—the mind does not have to carry out a detailed and term-by-term correspondence operation, as it has to in a purely conceptual or imaginary series, because the series is actual. It is just as if we had a rope whose parts are connected and contiguous and we wanted to draw the whole rope towards us; this can be done by just pulling the nearer end towards us and the whole rope will be pulled thereby: we do not have to pull each part of the rope. But if the rope is in several pieces, this operation cannot be carried out.[17]

Ṣadrā also criticizes philosophers in this connection on their belief in the infinity of disembodied souls saying that one can produce a structure in them by numbering them as one, two, three *ad infinitum,* and thus an actual, structured infinite would result.[18] Al-Sabzawārī rejects this criticism, saying that this structure would be extrinsic, not intrinsic to the souls,[19] but to my mind misses the point, since the structure, although extrinsic to the souls, will be intrinsic to the numbered series thus produced—an infinite actual number—and will indirectly affect the souls as well. Ṣadrā is, however, in indubitable contradiction with himself, since he affirms that an actual infinite is impossible only in things that occupy space and excludes from this not only intellects but even imaginative souls since imagination is non-spatial.[20]

Ṣadrā's example of the rope can also be taken as an implicit criticism of his teacher Mīr Dāmād who disallowed any force to the argument from correspondence on the ground that the difference between the two series is at the side of finitude and no matter how much the mind pushes it backward, it will only remain in the middle terms and would never reach the point of infinity.[21] What Ṣadrā's example of the rope glaringly brings out is that the series cannot be infinite because it is actual, i.e., existential and causally structured. Ṣadrā also seeks to support this contention by an argument from al-Ṭūsī,[22] which the latter seems to have contrived after the model of Ibn Sīnā's afore-stated argument, but which is highly dubious. According to this argument, which aims at avoiding the mental operation of detailed correspondence, every contingent is both an antecedent and a succedent, but if we count all the antecedents and succedents going backward all the way from now on, we will find that antecedents exceed succedents by one in the disputed side of infinity. Hence both series are finite. It is obvious that this can be so only if the present succedent is not counted; otherwise, they are equal. Al-Sabzawārī also criticizes this argument on the ground that the subject under discussion is the *causal vertical* chain, whereas this argument's subject is the *horizontal* chain of antecedents only.[23]

The third argument is based on necessity and contingency and states that if there is an infinite series of causes and effects, then all of them, taken as a collectivity, make one simple contingent which necessarily requires a cause. If this cause is also contingent, then it will be only a part of the total whole. But if it is necessary, that proves the finitude of the whole contingent series of which the necessary cause stands outside and of which it will be both a necessary and sufficient cause. An objection is raised against this argument. The objection asks why, if by cause is meant sufficient and complete cause, can the series not cause itself and still remain contingent, since it is dependent on its parts to cause the whole? Secondly, if by cause is meant efficient cause, why can one term in it not cause the whole, or, we can suppose an infinite number of causal chains each one acting upon others. Or, if the totality of the series has to be related to a necessary being, it is still possible to hold that the series of contingents is infinite but it is related to a necessary cause outside it. This last statement, of course, concedes the original argument for a necessary cause, but the reply to the first part, viz., why can the series not cause itself and still remain contingent, is that the argument has already supposed the series to be contingent and that, therefore, it cannot be a *sufficient* cause, while the sufficient cause is, therefore, outside it.

But our philosopher rejects this particular argument from contingency. Ṣadrā, who does not believe in the reality of a whole over and above its parts except where the whole is an organic unity like animal or man—in which case it is endowed with a specific form—finds a special difficulty in this argument insofar as it regards the series of contingents as a composite or compound whole. The difficulty is that if the cause is the cause of the whole, then many such so-called wholes come into existence only gradually, thanks to a succession of parts—like the pieces of wood made by a carpenter for a house, or, indeed, the world-process. Now, if the cause is not there when the first part comes into existence, then—since the cause is directly the cause of the whole—the effect, viz., the first part, precedes its cause or else there is a gap between the cause and its effect, viz., the later parts of the effect. Or, we say that each part of the whole comes into existence through a part of the cause. This will obviously make the cause a composite whole as well as the effect. This will destroy the supposed sufficiency of the cause—even if it has been supposed to exist outside the contingent series as its effect—because it becomes dependent on its parts. In that case, the contingent series may just as well cause itself, i.e., some of its parts may cause the whole, since we are no longer talking about an absolute and sufficient cause.[24]

Ṣadrā then strongly rejects that any whole which the mind may imagine becomes a real whole thereby, for a real whole implies a real unity and unity and existence are concomitants (*musāwiq*). But since existence is always individual, so is unity. Spurious or subjective wholes have, therefore, no existence. It is because of their belief in the reality of such subjective wholes that the latter-day philosophers were led to hold that a thing can cause itself. This is because they believed that the whole composed of the Necessary Being and the contingent beings is a real whole and since the Necessary Being is self-caused, they believed that this whole is also self-caused.[25] This point will be discussed again in Part II, Chapter I in connection with Ṣadrā's criticism of the same arguments to prove God's existence. Here it may be pointed out that in modern Western philosophy a similar view of the interdependence of cause and effect, viewed as "events" and being held together by the idea of substance has been held. On this theory, the whole world-process can be viewed as a series of events occurring in and held together by a continuing substance. This replaces the idea of different, discrete substances acting upon each other through causation. According to Ṣadrā, however, such a unity is purely subjective.

The fourth, fifth, sixth and seventh arguments[26] appear to be variants upon the second argument stated above (viz., that based on correspondence) and attempt to state in different ways either that, corresponding to the last pure effect, there must be a pure cause at the beginning or that the series may be divided so that the product of two finite parts must be finite. These are subject to the same objections as the second proof discussed before. The tenth argument seems to be the weakest of all. It says that the whole infinite series is either odd or even, that the odd is less than the even above it by one and the even is less than the odd above it. But a number that can be characterized by being less by one term is necessarily finite; hence the series is finite. Or it can be said that any given number may be increased or decreased by one and is, therefore, finite. This proof is rightly rejected on obvious objections seen in the second argument above.[27]

The eighth proof may be called the "hard-datum" proof. It states that unless there is an uncaused cause at the beginning, the entire series becomes void and cannot exist, just as when there is no first brick, which serves as the hard-datum or final support for all the bricks on top of it, the series of bricks is impossible.[28] This argument is sound and in its essence is the same as Ibn Sīnā's argument given above as the first argument. Finally, a similar argument is cited by Ṣadrā from al-Fārābī, viz., the ninth proof according to which, if each one of the terms in the supposed infinite series is such that it cannot come into existence unless a preceding one exists, then the entire series is impossible of existence. Hence we must suppose a first term which does not depend on another preceding one, *in order to make the series possible.*[29]

It should be noted that these two arguments and Ibn Sīnā's aim to establish that without a first cause, a causally structured series *cannot begin,* and hence *cannot come into existence.* This is different from the argument which is based on the impossibility of a simple (not causal) infinite—as in the case of infinite movement—e.g., that every series can be divided into two or it must be either even or odd, which we have previously characterized as dubious and of which Ibn Rushd's criticism appears to be effective.[30] But there is a stronger version of this argument given by Van den Bergh[31] and based immediately on al-Ghazālī, but ultimately on John Philoponus—like most of these arguments—viz., that if we assume an infinite series in the past, the present becomes impossible because, in order to reach the present—or, indeed, any given point in the series—an actual infinity will have been traversed, which is impossible. Ibn Rushd has criticized this argument by saying that it arbitrarily assumes an end to the series at the present or at any given moment, whereas what has no beginning cannot have an end either. But Ibn Rushd's criticism is ineffective, in my opinion, not so much because, as Van den Bergh says, there are finite times as well as infinite time, but because the real point in dispute is the other, infinite side in the past, and that side, being past and thus *actual,* must be finite. Ṣadrā has also mentioned this argument in *Asfār,* I, 3 (p. 153, lines 2–3), but his answer there is very weak, because after Ibn Rushd's restatement of Aristotle under the impact of neo-Platonism, Muslim philosophers like al-Suhrawardī and Ṣadrā also believed that whereas the vertical, causal series of Intelligences ending in God must be finite, the horizontal, temporal series may be infinite because it is not causal and involves only a temporal succession. But, as has been pointed out earlier in this chapter, the vertical cause does not operate in a vacuum and produce later terms of the series *de novo* and that is why these philosophers regard the preceding temporal series as *conditions.* These conditions, therefore, insofar as they become relevant to, and indeed part of, the cause, cannot be regarded as a mere temporal succession but become causally structured. Hence they cannot be infinite.

Finally, says Ṣadrā, all the effective arguments against the infinity apply only to the ascending series, i.e., the series going backwards, and establish only that there must be a first cause which itself is uncaused. They do not apply to the descending series, i.e., the series going forward. In other words, they establish only the finitude of causes, not of effects. This is because a cause behaves intrinsically differently from an effect, since a cause must actually exist if a series is to begin, but not vice versa, so that in the final effect all the preceding causes (1) exist, (2) exist together or simultaneously, and (3) exist in a causally structured manner. It is the conjunction of these three factors that forbids the infinity of causes. But not so with effects. In other words, the cause-effect relationship is an asymmetrical relationship. Ṣadrā states this view from his teacher Mīr Dāmād with tacit approval.[32] Al-Sabzawārī rejects this view on the ground that since the discussion here is about vertical causes, not horizontal conditions, the effects must also be finite and he accuses Ṣadrā of "being silent" on his teacher's opinion "perhaps out of respect." [33] As we have indicated, it seems that Ṣadrā does share this view with his teacher, although it is not clear whether he is thinking of vertical series only or of temporal conditions as well. As we have seen before in this discussion, there not only persists a constant confusion between the two but the distinction cannot, in fact, hold in the final analysis. We have seen Ṣadrā quoting with approval al-Ṭūsī's argument *in extenso* against the infinity of *temporal causation in the past.* If the notion of a vertical causation is adhered to rigorously, then, indeed, there is no causal series but only one Cause, God, and, given God, the whole of reality must instantaneously follow as His effects—not just the transcendental Intelligences, as al-Sabzawārī says—but the whole temporal sequence as well.

NOTES

1. *Asfār,* I, 2, p. 131, lines 21–22.

2. *Ibid.,* p. 131, last line–p. 132, line 9; see also al-Sabzawārī's comment No. 2 on p. 132.

3. *Ibid.,* p. 132, line 9–p. 134, line 6.

4. *Opera Metaphysica,* Vol. I, Istanbul, 1945, p. 435, last line ff.

5. *Asfār,* I, 2, p. 134, lines 9 ff.; p. 260, line 4 ff.

6. *Ibid.,* p. 134, line 17–p. 135, line 8.

7. *Ibid.,* p. 135, lines 9 ff. and al-Sabzawārī's note 1 on the same page.

8. *Ibid.,* p. 136, lines 2–12.

9. *Ibid.,* p. 136, lines 13 ff.

10. *Ibid.,* p. 137, line 7–p. 138, line 17.

11. *Ibid.,* p. 202, line 1–p. 204, line 7.

12. This is a basic theme of Ṣadrā; see Chapters I and IV of this Part.; but for the ambiguity over this issue see the *Introduction* and last part of Chapter IV.

13. *Asfār,* I, 2, p. 194, line 17–p. 201, end.

14. *Ibid.,* p. 204, line 11–p. 205, line 9; also *Asfār,* I, 1, p. 80, line 3–p. 81, line 2; see also the next chapter, Section B.

15. *Asfār,* I, 2, p. 206, line 10–p. 207, line 20; see also Ṣadrā's criticism of al-Rāzī on p. 207, lines 7–14 and his four criticisms of al-Dawwānī, p. 207, line 15 ff. It seems to me that his first criticism of al-Dawwānī, which states that it is no condition of a contradiction that the subject be a real unity, contradicts his own preceding criticism of al-Rāzī.

16. *Ibid.,* p. 144, line 4–p. 145, line 4.

17. *Ibid.,* p. 145, line 5–p. 149, line 14.

18. *Ibid.,* p. 152, para. 1.

19. *Ibid.,* al-Sabzawārī's note 1 on p. 152.

20. See below, Part III, Chapter III, esp. Section B on "Imagination"; also Chapter V of this part below, note 71.

21. *Asfār,* I, 2, p. 148, note 1.

22. *Ibid.,* p. 149, lines 15 ff.

23. *Ibid.,* p. 151, note 1; in his note on p. 149, al-Sabzawārī gives credence

to the proof of the theologians for the finitude of the past series—indeed, he regards it as "the soundest proof" for this thesis—on the ground that since each event in this series is temporally originated, the whole series must also be originated.

24. *Ibid.*, p. 152, line 8–p. 156, line 15.

25. *Ibid.*, p. 157, line 15–p. 159, line 12.

26. *Ibid.*, p. 162, line 2–p. 165, line 14.

27. *Ibid.*, p. 166, line 12–p. 167, line 7.

28. *Ibid.*, p. 165, line 15–p. 166, line 6.

29. *Ibid.*, p. 166, lines 7–11.

30. See above, p. 25, third line from the bottom; also Van den Bergh, *op. cit.*, Vol. I, p. 8, lines 12 ff.

31. Van den Bergh, *op. cit., Introduction,* p. xix, lines 28 ff.

32. *Asfār,* I, 2, p. 169, line 7, which is the end of the statements beginning on p. 167, line 8.

33. *Ibid.*, p. 168, note 3.

CHAPTER IV

CAUSE II: GOD-WORLD RELATIONSHIP

A. *Efficient Cause and Final Cause*

Aristotle had described God as both the efficient cause and the final cause of the universe: He is the efficient cause because He is the Prime Mover and sets the entire universe or, rather, prime matter, in motion and He is the final cause because the aim and purpose of the movement of the Universe is also God. God, however, does not make the universe as other natural causes make their objects, viz., by "pushing from behind," as it were, but by "pulling or attracting," since God exerts an attraction on the universe whereby it begins to move: He moves the universe as a beloved moves the lover. Muslim philosophers, like al-Fārābī and Ibn Sīnā do not apply the term "Prime Mover" to God but they use the term "First Cause" which is neither Aristotelian nor neo-Platonic but is, rather, a combination of the two, since this is nearer than either to the Islamic conception of God. But Muslim philosophers use the term "cause" or "efficient cause" (*fā'il*) both of God and other temporal or natural causes. This picture, however, becomes further complicated by the doctrine of existence propounded explicitly by Ibn Sīnā but which is implicit in al-Fārābī. According to this doctrine, matter and form alone cannot explain existence which is a third factor emanating from God, the source of all existence.

In the further development of this doctrine, particularly in the mystics Ibn 'Arabī and al-Suhrawardī, the "efficient cause" is lifted from the horizontal, temporal line of what naturalists call "causation" and is taken to the vertical line of causes, God and the Intelligences, as we have indicated previously. Ṣadrā takes over this doctrine and elaborates it: what are called natural, temporal causes are not real causes but only preparatory conditions, since they only cause movement or change and do not give existence to the effect which comes from God. Indeed, true cause is only that which not only gives existence to its effect but also continuity, so that it becomes inconceivable that an effect should last without its cause. The effect, therefore, has its being only *in* the cause, not outside of it, since the cause must be "present with (*ma'*)" the effect throughout the latter's existence. If a building can survive the activity of the builder, it shows that the builder is not the *cause* of the building but is only responsible for the movement of the building materials whereby these are arranged in certain positions; if an offspring can go beyond its parent, it is because the latter is not the former's real cause—which is God, the Giver of existence—but is responsible only for the movement of the semen to a certain place where the semen is further changed by other materials and grows.[1]

On this account, the only real cause or productive agent in the universe is God. But if we classify all temporal agents as actors, insofar as they produce movement, then actors are of six types. The first type is that which acts by nature as a fire burns or a stone moves downward by its natural power or propensity. The second type is that which acts under constraint as, e.g., when a stone is thrown upward contrary to its natural propensity. The third type of actor is that which acts under compulsion from the outside although its nature is to act freely, as, e.g., a man may do certain things by outside compulsion such as a threat or when he is thrown into water against his will by sheer physical force. The characteristic of all these three categories is that the actor acts without choice, either because of the nonexistence of choice as in physical objects or because of non-exercise of choice as in a man under external compulsion.

The fourth category is that of human actions which are characterized by free volition and choice. Such acts are preceded by will which is the result of knowledge or imagination accompanied by desire or appetition. In such cases, which constitute the field of characteristic human actions, the relationship between the basic power for action is equally related to action and non-action if we discount the knowledge-desire factor. Now Ṣadrā thinks that such actions, although they are certainly free in the sense in which the preceding three categories of action are not free, are still under compulsion if we take into account other factors such as strong motivations or other causes beyond the control of the agent. He reproduces the classical argument in favor of psychological-metaphysical determinism: since every volition is a temporal emergent (ḥādiṯẖ), it must have a cause. Its cause then is either another volition and so on to an infinite regress, or a nonvolition. In the latter case determinism is clearly imposed and Ṣadrā asserts with the Stoics that the human will is ultimately caused by the primordial universal will of God.[2] The same argument has been reformulated in modern times by those who hold physical or psycho-physical determinism (in terms of dispositions and physical environment, i.e., stimuli). But, as Ṣadrā will say in Part II, Chapter III, while discussing free will, if this is determinism, this is also precisely the meaning of human free will, for free will does not mean free will in a vacuum but within a context, and those free-willers are exercising in trivialities who deny this context. (Man can, of course, change this context—he can change the physical stimuli, i.e., his environment and, to an extent, even his dispositions—but this only means that he will create a new context, a new set of determinants for his actions). Human freedom has no other meaning—for it is in the human situation that he will be free within a determining context—but this certainly does not mean that man is not free or that this freedom is either farcical or meaningless. It is, indeed, farcical and meaningless to demand or attempt to supply any other kind of freedom for man.

The fifth and sixth types of actions differ from the fourth in that they are not the result of a deliberative choice and a conscious rejection of one alternative in favor of another. In this case, therefore, there is no conscious desire or will but the action proceeds directly from knowledge. But they are not involuntary or the result of compulsion but completely free in the sense that they flow along a single line without impediment from the nature of a free agent. This type of action is supremely characteristic of God but at the human level one may conceive of, for instance, a good person who does good by his very nature, not because he has no choice, but *as though* he had no choice. But still there is a difference between these two categories themselves. The first kind of action flows from the free agent by a "caring attention (*'ināya*)" and its result is in a sense outside the agent. At an imperfect human level we can illustrate it by the example of a man who stands on a wall but the mere idea or fear of a fall makes him actually fall.[3] This example was given by Ibn Sīnā to illustrate the influence of the mind upon the body and expresses the Stoic conception of the mind-body "sympathy," according to which when an event occurs in the one substance, a corresponding change occurs in another substance, not by mechanical causation but by "sympathetic" response.[4] But in the present context, Ṣadrā's example is not a good one because, as al-Ṭabāṭabā'ī points out, the man who falls from the wall also exercises a will not to fall, but his imagination and fear overwhelm and suppress that will. Further, what al-Ṭabāṭabā'ī does not say, the "caring attention" or *'ināya* is active whereas the example given here is of a passive fear. Ṣadrā also gives another example from human experience, which is also that of "sympathy," viz., if one imagines a very sour thing, one's tongue begins to water.

But these examples are drawn from the human experience which is imperfect. God's *'ināya* is perfect and arises out of His pure knowledge. That is why Ṣadrā, following al-Suhrawardī, replaces even *'ināya* by another concept, *riḍā,* or voluntary (but not 'volitional') assent and good pleasure. Again, a human approximation of this *riḍā* is when the mind, when engaged in thinking, creates ideas and thoughts voluntarily but without will in the sense of contemplating alternatives: the mind simply goes on creating ideas and this creativity is more akin to the activity of God. But this, again, is a relatively imperfect example, since the soul and its ideas are characterized by some kind of duality. God and His knowledge, as we shall see presently in the following discussion, and more fully in Chapter II of Part II, are not two things in any sense except in our conception of Him. Rather, God, by merely being what He is, gives rise to an ideal system of existence—which we may call His mind or the contents of His mind—and the contents of His mind, merely by being what they are, generate the universe without there being any second factor or change in His pure and absolute existence.[5]

In view of this transcendent and absolute reality of the ultimate and free principle of creativity as the cause, the world *in itself* has no reality at all apart from its Cause, and Ṣadrā condemns the naturalist materialists who hold that the world is self-existent and does not need a cause. On the contrary, in view of the titanic grasp of the cause over the effect, the effect can have its being only within the cause, not outside of it.[6] Ṣadrā also rebukes Ibn Sīnā and other Muslim Peripatetic philosophers who hold that the effect needs the cause for its existence but then comes to acquire a reality of its own.[7] For Ṣadrā, the world is real only when related to God; when not so related, it has no being whatever. Indeed, the world is not even *related,* it is a *pure relation* or manifestation, as we said in Chapter I of this part. He therefore describes the relationship of the world to God, not as a building is related to its builder or even as a writing is related to its writer, but as speech is related to the speaker: the moment the speaker ceases to speak, speech vanishes.[8]

Yet, Ṣadrā insistently denies that, on the view just stated, the instrumentality of the vertical contingents—the Intelligences—in causation must be rejected. He inveighs against the view that no contingent, be it an Intelligence or a body, may cause existence, since they are contingent and a contingent, taken by itself, does not exist, much less being the cause of existence of others. We shall see presently that Ṣadrā regards Intelligences to be intimately related with and manifestations of God's being, since, insofar as they exist, they share in Divine existence and, insofar as they have an essence, it manifests Divine Attributes—indeed, they are mere aspects of God Himself. Indeed, all existents share this Divine character in varying degrees—thanks to the systematically ambiguous nature of existence—and can, therefore, serve as secondary causes. In this context, Ṣadrā invokes an argument similar to the one he stated earlier (in Chapter II of this Part) in connection with the unreality of essence, but with a different emphasis.[9] He had said there that essences *by themselves* may not be described as either existent or non-existent, but when we take existential reality into account, we may say either that they exist—i.e., they have existential instances—or that they do not exist—i.e., they have no instance in existence. This is because reality (*al-wāqiʿ*) has different levels (*marātib*), and each of these levels has its own characteristics. A contingent, taken by itself, may not be said to be either an existent or a non-existent, but, in actual fact, it has existence, thanks to God. But when something does not exist at one level and exists at the other, existential, level, and the question is asked *absolutely*, "Does it exist?", the answer must be given in the affirmative. This is because privations or negations do not constitute positive attributes, whereas existence and its consequences do.[10] It will be noticed that this version of the argument is at first sight operating at something of a cross-purpose to the earlier version when he was discussing the existence of essences. But this apparent inconsistency is removed when we remember that Ṣadrā is talking about two different kinds of things in the two contexts. There essences, properly speaking, have only one level, viz., of non-being in themselves, and by themselves they cannot enter the existential level, for what exists are not essences but their instantiations. Here, on the other hand, a *contingent being*, although non-existent in itself, enters the existential field itself and not through instances, and the point Ṣadrā is making is that the Intelligences, although contingent *per se*, are nevertheless necessary in their actual existence. Ṣadrā has pointed this out several times in his writings. That is why the Intelligences are between God and the material world (which is truly both contingent and originated) and are, in fact, God's Attributes, since their contingency is merely conceptual, not real.

Just as God is absolutely free efficient cause without exercising choice and will as a human agent does, so His activity is purposive, but without His purpose being beyond and outside of Himself, as is the case with human agents. But in order to be able to conceive the nature of God's purpose, we must first analyze human purposiveness. A discussion of purpose involves a discussion of "that which is by chance" and the "unpurposeful" which are commonly believed to negate purposiveness. Now, purpose is discernible not only in humans, but also in nature, for every natural object has its natural behavior which is the result of its natural potentialities: a stone falls, air moves upward, fire burns. Many people think that nature cannot have a purpose because her actions are all on a single track and do not vary, whereas a purposive action varies according to purpose and is based on deliberation of the best means of achieving that purpose. This is surely not true for, if we suppose all human minds to be constituted alike, with the same motivations and same volitions, their actions would still be just as purposeful.[11] Further, it cannot be held that thinking and deliberation are necessary for an activity to be purposive, for often thinking takes place for its own sake and is purpose in itself, so that if we suppose that all purposive activity has to be preceded by thought, then all thought must be preceded by thought and this would lead to an infinite regress.[12] Again, in the case of settled habits of work, particularly those involving acquired and perfected skills, activity takes place without deliberation but certainly not without purpose.[13] Ṣadrā's last point can be supported by the consideration that such activity, although it may sometimes be described in popular language as mechanical or semi-mechanical, yet it is never regarded as divorced from purpose as in the expression "going through the motions of," which clearly indicates a lack of purpose or at least a lack of realization of purpose.

There are, therefore, natural as well as volitional purposes. Now, what is termed "by chance" occurs within the perimeters of purposive activities and has its rationale only within such activities. It can, therefore, be described as "accidentally purposive," although not wholly and essentially so. A man is digging a well and finds a treasure trove; this find is accidental or "by chance" to his real purpose, viz., digging a well, but is not accidental to his digging the place where the treasure trove was hidden. We call such things accidental because (1) we are ignorant of all causes that make up a chain, and (2) because they supervene upon an activity which had a different *rationale,* although, of course, the "accident" has its own rationale and end. This is basically different from sheer coincidence as, for example, when a sun-eclipse occurs when A sits down, although A's sitting down has its own rationale and the sun-eclipse its own, and neither of them is fortuitous.[14] Thus, the accidental and the essential differ only in their contexts and their rationales. If a person is taken ill by a consumptive disease and either gets cured by a doctor or dies, we do not regard the outcome as accidental, but if he gets interested in the medical art, acquires it, and cures himself and others, this is regarded as accidental since sick people generally are not expected to acquire the art of medicine.

Thus, the fortuitous turns out to be otherwise and is seen to have its own rationale. But there are certain activities which are called "unpurposeful." Now, an analysis of purpose in human action shows that the standard purposive activity has, as we said earlier, certain stages, viz., (1) the presence of an idea or knowledge, or, sometimes, a mere image; (2) an appetition generated by it; (3) a will or determination resulting in (4) action. But all these stages are not always necessary for an action to be purposeful: sometimes an action directly flows from knowledge (as in the case of God) or from a mere image (as in the case of non-rational human actions) without the intervention of appetition and will. Indeed, there need be no external action at all, in which case the mere image satisfies the requirement of purposiveness. A man may be bored by staying at home and may simply imagine a distant beautiful place and this image may satisfy him. Or, he may actually go to that place and this will constitute his satisfaction. A man may, again, wish to see a friend of his in a distant place, in which case a mere image or a mere getting there will not satisfy him. Now, we call certain activities unpurposeful or mere frivolities because we always tend to demand a rational idea as the *source* of such activities. But, as we have said, not all activity proceeds from a rational idea or knowledge and often an activity is initiated only by a compelling image, in which case it is purposive if it satisfies the demand of that impulsive image and it is illogical to demand that it satisfy a rational purpose. The action of a man who cracks his fingers or strokes his beard is thus purposeful and has its rationale in this sense, because there is no other rationale or purpose which is to be served by it but of which it fails to take account.[15]

Final cause cannot exist without the efficient cause. This is because the final effect of all purposive activity comes back to the agent. If a hungry person imagines the means of satisfying his hunger and then satisfies it, the end is the satisfaction of his own hunger. But if a person allegedly works for the pleasure of someone else, the result also finally comes back to him because *he* is satisfied, by pleasing someone else.[16] But most human purposes involve something else external to him as well—the vessel in which he realizes a value. A person who builds a house redeems the lack of a value, but satisfies it in a house which is external to him. Now, the idea or the image which impels him to action exists in him and it may be called an accident or an accidental form existing in him. Insofar, however, as it moves him to action, it is termed a purpose or a goal, while insofar as he is able to realize this value, it is called a good and a perfection. Insofar as it constitutes the term of his motion, it is called an end. Finally, insofar as the value is realized in something external to him, the purpose or the goal is called the form of that particular thing which has been actualized by the agent's activity.[17]

But at the level of God, a total identity of the efficient and final cause must be affirmed. God, in contemplating Himself, creates, by virtue of His very being as He sees it in Himself, a system of absolute good and ideal existence which overflows Himself. This system of existence has, therefore, its root and being in Him both as efficient cause and final cause. The ideal identity of the efficient and final causes would be conceded if we could suppose the separate and independent existence of a purpose. In that case, the purpose will be both purpose and efficient cause.[18] But since a purpose cannot exist independently of an actor, an actor can be conceived who will be both the efficient and the final cause, for the purpose does not go beyond His being. Aristotle held that God, in His utter transcendence, contemplates *only* Himself *and nothing else*, for if He thought of something else, His goal would lie beyond Himself and He would, therefore, become imperfect. Plotinus's One also transcended everything, but His transcendence is not the transcendence of exclusion but of inclusion: He transcends all because He includes all. The Muslim philosophers, therefore, held that in contemplating Himself, God implicitly contemplates everything, not *per se*—for *per se* He contemplates only Himself—but indirectly, since He is the source of all. Ṣadrā, therefore, affirms that in God's self-contemplation, an implicit and *per accidens* contemplation of the world is given and in His self-love the love for the world is included, since everyone who loves himself also loves all that positively flows from him.

If, however, God is the be-all and end-all to Himself, how can we regard Him as an actor and an actor with a freedom of purpose? The answer is that God is not just a being, an existent, but also has knowledge. Indeed, knowledge and existence, Ṣadrā insists, are aspects of the same truth and must co-exist at all levels of existence, even at the level of natural objects, for although these do not have conscious knowledge and certainly also do not have a will, they have a rudimentary level of knowledge commensurate with their rudimentary level of existence.[19] Their activity, as we have seen before, is purposive, although neither free nor volitional. Human activity has all three characteristics: purpose, freedom, and volition. Now, Ṣadrā affirms with Plotinus that God's activity is not volitional in the sense that it is not characterized by alternatives—for God there can be only one alternative, the best, commensurate with His being. But His activity is both purposive and free: it is true to say, "*If* God wills, He creates; if not, not," which is the mark of a free agent. It is true of God because it is no part of the truth of a conditional proposition that both its antecedent and consequent be also either true or false. We can say, "If it rains on the moon, its surface will be wet," but we know full well that it does *not* rain on the moon and the surface is *not* wet. This is a contrafactual hypothetical, but it is true because the point of significance is that it is applicable. Now consider the example of a painter who is gripped by an idea and he proceeds straightway to paint the picture. Actually, he cannot help painting the picture because he is totally gripped by the idea in his mind. Yet it is true to say, "If he wishes, he can paint the picture; if not, not." This is a hypothetical whose first part is actually necessary of realization, and the second part necessary of non-realization, but the entire hypothetical is still true. Now God's situation *vis-à-vis* His activity is of this kind, but the hypothetical is still true, "If He wills, He creates . . . ." This is because this sort of hypothetical indicates a free agent; it is not true of fire, for example, to say, "If it wills, it burns; if not, not." Hence God is characterized both by freedom and purpose.[20]

B. *God-World Relationship*

The question of God-world relationship can be conveniently dealt with in two parts. The first concerns itself with the relationship of the contingent to the Necessary Being and its subject matter is ontological in nature. The second deals with the problem of the relationship of the process of temporal emergence with the eternal or supra-temporal and is centrally related to the question of movement and time. Ṣadrā's system of thought is particularly rendered suitable for this division because of his doctrine of the distinction between the vertical causation and the series of temporal antecedents and he has, indeed, dealt with the two questions separately. We shall discuss the second question in the next chapter, which concerns movement and time. The subject of the present discussion is the causation of the vertical contingent by the Necessary Being or emanation of the former from the latter. This discussion, wherein Ṣadrā attempts a synthesis between the Muslim philosophers' theory of emanation and Ibn 'Arabī's doctrine of "descents (*tanazzulāt*)" of the Absolute Being, is highly delicate and complex and, to my mind, beset with certain difficulties of a serious nature. In any case, we shall first follow Ṣadrā's own analyses as accurately as possible, trying to fix the meanings of certain basic but somewhat slippery terms and then say something by way of criticism.

Before describing the procession of existence from God, we must re-emphasize the status of essences. Since essences are *nothing* in themselves, they cannot be characterized by causation or emanation; they cannot be caused, let alone caused to exist. This is because that which is nothing in itself cannot receive existence from anything, including God.[21] The common philosophical view that in a real existent existence and essence are *factually* conjoined is an error, because what exists as a contingent is a simple mode of existence (*naḥw al-wujūd*), which in turn causes essences to arise in the mind. It would be a sheer mistake to imagine that existence and essence are conjoined in real existence as a certain body may be conjoined with "black," for example. Although a body is a primary existent and "black" exists only as its accident, yet "black" has a being of its own, if only a secondary and attributive one. But essence has no being at all—either primary or attributive.[22] Essences, in fact, are nothing "to be spoken of." Even when we negate existence of them, this negation is not a part of them, so that it might be suggested that they are *something* of which existence is being negated.[23] For, even when we assert non-existence of them, some kind of existence—in the mind—is conferred upon them. In themselves, they are non-distinct, immersed as they are in the limbo of darkness and their distinctions arise only in the mind, when they are invested with mental existence.[24] Ibn 'Arabī said that although essences have no real existence (*ma'dūmāt al-'ain*), yet their effects and consequences are real. This is true only when we mean by "real" "being in the mind," for in objective reality there is no trace of them or their effects.[25] In view of this, it would be more correct to say, "such-and-such existent is man," rather than saying, "essence of man exists," or even "essence of man has been instantiated—in such-and-such." [26]

But with all their utter vacuity, essences have something to do with real existence, viz., they are caused *in the mind* by the latter. They, therefore, differ from such general notions and secondary intelligibles in the mind as "contingency," "something," etc.; for whereas nothing corresponds in existential reality to these latter, to essences there corresponds an existent, or, to be more precise, this-and-this sort or mode of existent (*naḥw min anḥā' al-wujūd*).[27] Indeed, essences can be defined as functions of existence *in the mind:* "That which is witnessed is existence but that which is understood is essence." [28] Essences, therefore, have consequences *in the mind* for and effects upon existence, and vice versa. They are, therefore, real in this sense. Indeed, as we saw in Chapter II above on Essence and as we shall again see presently, essences have a transcendental reality as well: They "appear" in God's mind as well, not as part of or existing alongside of or even "in" His being, but in the sense that they arise in His mind as caused by His existence, just as mundane essences are caused in *our* minds by external existence. Indeed, it is the contingent essences that are responsible for evil and non-perfection and non-being in the world, for existence as such is pure goodness and perfection.[29] To deny the reality of essences *in this sense* is, therefore, either to deny evil or to attribute it to God, the Pure Existence.

Essences, therefore, cannot be caused; what is caused is the modes of existence, although this causation also indirectly affects essences insofar as they arise in the mind. In other words, to attribute causation or existence to essences is a pure metaphor.[30] Let us now see how existence proceeds from God and in what sense God can be said to be a cause. We have seen earlier in this chapter that an efficient cause is "together with" and "present in" its effect, i.e., that whereby it exists and that whereby it is a cause is one and the same thing. Now, this is most eminently true of the First Cause, since it has no trace of duality of nature, being pure and absolute existence. Hence the absolutely and simply existent, by merely being what He is, produces His first and only effect. But just as this First Cause is simple, so is its effect, i.e., its effect does not have two aspects, one as a being and the other as an effect, but its being consists wholly in being an effect.[31] This first effect is what Ṣadrā will describe later as the "first self-manifestation" of God to Himself at the level of self-knowledge and as the "self-unfolding existence (*al-wujūd al-munbasiṭ*)," thanks to which every being has existence and which, in a sense, behaves like matter to all existents. But in the meantime an important difficulty has to be resolved and the relationship between the First Being and other beings has to be further clarified.

The difficulty is that, despite its insistence on the Unity of God, this account has shown a duality in Him—the duality of cause and effect, and, further, by the same token, has put God's being in the category of relation since cause and effect are relational concepts. The reply is that the category of relation, being one of the categories, pertains to the domain of essences or pure concepts, while God is pure existence, having no objective essence at all. As pure existence, He cannot be captured by a human mind, which captures only essences. The human mind, therefore, after all its rational efforts, cannot do better than stating, with an uneasy "sense of embarrassment (*bi ḍarb min al-dahsha*)" that the causal influence of God is by virtue of His very being and that the effect is, in this sense, internal to Him. The embarrassment of reason itself is both natural and rational, since reason aims at something higher, viz., unity of God, than what it can successfully achieve, viz., the assertion of God's causal activity by virtue of His very being. In the final analysis, there is no proof for God's uniqueness and unity except God Himself who, witnessing the self-conscious failure of reason, fulfils it by His sheer grace.[32]

Indeed, the cause-effect concept does not really apply to God. The situation, rather, is that which is usually characterized by emanation but even that word, taken in its banal sense, is misleading, for it also implies some kind of relation between entities. The causation under question is *dynamic causation,* which is a process, not a relation between static entities: Given God, "to exist," as a verb, becomes applicable to things. But since it is God who originally exists, all other things exist by virtue of His existence. All existence is, therefore, God's existence in a basic sense and all else is a farce. Yet, everything else also, in a sense, exists really since the verb "to exist" is applicable to everything in a real, not metaphorical, sense. This is the meaning of the systematic ambiguity of existence. We shall explain presently how this is so. Here an illustration from the phenomenon of numbers may be in place to help understand this relationship. Ṣadrā then states the age-old theory of numbers to explain the rise of many from the one, but states it in terms of his own doctrine of systematic ambiguity of existence and subjective character of essences.

If we regard unity or oneness in itself, with the condition that nothing further is added to it (*bi-sharṭ lā shai'*), it is number one, entity by itself. Similarly, if we regard existence as such, by itself, it is the first Existent, God, an entity by Himself. But if we regard unity as a comprehensive nature (its comprehensiveness, we note, is not in the sense in which a whole comprehends its parts, nor yet in the sense in which a universal comprehends its particulars—not the first because a whole does not apply to its parts, nor the second because a universal has no real existence), then it *is* all the numbers, including one, for it is the recurrence of unity that creates all numbers. Similarly, if we regard existence as a comprehensive (not general or universal) nature, it *is* all things. Further, each level of number, when created, is a simple (not composite) species or a simple mode of number, wherein matter and form, genus and differentia are identical, since the difference in various numbers is produced by unity itself, i.e., *that which is the principle of their identity, is the very principle of their difference.* This is what is meant by systematic ambiguity (*tashkīk*). Exactly so, in the realm of existence, each existent, e.g., an Intelligence, a man, a horse, etc., is a simple mode of existence. Again, each level of number, although in itself it is only a mode of number, generates certain characteristics and properties *in the mind,* i.e., the mind extracts them from it. Similarly, in the case of existence, each mode of existence gives rise, *in the mind,* to certain properties we call essences.[33] The difference, of course, between the phenomena of existence and numbers is that whereas the former is real—indeed, it is the only reality—the latter do not really exist but only have a conceptual order of existence. The second important difference between the two is that whereas numbers are created by the *recurrence* of unity, existents are not created by the recurrence of existence: existence, by being what it is, a unique reality, *is* all things. God does not repeat or manifest Himself again and again to produce modes of existence; His one primordial self-manifestation creates them all.[34]

Ṣadrā's theory of the process or the order of the universe, both in its existential and essential aspects, from God, rests squarely on the doctrine of Ibn 'Arabī and, in his attempt to synthesize it with the Muslim Peripatetic view of the relationship of God with the universe, he comes to modify the latter, seriously in some respects. When God, as Necessary Existence, reflects upon Himself, the first effulgence from His being takes place. This is what Ṣadrā meant while discussing the first effect of God. This effulgence or effect is, in a sense, identical with God Himself as pure existence but as being the result of His self-reflection, it is something different as well. But it is not to be understood as being separate from Him—indeed, it is not really an *emanant* or an *effulgent,* but rather an act, an act of self-reflection so far as God is concerned and an act of pure effulgence so far as it itself is concerned. Yet it can be hypostatized: it is nothing but real existence, the stuff of which all existents are made. It is called the self-unfolding existence (*al-wujūd al-munbasiṭ*) and, in a sense, behaves vis-à-vis all existents as matter behaves vis-à-vis all material objects, except that while matter is pure potentiality, it is pure actuality.[35] God Himself, in

His transcendent unity, is unknowable, but this being is knowable, after a fashion (by intuition, not by the reflective mind which knows only essences), since it exists in and with and as the basis of all things. Taken in itself, it is absolute and modeless but exists in all modes—with the eternal it is eternal, with the temporal, temporal; with the necessary, it is necessary; with the contingent, contingent; with the stable it is stable, with the transient, transient.[36] Yet, it is self-same all through and no modalities touch its intrinsic character; it is God's witness in all things. It is the shadow (*ẓill*) of God in all things and when this shadow casts itself upon the in-themselves-non-existent essences, the world comes to be constituted—the world of contingent existents. Ṣadrā speaks of it sometimes as an hypostasis, sometimes as an act, and sometimes as a relation mediating between God and the world of contingency: [37] apparently it is a hypostasis or a substance with reference to each existent as its existential root or principle; it is a relation between God and the world of contingency *as a whole* and, finally, it is an act of self-reflection on the part of God as well as a pure relation to Him in His mind.

But it is as an hypostasis that it plays the most important role in the ontology of Ṣadrā and Ibn 'Arabī. Ṣadrā even describes it as the first emanant from God. If the Peripatetic philosophers hold that the first emanant from God is the First Intelligence, this is only a general and vague statement which needs further specification. The truth is that the First Intelligence is the first emanant only in comparison with the rest of *particular* beings which exist in separation or quasi-separation from God, and is itself the result of the conjunction of this self-unfolding existence *with an essence* and is the former's first determination, as all particular beings are, in turn, its incessant determinations. But the self-unfolding existence is not separate from God, as we have seen.[38] There is, therefore, no real contradiction between this view and that of the philosophers.

Indeed, each particular determination of the self-unfolding being necessitates the attachment to it of an essence—in the mind. This is the meaning of contingency or contingent existence. When this self-unfolding being enters the realm of contingency and through its self-determination beings with essences arise, it is called "the Breath of the Merciful (*nafas al-Raḥmān*)," a term which also comes from Ibn 'Arabī like the term "self-unfolding existence." This substance—the Breath of the Merciful—is the self-unfolding being insofar as it gives rise to contingent beings and manifests essences. The factor that generates this change in the self-unfolding being and brings it down from the level of pure existence is again in the mind of God.

God, who, as pure existence, had generated the self-unfolding existence, creates by a second reflection or effulgence upon Himself, a multiplicity of attributes—life, knowledge, power, etc. In other words, what the first stage of Divine Consciousness had adumbrated as a unity and contained in an implicit manner, now becomes explicit at the second stage of self-consciousness. These detailed contents of the second level consciousness are at once the attributes of God and the Ideal Essences of the created world. There is, however, a vital difference in the results of the two self-reflections. The first reflection—of existence—had reflected or irradiated the "outward" of God, which is pure existence; the second reflection remains the "inward" of God. This is because of the principle that existence is the reality while essences, as concepts, are confined to mental existence.[39]

But with this second effulgence, a change occurs in the first one as well which cannot fail to be influenced by the second event; and although it retains its character of existence, it becomes infected with essences. Ṣadrā describes this new substance as the highest Intelligible Substance which, by casting a shadow upon the temporal world, generates the primary substance, pure matter. The principle involved here is *that the higher a substance is in the Intelligible Realm, the lower is its shadow in the material realm,* and since the Breath of the Merciful is the highest substance in the Intelligible order, its shadow in the material order is the lowest. Whereas the Breath of the Merciful represents the highest degree of actuality in the contingent order of things, primary matter represents the zero level of actuality and is, indeed, pure potentiality.[40] But since no substance is conceivable without attributes and, indeed, primary matter itself becomes existent only through attributes or forms, so is the highest substance, the Breath of the Merciful, inconceivable without attributes. Indeed, God Himself has been seen to exhibit attributes in His own mind. Just as God's being, in conjunction with His attributes, becomes His Names—the Living, the Knowing, the Powerful, etc.—so does this supreme substance, when conjoined with specific attributes like the Intellect, Reason, Perception, Nutrition, etc. become specific substances, like Intelligence, man, animal, plant, etc. Indeed, attributes and essences are the principle of diversity (in the mind), whereas existence is undifferentiated unity (in reality). Just as in the contingent existents there is nothing but a contingent existence which, when it comes into relation with a knowing mind, generates a multiplicity of concepts and essences, so, in the case of God, there is nothing but an absolute and pure existence which *in His mind* generates a multiplicity of attributes. The difference is that whereas in contingent existents (except man), there is only existence without (at least conscious) knowledge, in God both existence and knowledge coalesce—hence the necessary rise of attributes in His mind.[41]

Ṣadrā is well aware that this Ibn 'Arabian doctrine is a violent affront to the Peripatetic philosophers who vigorously deny any real attributes to

God over and above His being, which they define as pure existence without essence, since in their view, the addition of essence to existence in God would make Him contingent, and who, therefore, seek to explain away God's attributes either as relations or as negations and loudly proclaim that God's attributes are absolutely identical with His existence and have no being beside it. Further, such a view as Ṣadrā's would render their principle of emanation—"From the One only one can proceed"—(on the basis of which they affirm the emanation of the First Intelligence from God) totally void since on this view both God and the first emanant—the Self-Unfolding Being or the Breath of the Merciful—are said to possess both existence and essence. In his reply, Ṣadrā declares that what has been revealed by an authentic and direct intuition can never be contradicted by true reason and that, if a contradiction appears, then reason has not been used correctly.[42] His rational defense[43] of his view consists in pointing out that the philosophers also agree that attributes like life, knowledge, will, and power are assertable of God but that these are mere human concepts, while in God there is nothing but existence, pure and simple. Ṣadrā affirms that this is true and that, in fact, this confirms his own view of essences being only in the mind. But when they exist in the mind, they are *real at that level* and each essence and concept has its own content different from others. This explanation, however, does not really meet the point since, according to the philosophers, God's attributes are in the *human* mind, according to Ibn 'Arabi and Ṣadrā, they are in *God's* mind, which has, indeed, among its contents, essences of contingents as well since these latter are only modes and combinations and permutations of the Divine attributes themselves. The philosophers also, it is true, hold that in contemplating His own existence God knows everything—all essences—but they contend that these are merely implicit in God's existence and have no explicit existence there. But Ibn 'Arabi and Ṣadrā, by distinguishing a second level of consciousness in God's being—the level of differentiated attributes and essences—have attributed a real multiplicity to God, i.e., in His mind. This is the crux of the problem according to the philosophers' point of view, and Ṣadrā's insistence that attributes and essences only exist in God's mind and have no place in His absolutely existential level cannot save his doctrine from the attack of the philosophers.

Nor does this theory seem to me to accord with Ṣadrā's basic view that essences are mere negations of existence, "pure darkness," absolutely unreal and, indeed, source of all evil. How can these essences, then, become part of God? Further, what difference remains between the necessary and the contingent being since in his own view, contingent essences have their being only in the mind while now it turns out that God's attributes—His essences—are also only in God's mind? Indeed, it is not without irony that according to the philosophers essences have an objective and positive reality in the world of contingency, besides existence, but they exonerate God of all essence. But Ṣadrā, who has relentlessly criticized philosophers for believing in the objective reality of essences in the contingents and contaminating pure existence with them—indeed, of giving priority to them over existence—and has untiringly affirmed the non-being and utter inanity of essences, ends up by making them the veritable contents of God's mind.

One positive consequence of this stand, which is, of course, also the real purpose of Ṣadrā's manipulation, is the reduction (or elevation) of the transcendental Intelligences of the philosophers to the status of the Attributes or Names of God. The philosophers had given these Intelligences, as contingent beings, a being separate from that of God and had often identified them with Angels. But very often they had also spoken of these Intelligences, particularly the Active Intelligence, as a veritable God or substitute for God in relation to the mundane world. This is one of the points of major attack upon the philosophers from the orthodox theologians. In Ṣadrā's system, the Intelligences become in a sense part of Godhead; but, inasmuch as Attributes may be distinguished from the "Being of God," in His mind, they are on the borderline between God and the world and are also instrumental on God's part vis-à-vis the temporal world.

It also remains something of a problem throughout this discussion as to what is precisely the locus of contingency. We are frequently told that in being or existence itself there is no contingency and multiplicity which are due to its infection with essences which are truly contingent. Of course, the infection of being with an essence is not itself a contingent fact, but arises out of the very nature of being or existence which, by virtue of its procession from absolute existence, necessarily assumes the character of contingency. But Ṣadrā constantly reiterates that, of the two, existence and essence, contingency belongs to essence which is responsible for the static multiplicity of mutually exclusive forms, while existence is simply a flow of pure being.[44] On the other hand, essence in itself, as pure non-being, is *nothing* to be referred to or spoken of and when it is said to be a contingent, it is already invested with a kind of existence—albeit mental existence only, as we have seen above.[45] An essence is a paragon of privations and negations: it is neither existent nor non-existent, neither eternal nor contingent, neither a cause nor an effect, for all these attributes belong to existence alone.[46] It is the non-necessary existent that is, properly speaking, contingent, not an essence in itself.[47] It is, then, a particular being, a mode of existence which is contingent and its contingency is due to its being conjoined with an essence (which in itself is not a contingent), i.e., due to its capacity to *become conceptualized in the mind.* It is, then, something of a mystery why God does not become contingent because of His conceptualization in His own mind, at least. Ṣadrā, however, will assure us in Chapters I and II of Part II (pages 128 and 141 below) that essences and attributes in God's mind cannot be characterized by contingency since contingency is the mark only of limited essences; God's attributes, being unlimited and infinite, are as necessary as His existence.

A somewhat older Indian contemporary of Ṣadrā—a sworn critic of Ibn 'Arabī—Aḥmad Sirhindī, when faced with the same problem of contingency, had refused to accept Ibn 'Arabī's doctrine that God's attributes were the materials from which the contingent world was created and endowed with existence. Sirhindī held that while God's attributes are real and are identical with His Existence, the essences of the contingents are the very opposites or negations of these attributes: God has being, life, knowledge, power; the essence of a contingent is characterized by non-being, non-life, ignorance, and impotence. But God then redeems the contingent through His positive attributes by casting their shadows upon the former. It is obvious, however, that Ṣadrā would never accept the principle of moral dualism introduced by Sirhindī.[48]

Indeed, we must not imagine that Ṣadrā's investing God's mind with essences is fortuitous or that he blindly or mechanically follows Ibn 'Arabī in this respect. It is, I think, a consequence of a central theme of Ṣadrā's philosophy, a theme which may be said to be the main purpose of his whole philosophic system, viz., the doctrine which he calls the "special doctrine of God's Unity (*al-tauḥīd al-khāṣṣī*)." This doctrine states in sum—as has been indicated in Chapter I of this Part and as we shall elaborate further in our discussion of God in Chapter I of Part II of this book—that, in the realm of diversity and multiplicity, a real unity exists while, conversely, in the realm of absolute unity, multiplicity exists in an "eminent," "ideal," or "simple" manner. This is the doctrine of unity-in-diversity and diversity-in-unity (*waḥda fi'l-kat͟hra wa'l-kat͟hra fi'l waḥda*). He condemns those materialist atheists who recognize only a disjointed multiplicity in nature and do not recognize the presence of one Existence-principle, one God in it, as we have seen in Chapter I of this Part; he also declares gravely erroneous the views of those mystics, who even in the realm of contingent multiplicity only see a unity and deny the existence of diversity, where every existent is, in fact, unique; [49] thirdly, he denounces those immanentist "ignorant sufis" who think that God exists only in His manifestations or modes—in multiplicity—and that He has no transcendental existence in Himself as absolute existent.[50] Finally, he sharply criticizes philosophers for holding that God is so transcendent that, in His pure and simple existence, there is no room for the world even in an "eminent" and simple manner. This is why he vigorously criticizes the philosophical doctrine of abstraction in all possible contexts, as we have seen in Chapters I and II of this part and shall elaborate in Part III (particularly Chapters II and IV) while dealing with his theory of knowledge. According to Ṣadrā, the higher does not "abstract from" or negate the lower forms of existence but absorbs, includes, and transcends them: they exist in it in a simple manner. That is why, while characterizing God, he enunciates the principle, "a simple being is [i.e., includes] all things (*basīṭ al-ḥaqīqa kull al-ashyā'*)." There is, therefore, no question but that God *includes and transcends* all things—mundane and supra-mundane. The tension that arises here is between his pronouncements on the utter inanity of essences and his investing God's mind with them. It is not without interest to note that *in this respect,* Ṣadrā's doctrine in effect amounts to the same as Sirhindī's.

NOTES

1. *Asfār,* I, 2, p. 213, lines 5 ff.

2. *Ibid.,* p. 220, line 13–p. 223, line 8.

3. *Ibid.,* p. 223, line 9–p. 225, line 3. Ṣadrā illustrates all the six categories from the phenomena of human actions, p. 225, lines 4 ff.

4. *Ibid.,* p. 225, lines 14–15; al-Ṭabāṭabā'ī's note on p. 223.

5. *Ibid.,* p. 225, lines 5 ff.; *ibid.,* p. 224, line 18–p. 225, line 3; p. 220, lines 5–10; p. 226, line 5–p. 229, line 7.

6. *Ibid.,* p. 214, lines 12 ff.

7. *Asfār,* I, 1, p. 80, lines 2 ff.

8. *Asfār,* I, 2, p. 216, lines 3 ff.

9. *Ibid.,* p. 216, line 19–p. 219, line 6.

10. For the discussion of essences and their being neutral to existence and non-existence, see note 2 of Chapter II above.

11. See the discussion, *ibid.,* p. 253, line 17–p. 259, line 20, particularly on this point, p. 257, lines 1–8.

12. *Ibid.,* p. 257, line 8; p. 253, lines 7–8.

13. *Ibid.,* p. 257, lines 9–16.

14. *Ibid.,* p. 255, last line–p. 256, end.

15. *Ibid.,* p. 251, line 7–p. 253, line 14.

16. *Ibid.,* p. 270, line 15–p. 271, line 15.

17. *Ibid.,* p. 268, lines 1 ff.

18. *Ibid.,* p. 263, lines 4 ff.; p. 273, lines 1–12; p. 281, line 8–p. 282, line 5; p. 272, lines 4–11.

19. *Ibid.,* p. 282, line 6–p. 285, line 9.

20. *Ibid.,* p. 224, lines 16 ff.; p. 216, lines 12 ff.; *Asfār* III, 1, p. 309, line 9–p. 310, line 3; p. 318, lines 13 ff.

21. *Ibid.,* p. 287, lines 4 ff.

22. *Ibid.,* p. 289, lines 16 ff.

23. *Ibid.,* p. 288, lines 4–6, lines 20 ff.; see also Chapter I above.

24. References in the three preceding notes.

25. *Ibid.,* p. 288, last line ff.

26. *Ibid.,* p. 290, lines 2–3.

27. *Ibid.,* p. 290, lines 13 ff.; see also Chapter II above, reference under note 15.

28. Cf. Chapter I above, note 9; *Asfār,* I, 2, p. 294, lines 8 ff. (quotation from Ibn 'Arabī).

29. *Ibid.,* p. 350, lines 12 ff.

30. *Ibid.,* p. 290, lines 8 ff.

31. *Ibid.,* p. 299, lines 8 ff.

32. *Ibid.,* p. 301, line 6–p. 303, line 3.

33. *Ibid.,* p. 308, lines 8 ff.

34. *Ibid.,* p. 357, lines 2 ff.

35. *Ibid.,* p. 328, line 1–p. 330, line 1; p. 331, line 6–p. 333, line 1; p. 340, lines 11 ff.; p. 357, lines 1 ff.

36. *Ibid.,* p. 328, lines 1 ff.

37. References in note 35 above.

38. Especially *ibid.,* p. 332, lines 3 ff.

39. Reference in note 34 above.

40. See the whole important discussion, *ibid.,* p. 312, line 4–p. 318, line 4, particularly p. 312, line 12–p. 313, line 4.

41. *Ibid.,* p. 313, line 5–p. 315, line 1.

42. *Ibid.,* p. 315, lines 2–18.

43. *Ibid.,* p. 315, lines 19 ff.

44. In addition to numerous passages referred to before, see *ibid.,* p. 320, lines 1–11, and p. 339, line 7–p. 341, line 10.

45. See references in Chapters I, II, and the present chapter—this is, indeed, the most fixed point in Ṣadrā's thought.

46. Self-same reference as in the preceding reference.

47. *Ibid.,* p. 312, lines 1–5; and passages referred to in Chapters I, II above, and the present chapter. The trouble seems to arise from the concept "contingent" or "contingency." On the one hand, contingency is said to come to the contingent being from essences, since *all* existence is in itself one and necessary; on the other, essences-in-themselves cannot be said to be even contingent since they are mere "nothing." But the conjunction of essences with *particular* existents results in contingency.

48. See my *Selected Letters of Shaikh Aḥmad Sirhindī,* Karachi, 1968, *Introduction,* Chapter II.

49. See Section D of Chapter I above; on the reality of multiple contingents, see especially *Asfār,* I, 2, p. 318, lines 7 ff.

50. *Asfār,* I, 2, p. 345, lines 3 ff. and the important note 1 by Sabzawārī on the same page.

CHAPTER V

MOVEMENT, TIME, AND WORLD-ORDER

A. *Movement*

Ṣadrā's theory of movement is something novel in the history of Islamic thought and rests on the concept of a continuous structure of spatio-temporal events. Solid bodies are liquidated and analyzed into a factor of pure potentiality of movement called matter and an actualizing factor, called "physical form" or "bodily nature" which is continuously changing and giving rise to a continuum which is spatio-temporal in the sense that neither space nor time exists independently but both are integrated functions or aspects of this continuum of movement. Further, this movement is unidirectional and evolutionary, resulting in ever higher forms of existence until material existence reaches the stage where it rises beyond the realm of space-time: this movement is called "movement-in-substance" (*ḥaraka fī'l-jawhar*) where the very substance of bodies is subject to change as opposed to the merely qualitative change—i.e., in terms of size, shape, or other qualities—and where this latter form of change is reduced to the former. But before discussing these substantive points, the objective existence of movement *as a process* has to be established and this calls for a correction of certain statements emanating from Ibn Sīnā, the High Priest of Islamic Peripatetic philosophy.

Ibn Sīnā says that, with regard to movement, two ideas may be distinguished. One is the concept of movement as a continuity, i.e., the *passage* (*tadrīj*) of motion from one point to another or from the beginning to the end *as a whole*. This can exist only in the mind, since the mental picture conserves the various points that a moving body has traversed involving rise and decay of passage-instants and constructs these into a unified *present* whole. The second, which is actually observable in the external world, is an *unchanging, permanent* condition of the moving body, the condition, viz., of being *somewhere* between the beginning and the end. This second view does not involve the notion of change, since it merely sees the object at some space-point at a time-instant. The first view is called the passage (*qaṭ'*) view, the second the "medial (*tawassuṭ*)" view. According to Ibn Sīnā, it is the first, subjective, view which gives rise to the idea of time as an extension, since the observation is concerned only with time-instants.[1] But Ibn Sīnā refused to call time as an extension unreal or fictional, since its basis lay in our experience of the external world.[2]

Ṣadrā's teacher, Mīr Dāmād, criticized the view that movement as a process was subjective. He argued that if the idea of a *continuous process as a whole or a unity* is inconceivable, then it can exist as little in the mind as in the outside world. But that it is not only not inconceivable but can be actually experienced is shown by a body extended in space where its parts are continuous and yet the whole is also given. Just as in time, one part succeeds another, so does in space one part of a body succeed another. The idea of a gradually unfolding process is not antagonistic to its existence *as a whole* in time which is also an extended unity, although of course it cannot exist in a time-instant.[3] Ṣadrā accepts his master's view and gives several reasons why Ibn Sīnā's statements must be interpreted to accommodate the objectivity of movement as process, one of them being that the subjectivity view contradicts certain other statements of the philosopher.[4] It is surprising, however, that al-Sabzawārī in his commentary does not accept Ṣadrā's position and insists on the subjectivity of the passage-view of movement, although it appears to be cardinal for Ṣadrā's fundamental theory of "substantive movement," which al-Sabzawārī certainly accepts.[5] For, otherwise, it is not at all obvious how one can erect a theory of an objective space-time continuum. It is true, as we shall see, that for Ṣadrā and al-Sabzawārī, the essence of the world is change and newness, but it is this change and newness that, *as a process*, makes the continuum possible.

Traditional philosophy holds that movement, being a stable condition of flow (*ḥāla sayyāla*) which creates a continuous process *only* in the mind, needs a substrate to support it, this substrate being at once something stable and moving, i.e., being in a sense actual and in another sense potential since its actualization consists in movement. This view, of course, holds that movement occurs in accidents only, i.e., place, size, quality, etc. It follows also that movement, being confined to accidents, can never produce a difference in the essence or species of the moving body although, as we shall see, this movement does produce specific differences in the accident (e.g., black) in respect of which movement occurs *to* the substratum.[6]

However, Ṣadrā goes on to say, since motion means *moving* as a verb, i.e., a "continuous renewal and lapse (*al-tajaddud wa'l-inqiḍā'*)" of the parts of motion, it is impossible that its immediate cause should be something with a stable or enduring being. For, a stable or enduring entity will contain in itself the passing phases of movement *as a present fact,* and this togetherness of all passing phases would amount to stability, not movement. Movement, therefore, cannot be established on the basis of a stable entity. Such an entity can have a stable *essence,* but not a stable *being* which must consist simply in change and mutation. *There is, therefore, beneath the change of accidents, a more fundamental change, a change-in-substance*—thanks to ever-changing material forms—to which, in fact, all changes in accidents are finally traceable.[7] All bodies, be they celestial or material, are subject to this substantial change in their very being and this proves that the entire spatio-temporal world is temporally originated insofar as its existence is ever-renewed every moment.[8]

This view modifies the traditional in three respects. First, it can no longer be held that movement needs an enduring substratum unless we are talking about the static *essence* of the immediate cause of the movement, not of its real being, which must be renewed every moment. The essence is static because it yields the *concept* "that which constantly renews itself as the basis of material nature and causes movement in nature"; [9] or else we mean by movement accidental, not substantive movement.[10] Secondly, as we shall see shortly, even the substratum of the accidental movement cannot be a stable entity in the traditional sense, for, the substratum of accidents can now be conceived only as body in a general sense, i.e., as a species, not as a definite piece of body, as subjected to a constantly changing bodily or material nature or instant-form. Hence the "enduring" entity for accidents can be only the process or a part of the process viewed as a unity. But truly speaking, accidental change is itself traceable to substantive change, wherein nothing endures except change. For, in that change, movement and that which moves are identical.[11]

Thirdly, what has been called above "the immediate cause of movement," i.e., that which is self-moving and causes all accidental movements, is precisely the nature with which body or matter is endowed or, rather, it is the specific nature which is commonly held to create real species—heavens, man, animal, plant, mineral. It is this nature which is constantly subject to change and with it all accidents change as well. Traditional philosophy regards this nature as stable, but as a producer of change; and it is held that movement is either the result of nature (as when a stone falls) or constraint of nature (as when a stone is pushed up) or free volition. But it is obvious that all movement is finally due to nature for even in volition the body moves only because it has a nature. Further, Ibn Sīnā and other philosophers admit that nature does change in order to give rise to movement, but they insist that this change comes upon the nature of the body from the outside in terms of the renewal or emergence of the degrees of distance of the moving body in respect of its goal.[12] They also talk about a double series in movement, viz., the basic movement itself and the successive degrees of the body's approximation to the goal and assert that each of these two series, together with the stable nature of the body, gives rise to the other series. But this method of explaining motion and linking the moving with the stable is utterly insufficient, for the question is: how does the movement itself start? The two series and their interaction may be helpful in discovering or describing the *characteristics* of the movement but they cannot explain their own genesis, which must lie in the nature of the body itself. Hence the nature of the body must itself lie in motion.[13]

If nature is in constant flux and every moment we have a new body with a novel form, the question is: whence arises the idea of unity of a "thing" and the idea that a certain thing is, e.g., an animal or a plant. The answer is that in any given "thing" the constantly changing forms are so similar that we *imagine it* to be the same and subsume it under a stable, static concept, for example, man or plant. This is because concepts or essences are static and serve to describe certain properties which enable a certain set of them to be invested with "thingness", i.e., an enduring entity. It is only when the culmination of forms reaches a certain crucial stage, as e.g., plant, having exhausted its own potentialities, moves into the higher animal kingdom, that we realize that a change has occurred. Otherwise, this change is imperceptibly taking place all the time.[14] But man can experience this change within himself if he examines his own consciousness with sufficient subtlety and acuteness and can see that the absolutely changing is the absolutely stable and can visualize the possibility of his finally transcending this spatio-temporal realm and becoming a member of the divine order, since all this change is rooted in and manifestation of that order itself. Existence which is God Himself has a natural impulsion toward taking ever new forms.[15]

A "thing" for Ṣadrā is, therefore, a particular "structure of events," thanks to the continuity of movement and the similarity of infinitesimal forms which permit the subsumption of a particular event-system under a mental concept or essence. In reality, there is nothing but a flow of forms and since this flow is unidirectional and irreversible, each successive form "contains" all preceding forms and transcends them. The movement is from the more general and indeterminate toward the more definite and the more concrete: this process resembles the rise of ever more concrete species and individuals from the general and indeterminate being of genuses, thanks to the emeregnce of successive differentiae.[16] Ṣadrā explicitly rejects the atomism of Kalām-theology supported by al-Rāzī, because, by postulating movement by jerks or "jumps" (*ṭafra*)," this theory denies the reality of continuity and process.[17] Whereas in Kalām atomism, therefore, a "thing" is made up of discrete atoms, for Ṣadrā a "thing" is a particular segment of this continuous process regarded as a particular "event system" for purposes of description.

At this point emerges the importance to Ṣadrā's doctrine of the objective existence of movement as process which al-Sabzawārī does not accept. For Ṣadrā, an event-system, although it is a part of the process of reality, is not subjective and arbitrary: a "thing" is a real individual having a validity of its own, whereas for al-Sabzawārī, what is real is only the flow or movement of a ceaseless succession of rising and decaying forms, segments of which the *mind* somehow carves out for inspection and description, but this mental operation has really no validity,[18] although quite often al-Sabzawārī accepts the language of his master and calls a particular space-time extension a "real unity" and a "real individual." [19]

We now come to a more detailed consideration of how movement can be said to occur in the accidental categories of quality and quantity so that we may prove from this the existence of substantive movement or movement in the category of substance itself. A preliminary remark may be in order here. We have indicated earlier (and this will be elaborated here) that movement in accidents is, in the final analysis, linked with and consequent upon substantive movement. It is, therefore, as irreversible as the latter. But it is obvious that qualities not only increase but decrease: cold changes into hot and vice versa; black becomes white and vice versa. Yet Ṣadrā insists that all qualitative change is towards perfection and is unidirectional, like,[20] and indeed consequent upon, movement-in-substance. Ṣadrā himself appears to have left this point unexplained, but al-Sabzawārī thinks that while traditional philosophers hold that accidents are not really "changed into" but simply "replace" each other, a consequence of Ṣadrā's doctrine is that they "change into" one another. But along with this change, which is purely external and bidirectional, there is an inner, "essential" change in qualities which is unidirectional.

The first point to note is that in the case of motion in accidents, the substratum of movement is not the accidental categories themselves but the substance itself: when "black" increases in intensity, it is not the case that "blackness increases" but that "the body increases in blackness." This view held by the philosophers is correct and indicates that the substance itself changes *in respect of blackness*. For, if the subject of increase were blackness itself, then either the original blackness still remains or does not remain. If it does not survive, then obviously it cannot be the subject either and another, new blackness has arisen. If it remains intact, then no increase, no movement has taken place in it. But if it remains and a quantum of new blackness has been added to it, then a new addition from the outside, as it were, has occurred and the original blackness has still not changed. This shows that when blackness increases, a new black comes into existence which the original black has changed into, and it is the substance itself which moves from one grade of blackness to another. That is why the philosophers hold that in qualitative change an infinite series or species of, for example, black arises, each replacing the other in succession but that this infinity is potential, i.e., infinitely divisible by the mind. The philosophers, therefore, assert that, in its intensification in blackness, it is not the case that the body has two blacks, the original and the additional, but an entirely new species of black.[21]

On this account, if the question is asked: What constitutes continuity in view of the fact that nothing original of the quality remains but there are only ever new species arising?, the answer is that the substratum continues and also continues to change. This picture is certainly different from that of the Kalām atomism which does not allow any continuity. But this philosophical doctrine has also to be further modified since it does not make for the qualitative change *as a process* inasmuch as nothing original in terms of black quality is allowed to remain. Let us imagine that a point, for example, the head of a cone, races over a surface. In this case, there is a single point that persists throughout the time of motion and there are other points, i.e., those on the surface with each of which the former becomes successively identified. In the example of the intensification of blackness, therefore, we must suppose that there is an original blackness which identifies itself with points of ever-increasing blackness and gives them a kind of unity. The unity may be weak since, as we have said before, the original is like an indeterminate genus and concreteness belongs progressively to the emergent species which alone possess existential reality, but it is enough to enable the whole to be subsumed under the concept or essence "black".[22] It follows from this that the substratum of qualitative change—in this case, of black—is not just body but body with *some* degree of black.

This conclusion is important for clarifying the problem of quantitative change, since a great amount of difficulty has been experienced with regard to it. The reason is that when a certain quantity increases (or decreases), the original quantity is no more in existence and when the quantity is destroyed, that which is quantified, i.e., body, is also destroyed. For this reason, al-Suhrawardī and his followers denied movement in the category of quantity altogether.[23] Ibn Sīnā also experienced difficulty in quantitative change in organic bodies, particularly in animals and plants, because he thought no persisting factor could be located in these bodies. Ṣadrā quotes a lengthy passage from Ibn Sīnā where he mentions many successive alternative possibilities, but rejects them all and ends in a prayer that God may bestow a satisfactory solution upon someone who persists in his thinking endeavor, and with the admonition that one must not despair of finding an answer.[24]

Ṣadrā offers two solutions for these two difficulties, one felt by al-Suhrawardī with regard to inorganic quantities and the other felt by Ibn Sīnā (whom he will criticize again on this point below in Part III, Chapter I, note 28) about the unity of organic body in plants and animals. His solution to the first difficulty on the analogy of the quality of blackness is that the substratum of quantitative change is matter plus *some* quantity, not a definite quantity [25] or, in other words, matter clothed in bodily form. For, continuity or extension, i.e., the capacity for dimensions, is the differentia of body as such and with it body *as species* comes to be constituted. This is called "natural body (*al-jism al-ṭabī'ī*)" as distinguished from "mathematical body (*al-jism al-ta'līmī*)" for which definite dimensions are necessary. Now, the substratum of substantive change and all qualitative and quantitative change, according to Ṣadrā, is the former—a bodily form—plus *some* quantity and quality, but not a definite quantity and quality, for with a definite quantity and quality, the body will become "mathematical." [26] This "some quantity and quality" is that quantity and quality which is the "common factor (*qadar mushtarak*)" in the successive phases of change and persists through them.[27] What makes this assumption necessary is *the fact of the continuity of the process* which, as we have seen, integrates and bestows unity upon the phenomenon of movement. If there were no continued unity of the process, it would be correct to assume that nothing of the original black or original quantity remained in the substratum. The real substratum is, therefore, the continuity of the process itself. Those things which are subject to change and continuous replacement in this process are the definite quantities and qualities (as opposed to quantity-in-general and quality-in-general which do not change) which we have described earlier as the potential infinity of qualitative and quantitative species between the beginning and the end of the movement.[28]

To recapitulate, from the complexity of our philosopher's statements, the following points seem to emerge clearly. All movement is essentially evolutionary and undirectional. All movement has the effect of producing an individual process—entity whose unity is assured by a substratum and an indeterminate quantity or quality which behaves, vis-à-vis the progressively emerging infinity of determinate quantities and qualities, as a genus does vis-à-vis concrete species. The substratum is something nebulous (matter or bodily nature); the persisting unity is something indeterminate like a genus; the infinity of emergent species within the movement is concrete but only potential in the sense that they are mentally divisible *ad infinitum*, but the resulting unity is objective and strong, a unity of the process-entity or the event-structure as an existential individual.[29] For grasping the full significance of these conclusions we must await Sadrā's doctrine of substantive movement, and the following solution of Ibn Sīnā's problem will hold a definite clue to that doctrine which rests squarely on Ṣadrā's theory of existence.

Of course, the answer given above to al-Suhrawardī would also hold good for Ibn Sīnā since the required persisting substratum is only body-in-general (*jism muṭlaq*), not a body in particular. This is as true of organic matter in plants as of inorganic matter.[30] But Ibn Sīnā's tribulations are due to the fact that he did not fully realize that, in the scale of evolution, every higher differentia contains the lower ones as its potentiality or matter, and is itself equivalent to concrete existence. In our discussion of essence in the second chapter of this first part of the book, we have established the differentia-existence equivalence. Therefore, in a plant, body behaves as matter and "is capable of growth and decay" as differentia. So long as the differentia remains, the being of the plant will remain intact and any changes in its body or matter-principle will not affect it. Thus, with growth or diminution of the body, the body-individual i.e., the *definite* quantity of the body will be destroyed, but the differentia "capable of growth and decay" will remain intact since the differentia has ensured that *some* body will remain as its part. So is the case with animal vis-à-vis plant: as long as the animal differentia, viz., "capable of perception and locomotion," remains, animal will remain intact despite a thousand changes in its body. The existential identity of all higher forms of existence is ensured by their respective differentiae.[31]

It may be noted that the language in which Ṣadrā has formulated this last point appears confused and even contradicts his answer to the first point. We recall that he had said there that the unity of movement in quantity and quality is, in part at least, due to the persistence of the body-in-general and/or quantity or quality-in-general. But now: "capable of growth is the plant's differentia whereby its being is perfected, since its perfection (i.e., concrete existence) is not due to its being a body alone which is only its principle of potentiality. Hence, there is no doubt that the change of bodily entities cannot cause change in the substantial being of the plant itself *since body is taken in it only as body-in-general. . . .* Thus it [the plant], *insofar as it is a natural body-in-general is destroyed as an entity,* but insofar as it is a body capable of growth, is not destroyed, either itself or even its part for its part is nothing, but *body-in-general.*"[32] Yet, there is no confusion or contradiction if we take the body-in-general and the quantity or quality-in-general spoken of in the first point (as we have, indeed, done) in the sense of *genus,* while we regard the body-in-general in the first two cases in the present passage as meaning the *matter-principle* (as, indeed, we have done in the preceding paragraph), and we take the same expression in its third occurrence in this passage as, again, meaning genus. The context makes it very clear, but the expressions are highly confusing. Such instances abound in Ṣadrā but only occasionally become as acute as this. It is clear that where body-in-general is said to persist and give unity it must mean genus because genus is an inalienable part of differentia; but where it is said to be alienable without affecting the differentia, it must mean matter as principle of potentiality; for when the potentiality is actualized, it dies or, if it is an existent in itself, as, for example, body vis-à-vis plant, its fate becomes indifferent to that of which it has been the potentiality but which is now actual—the higher differentia. (For the difference between genus and matter, see Chapter II above on Essence.)

The fact that, in evolutionary movement, both change and identity are preserved by the emerging differentia which is equivalent to existence, shows that, in the final analysis, substratum-form account is not important for Ṣadrā but essence-existence account. This is because substratum-form account is not sufficient in explaining evolution or change in terms of emergence. It is true that in all change there is some kind of "enduring" substratum but this condition can be satisfied with a body or matter which may become individuated by *some* form, not any definite form. The philosophers themselves admit that in a change where one form or nature is succeeded by an entirely different one, as, for example, when water becomes air, the identity of the primary matter is preserved by *some* form, not a definite form. If this is the case with primary matter which is pure potentiality, a general-bodily-form can *a fortiori* be preserved because it is already actual and not pure potentiality.[33] But in order to explain evolutionary change, we have to cast the story of movement not in substratum-form terms but in terms of the principle of existence which, as we know by now, is characterized by "systematic ambiguity (*tashkīk*)," which means a progressive unfolding of existence at ever different levels and which, therefore, permits ever-emergent newness with the retention of identity. For existence, as we recall from Chapter I of this Part, is that principle "which by virtue of being self-same becomes different." Let us resume the story of movement in black color.

As we have seen, the Peripatetic philosophers held that when black color intensifies, it is still a continued unity from the beginning to the end, but at every moment during its movement it is different in the sense that it is capable of yielding a different form to the mind, even though, as we have seen, these forms may appear indistinct in normal material objects due to the close similarity of forms and, therefore, a material object appears identically the same. We have also seen that these forms are potentially infinite. From this, two conclusions follow. First, that existence is the primordial or objective reality while forms or essences are subjective, i.e., they appear only in the mind. For, if essence should be regarded as the objective reality and existence something arising in the mind, as later philosophers from al-Suhrawardī onwards have held, then the infinity of forms or essences would have to be an actual infinity, not merely a potential one, which is impossible since a structured infinite can never be actual. Secondly, because an infinity of progressive forms or essences can be yielded by this existent, viz., black body in the mind, it follows that this existence is in perpetual movement towards its goal and, despite its unity, has an infinity of individuals (*afrād*) succeeding one another, not as atomic and discrete events but as a continuous process.[34] As we have seen before, unity-in-process can be verified by our own conscious history as an individual and by sinking into our own selves where consciousness reveals a constant stream or flow of existence and proves that each one of us is one individual, yet never the same individual at any two moments. Ṣadrā also quotes an author, whom he does not name, to this effect.

That the human body is in constant flux from embryo to old age is an old idea and Van den Bergh has cited some very interesting passages on the point from Plutarch and Seneca.[35] Ibn Sīnā used this flux of the body to prove the non-materiality of the soul which explains abiding human identity throughout and despite physical change. Al-Ghazālī and Ibn Rushd both reject this argument on the ground that even in plants and animals this identity remains despite the fact that they are in constant flux.[36] Ṣadrā differs from this view in two important respects. First, according to him, the entire human being, i.e., both body and mind are in flux, not just the body. Indeed, the example he has explicitly given is of the flow of consciousness, not of the change in the body. Secondly, the flux does not mean simple change but a developmental change where the moving entity progressively realizes perfection until, as we shall see in Chapter V of Part III on eschatology, both soul and body attain an eternal existence.

This is precisely what is meant by Ṣadrā's doctrine of "continuous movement (*ḥarakat al-ittiṣāl*)" where both identity and change are present and are guaranteed by the principle of existence which by itself manifests itself in ever-changing forms and yet remains the same. In the case of black we may say that, in intensification, existence of the black object continuously seeks to perfect itself, by passing through ever new and progressive manifestations of black. Hence, says Ṣadrā, "persistent existence is absolutely identical with changing existence and is also absolutely identical with each of its (infinite) instant-manifestations. . . . Therefore, if we say that it (i.e., black existence) is one, we will be right; if we say it is many, we are equally right. If we say that it persists identically from the very beginning of change to the end, we shall be speaking the truth; if we say every moment it is a new emergent (*ḥādith kulla ḥīn*), this will be equally true." [37]

The same argument from change-in-unity which applies to accidental categories must also apply to the category of substance and it must be conceded that existence moves from one essence to another while retaining its identity. Just as, that is to say, a substratum passes through infinite accidental forms (color, quantity, etc.), so must it be admitted to pass through an infinity of *essential* forms (mineral, plant, animal, man).[38] Ibn Sīnā accepted movement in accidental qualities but rejected movement in substance. His argument is that an essence, as opposed to an accident, is incapable of being "more or less"; a black may become more black or less black but man cannot become more of man or less of man, for man is just man, neither more nor less. This is why whereas accidents accept change, an essence can only be replaced by another essence, for example, essence of plant cannot become more of plant or less of plant but can be replaced either by form of animal or of inorganic matter. If a substance were capable of increase and decrease, then, while it increases or decreases, either the species remains the same or not. If the species remains the same, then there has been no change in the substance but only in its accidents; but if the species changes, then a new substance has arisen and the earlier one has been destroyed. Thus between every two substances, there will be an actual infinity of specific substances, which is impossible. Hence there can be no change in substance at all.[39]

"This argument," says Ṣadrā, "rests on dogmatism and fallacious thinking rooted in a confusion between essence and existence and between the potential and the actual. If in the statement: 'either its species persists during intensification' by 'persistence of species' is meant its *existence,* then we choose that it does persist because existence as a gradually unfolding process has a unity and its intensification means its progressive perfection. But if the question is whether the same specific essence which could be abstracted (by the mind) from it previously still continues to exist—then we choose to say that it does not remain any longer. But from this it does not follow that an entirely new substance, i.e., existence, has arisen; it only means that a new essential characteristic (or specific form) has been acquired by it (i.e., by existence . . .). That is to say, this substance either has been perfected or has retrogressed (the latter, however, does not actually happen) in the two modes of existence and hence its essential characteristics have been transmuted. This does not mean that an *actual* infinity of species has arisen (just as it did not mean in the case of black that an *actual* infinity of black colors had arisen); it only means that there is a single, *continuous,* individual existence characterized by a *potential* infinity of middle points in accordance with the supposed time-instants in the duration of its (moving) existence. . . . *There is no difference between the qualitative intensification called 'change' and the quantitative intensification called 'growth'* [*on the one hand*] *and the substantive intensification called 'emergence (takawwun)'* [*on the other*] *in that each one of them is a gradual perfection, i.e., a movement towards the actuality of* [*a new*] *mode of existence. . . .* The claim that the first two are possible and the third is not possible is pure dogmatism without any proof, since the objective reality in everything is existence while essence is merely secondary or derivative as we have recurrently pointed out." [40]

It should be pointed out that there is a considerable ambiguity of expression in Ṣadrā as to what is persistent and what is subject to change in movement: is it existence or essence? Sometimes he says that essence or form remains stable while existence moves to a higher degree of reality and actuality,[41] while at other times we are told—as in the preceding quotation—that existence remains stable while essences change. This has been noticed by al-Sabzawārī. Yet, as this commentator explains, the ambiguity is more in expression than in fact.[42] As for existence, since it is the only primordial and objective reality, it remains the same and God, being absolute existence, possesses absolute identity as well. But in contingent existents, although existence still remains the same, it yet becomes a *mode* of existence, i.e., it becomes confined to an essence *in the mind*. This modal existence (called the Breath of the Merciful in the preceding chapter), by passing through different and successive modes or phases, moves towards the absolute existence, viz., God. In each mode it is, therefore, different, yet the same, and this is what the principle of "systematic ambiguity" means. Essences are not systematically ambiguous, but each essence, concept, or meaning is what it is and is, therefore, static, incapable of change. But in each different mode of existence, a different complex of existential reality plus a subjective essence emerges and at each moment a modal existent yields a different form or essence to the mind. Hence one essence is continuously being replaced by another, thanks to ever-emerging modes of existence, which constitute the existential continuum. Essences can, therefore, be said to be stable *because they are static*. But there is also another more or less Pickwickean sense in which an essence is said to be stable. When, in a given object, the change in essence is imperceptible or infinitesimal, the broad range of form or essence remains *apparently* the same as a common factor between the beginning and the end of movement within that object which continues to be subsumed under a stable concept, for example, a stone, a plant, or an animal, etc.

Ṣadrā seeks to derive his evidence par excellence for substantive movement from the statements of phiolsophers themselves regarding the movement of the heavens. The heavens, according to Ibn Sīnā and others, move eternally because their souls create a continuous succession of ideas or images which necessitate the occupation, by the body of the heavens, of successive positions, and, thus, each idea-position complex is succeeded by a new idea-position complex *ad infinitum*. Two conclusions follow from this view. First, that ideas or forms in the souls of the heavenly body are subject to continuous change precisely in the manner we have defined substantive change, viz., the continuous and infinite rise of forms or essences in a body. Secondly, it follows that positions (with other characteristics) define the very mode of existence of a body: they are either identical with this mode of existence or flow from it necessarily—just as, for example, heat flows necessarily from fire. This being the case, a change in position and in other qualitative and quantitative characteristics of a body is necessarily indicative of substantive change, i.e., change in the very mode of existence of a body. Heavenly bodies are, therefore, subject to substantive flow and change as much as any other body and cannot be eternal as philosophers have held them to be.[43]

A crucial difficulty in this philosophical account, which Ṣadrā exploits to his own advantage, is that the occupation of successive positions by the heavenly bodies during their ceaseless revolutions is declared by the philosophers to be "natural" since heavenly bodies are free from constraint, contrary to sub-lunar bodies which, when they occupy their natural position, do not move away from it except under constraint. Now, says Ṣadrā, if this is the case with the heavenly bodies, this is clear proof that the very nature or substance of the heavenly body consists in ceaseless change, which is nothing other than movement-in-substance. Ibn Sīnā and his followers do not, however, accept this consequence and say that the heavenly body only requires a position-in-general, not particularly this or that position, and that particular positions only arise because the nature or species of movement cannot be preserved except through particular positions. But this is not correct because in the philosophers' own view the purpose of nature is not to produce something general—or universal—but an existential particular. That is why in their discussion of categories, they say that the primary substance is a particular existent and that universals are only secondary substances. It is, therefore, not correct to say that the heavens move in order to seek a position-in-general. Also, the reality in everything is not essence or a universal—which is only subjective—but particular existence. The fact and nature of the ceaseless revolution of the heavens, therefore, prove the existence of substantive change in them.[44] But if the substance of the heavens is fluid and unstable, how much more so will be the nature of other bodies?

It is clear from this account that, since the image-position complex of the heavens is in perpetual flux, both the body and the soul of the heavens is subject to change and that the unchanging and eternal part of the heavens is only the Intelligence which ultimately moves the soul-body complex. Indeed, all souls, insofar as they are souls, i.e., have contact with the body, are subject to substantive movement, according to Ṣadrā. But if this is the case, a crucial difficulty arises for Ṣadrā as well, who, as we shall see later in Part III, Chapter III (Section B), and Chapter V of this work, also affirms that the imagination of the heavens is the repository of stable, unchanging images called "The World of Symbols or Images ('Ālam al-Mithāl)," argues at length against Ibn Sīnā to prove that an image is non-material and holds that even undeveloped human souls which have not passed from imagination to pure intellect as well as animal souls are non-material and hence survive the death of the material body.[45] It is true that Ṣadrā says there that images are not in a material body but in a symbolic or pneumatic body which has no spatial location and is not liable to material flux, but then the images in the heavenly souls should not be subject to flux either. In sum, the theory of substantive change in the heavenly bodies and souls, upon which Ṣadrā builds their temporal emergence and denies their eternity, is in conflict with his doctrine of the World of Images.

To resume our account of the substantive movement of the heavens: since the body of the highest heaven is subject to change, it follows that that body and its revolution is not the creator of time, as the Aristotelians hold, since it is itself within time. With Plotinus, therefore, Ṣadrā holds that time is created by the Universal Soul or the soul of the highest heaven. This world-soul, according to Ṣadrā, has two aspects: by its intellect-oriented aspect, the soul creates time as a unity, while by its body-oriented aspect, it creates time as a succession. Plotinus, however, rejected the Aristotelian idea that time is the measure of movement and affirmed, on the contrary, that movement is the measure of time.[46] Ṣadrā parts company here with both Aristotle and Plotinus and regards time as the measure of movement—not of the external movement or revolution of the heavenly body which, as we have just said, is in time itself but of the fluid physical nature or *substantive movement* of the heavenly body. Precisely in what manner time is the measure of this substantive movement, we shall see in the following section. But it should be noted here that, whereas for Plato the body of the heavens is kept intact by the soul although in itself it is liable to flux just as any other body, for Aristotle that body is in itself unchanging and stable in nature—made as it is of a fifth element called ether—and hence does not need a soul to keep it together. For Plotinus, again, the incorruptible and stable nature of the body of the heavens is due both to the perfect nature of that body and to the nature of the soul that created it. Muslim philosophers, as usual, combine Aristotle with Plotinus (as Plotinus had combined Aristotle with Plato) and admit both that the constitution of the heavenly body is of a fifth element and that the heavenly bodies are ensouled. Ṣadrā absolutely rejects the idea of the indestructability of the heavenly body which, for him, has the same fluid nature as the earthly bodies and affirms that even its soul—insofar as it is soul—is liable to this flux and the whole is kept by the transcendental Intelligence.

It will be objected against me, says Ṣadrā, that I am guilty of deviation from tradition in recommending that substance itself moves and is unstable, while, according to philosophic tradition only movement and time have that nature. It is true, he says, that an intelligent person does not deviate from tradition if he can help it, but there are strong reasons in this case to break with tradition or what is held to be tradition.[47] Now, the sharp distinction between essence and existence has led to the establishment of substantive change and whereas the very essence of time and movement consists in change and renewal, in the case of natural forms, their essence is static but their existence is in perpetual flux. Just as in the case of white there are three distinct factors to be taken into account, viz., becoming white, whiteness, and that which becomes white, the first denoting the process or movement, the second that *whereby* a thing becomes white, and the third that which becomes white, so with regard to substantive movement there are three things or factors. The first is the fact of movement itself, the second that whereby or in respect of which there is movement, viz., bodily nature or natural forms, and the third that which so moves and that, as we have indicated, is matter.

Nor is it true to say, Ṣadrā continues, that "no sage before me has talked about change in substance. For the First Sage who has made statements to this effect is God Himself, who tells us in the Qur'ān: 'When you see the mountains, you think they are stable but they are [in fact] fleeting just like clouds'; [48] 'These people [Muḥammad's opponents] are in doubt about [Our] renewed Creation'; [49] '[The day] when the earth shall be changed into non-earth'; [50] 'We shall change your likenesses and cause you to be re-created into what you do not know,' " [51] etc., etc. Ṣadrā here quotes a host of similar verses of the Qur'ān and understands them in the light of his own doctrine. Elsewhere also he illustrates the constant renewal and continuous change of all modes of existence by the famous Qur'ānic verse, " 'He [God] is every day in a new mode'." [52] It is to be noted that the modern Indo-Pakistani Muslim philosopher, Muḥammad Iqbāl (d. 1938), who also taught the philosophy of dynamism and creative change in terms of vitalistic thought, quoted the last-mentioned Qur'ānic verse in his *Reconstruction of Religious Thought in Islam*.[53] It would be worthwhile to find out whether, and if so, how far, Iqbāl was influenced by Ṣadrā's thought which he had studied for his doctoral dissertation.[54]

B. *Time*

Ṣadrā rejects the view that time is an independent, self-subsistent entity. In view of his doctrine of substantive movement, he defines time, not as measure of movement as Aristotelians do, but as "measure of [physical] nature in as much as it [moves and] renews by itself." Time, therefore, far from being an independent existent "in" which events occur, as in a container, is part of this process. It is an extension or dimension (*imtidād*) of physical nature, just like other three spatial dimensions.[55] "Time is related to the physical nature (or form) in respect of its time-dimension just as spatial magnitude is related to the bodily nature (or form) in respect of its space-dimension." [56] Whoever reflects a little on the nature of time knows that it has no reality except in the observer's mind. It is not a quality which externally characterizes body like black and white but arises only through mental analysis. Since it does not exist externally, it cannot be described as "arising" or "passing," attributes which characterize physical nature itself, thanks to its perpetual, substantive movement. It is, therefore, odd that Peripatetic philosophers have attributed these qualities to it, as though it were an independent existent.[57] Indeed, just as spatial magnitude has no indepedendent existence apart from a body, so does time have no independent existence apart from it: The measure and the measured are the same.[58]

What Ṣadrā is concerned to show in these statements is: (1) that just as all body or "physical nature" has a spatial magnitude, so it has an inherent time-dimension, thanks to substantive movement, and that time does not attach itself to it "from the outside"; (2) that since this movement is continuous, the entire physical field is a spatio-temporal continuum; and (3) that this continuum is an evolutionary process which has, as its goal, the attainment of a level of divine existence which is free from change and mutation, and hence beyond time. Al-Ṭabāṭabā'ī, Ṣadrā's modern commentator, suggests on the basis of this interesting language, that we have here a form of the theory of relativity of time and that for Ṣadrā time is a "fourth dimension." [59] Ṣadrā does not actually say that time is relative, although the idea that everything has an inherent and unique movement-time factor, in conjunction with Ṣadrā's doctrine of *tashkīk* or relativity of being, may be manipulated to yield some such inference.

The absolute standard of time is the movement of the outermost heaven—the movement, that is, in the substance of that heaven which produces the visible circular motion in terms of endlessly successive positions. As we have seen towards the end of the previous section, the Intellect (being the Divine Logos) is the creator of time, while the soul-body complex of the heaven is its primary recipient, for time is an inherent function of a body, and the soul, insofar as it is attached to the body, is also like a physical form. Since, as we have also seen above, time itself does not change or arise or pass—being a subjective entity—it is called "eternity (*sarmad*)" when related to God or Intellect, "perpetuity (*dahr*)" when it is related to heavens and "time (*zamān*)" when it is related to things that come into existence and pass out of existence. It is, however, obvious that it is not quite consistent on Ṣadrā's part to locate the standard of time in the outermost heaven, for substantive movement is not a peculiarity of the heavens but of *all* physical nature and this substantive movement is not intermittent but continuous.

Time, as a subjective analytical factor, is eternal and has no beginning, just as substantive movement is eternal and without a beginning. As for God and the Intelligence, they are beyond successive or serial time. All other beings, including souls, are within time since they are subject to substantive movement. Time is eternal because whatever is conceived to be "before" time necessarily turns out to be in time, since "before" in this context must involve time. The very temporality of time, therefore, involves the eternity of time.[60] Time, in this respect, is different from space, according to Ṣadrā, since the "limitedness" of space does not involve space beyond space. Of course, "beyond space" can exist as an image or an idea in the mind, but this does not mean real space; with regard to time, however, the mere idea of a "time before time" involves real time because the reality of time is only in the mind, as we have said.[61] There is something queer about this argumentation: although the idea of time arises only through a mental analysis, nevertheless, time is a function of substantive movement which is not subjective but real. It would, therefore, follow from this account that the eternity of (substantive) movement is *inferred* from the impossibility of conceiving a time before time. Otherwise, there is no difficulty in conceiving a beginning for movement, for we can conceive that the world-movement *starts after it was not there* since there is no *a priori* reason or rational necessity for the beginninglessness of movement.

Although the notion of time arises from a mental analysis, yet its status is different from that of an essence which also arises from a mental analysis of a concrete existent into essence and existence. Whereas essences are "nothing positive" by themselves, time is something positive and has a "peculiar existence" [62] of its own, and, of course, has an essence as well. It is on the basis of this distinction between the essence and existence of time that Ṣadrā seeks to solve the difficulty that time is something merely relational (*muḍāf*). What is relational is the essence or concept of time which is "a non-stable and continuous extension or quality." Hence the *concept* of time is relational. But the *existence* of time i.e., every point of time, is an existential fact or reality and is not relational, i.e., its reality is not exhausted by relationality.[63] When Ṣadrā says that time is "not an objective reality," he, therefore, means that it is neither an independently existent reality nor yet like physical qualities as black, round, etc. But it is a reality in the sense that it "measures movement" and its reality is no more or less than the reality of movement *as measured*. But since "measured" adds nothing to the reality of movement, time is, in that sense, not real, i.e., non-existential: it is only something that is calculated just as space-dimensions are no more than calculations.[64] It is because of this that movement—which is real, and time—which is not real, are said to have similar characteristics. Just as we distinguished at the beginning of the preceding section two aspects of movement, viz., its passage from one point to another (*tawassuṭ*) and its continuity (*ittiṣāl*), so, in the case of time, a "flowing moment (*ān sayyāl*)" which "persists through" may be distinguished from time as a continuity (*zamān muttaṣil*).[65] But we must not attribute to time—a mere measure of movement—existential characteristics of movement, viz., "arising (*ḥudūth*)" and "passing away (*'adam*)" because that which arises and passes away is movement or, strictly speaking, physical reality.

On the controversy between theologians and philosophers over the question of the eternity of time and the world, Ṣadrā recounts several arguments of the theologians against eternity and refutes them. Whereas his refutations are essentially borrowed from al-Suhrawardī almost verbatim, his positive solution of the problem rests squarely on his doctrine of the substantive movement which allows him to say, on the one hand, that the world as a process is eternal and, on the other, that the world is temporally originated in the sense that everything in it is changing continuously in its substance and hence cannot last even for two moments, let alone be eternal. Among the specific arguments against eternity is one which says that an infinity in the past, which is actual, is impossible. Ṣadrā's reply, which is taken from al-Suhrawardī[66] but which comes originally from Ibn Rushd's reply to al-Ghazālī,[67] is that in things which exist successively and not together or simultaneously, there is no harm in infinity because there is no existing whole. The trouble with this reply seems to be that the past, being actual, does exist in some sense. But a more serious objection against eternity, Ṣadrā's second, is that if an infinite past has to be traversed in order to reach the present, the present will be impossible since an infinity can never be traversed. Ṣadrā's reply, again borrowed from al-Suhrawardī, is that if the present were dependent upon an "unrealized infinite," it would be impossible but since the past is realized, the present is possible. It is obvious that, besides there being a contradiction in the term "realized infinite," this reply also contradicts Ṣadrā's reply to the first objection, for that reply consisted essentially in the assertion that the past is *not* actual or realized.

On the whole, the entire defense of Ṣadrā of the eternity of time seems to me very weak. However, in his discussion of the last and eighth objection of the theologians, he gives a good account of the real weakness of the theologians' stand and then brings his own doctrine of substantive change into play. This famous theological objection is formulated as follows: "The world is never free from temporal emergents, but that which is never free from temporal emergents is itself a temporal emergent. Therefore the world is temporally originated." Ṣadrā criticizes the phrase, "that which is never free from temporal emergents," saying that if it refers to the totality of emergents, this is fallacious because the "totality" has no existence over and above the individual items." [68] It is, indeed, difficult for most theologians to precisely formulate the point at issue and hence they become confused. For when a theologian says that the "world is originated" and is asked what he means by "originated," he does not know what to answer. For if he says that "originated" means "it is not self-sufficient but depends upon God," he finds that his opponent agrees precisely with this. But if he says he means "it was preceded by time," he finds that he himself does not believe this, since for him, as well as for the philosopher, time cannot be preceded either by time or by mere nothing. And both hold that only God precedes the world and time, this "precedence" not being temporal but essential or logical. The dispute, then, turns out to be verbal, unless the theologian comes out with some statement which says that the world depends *not only* upon God's being but, say, upon His Will as well—in which case he becomes guilty of a form of polytheism.[69]

The essential point here is that even the theologian cannot hold that time is originated, i.e., that there was time before time. This is correct, for even al-Ghazālī had taught that time is generated and originated but that there was no time before time even though he held that there could be an empty time when there was no world.[70] But, surely, this is admission of the "eternity" of time—which is, in any case, a tautology—and if time can be "eternal" in this sense, why not the world? It is obvious, however, that "eternity" in this context is not equivalent to "infinity" in the past but simply means "co-extensive with time." And the crux of the matter between Muslim theologians and philosophers is not eternity in this sense but the question of infinity in the past, i.e., the beginninglessness of the world. It is strange, however, that, in this context of infinity of time, Ṣadrā accepts the existence of an infinite number of souls, which he had emphatically denied in his discussion of the finitude of the causal series and had accused the philosophers of holding this view.[71]

Ṣadrā then seeks to vindicate the theological preposition, "the world is [temporally] originated" on the basis of his own doctrine of substantive movement. Since everything moves in its very substance and nothing remains the same for two moments, everything, i.e. every event, is a temporal emergent. The world is, therefore, a temporal emergent (although the entire process is without beginning and without end). The conclusion is, of course, based on the further premise that a "whole" like this has a reality over and above its parts. This, in turn, is vindicated by his principle that continuity (*ittiṣāl*) bestows a *real* unity upon a thing and that a "thing", although it is structured by an infinity of spatio-temporal events, is, nevertheless, one. Still, it is difficult to see, why the world, since its movement is continuous, cannot be regarded as unoriginated more especially because the process is not and cannot be a finished product since it is infinite at both ends.

In this context, Ṣadrā also reinterprets John Philoponus' famous argument for the creation of the world from the finitude of the potentialities of all bodies. Al-Suhrawardī had criticized this argument by saying that although the world by itself may be finite in its power of existence, nevertheless, since God is its cause, He may cause it to exist forever so that its eternity of existence is borrowed continuously from its Cause and is not inherent in it. Ṣadrā comments that this is possible only in the sense that every moment a new power comes into existence in a body and this entails that every physical reality undergoes movement in its substance and then declares, "This is the view that the world [continually] comes into existence and passes away, i.e., that every individual [event] in it is preceded by a temporal non-existence—a temporal non-existence which is an eternal fact. And this is the real intent of those [who hold that the world is created and] who belong to one of the three religions—Judaism, Christianity, and Islam." [72] It is obvious, however, that John Philoponus, who did not believe in substantive movement, simply intended to prove that the world is finite in its existence, i.e., just as it was created in the beginning, it will be necessarily destroyed at the end.

C. *World-Order*

The perennial problem of classical philosophy has been to explain diversity and change in terms of a unitary, unchanging principle and to establish an intelligible relationship between the two or, in other words, between necessity and contingency. Plato found this explanation in the two aspects of the world soul, the "Same" and the "Different," in his *Timaeus* and in the "Realm of Ideas" and the "Realm of Material Nature." Aristotle explained this link in the relationship between an unmoved Mover and the world of matter mediated by the perpetual circular motion of the heaven. According to the Muslim Peripatetics, this mediation is made possible by the fact that the circular motion of the heaven, being eternal, is related in this aspect of eternity to God or the Active Intelligence, on the one hand, and, being movement and change, is related, in this respect, to the temporal world of change, as the latter's cause. In its aspect of eternity, this circular motion does not need a further temporally originated cause because movement and change is its *very essence,* and something whose essence is movement does not require a temporal mover but only an unmoved mover.[73]

Since, however, the heaven—the substratum of this eternal movement—is eternal according to the philosophers in both its body and soul, Ṣadrā, who believes that the heaven itself is subject to perpetual substantive mutation, rejects the account given above of the movement of the heaven and its mediation between the changing and the changeless: the perpetual change of positions of the heavenly body is only an outward symptom or effect of its inner, substantive instability and constant mutation.[74] Ṣadrā then gives his own explanation of the origin of continuous and eternal movement in terms of the substantive change of all physical nature. This physical nature, whose eternal and unchanging idea—the Platonic Paradigm—exists in the mind of God, is such that, *when it exists,* it necessarily exists as subject to change and evolutionary mutation. Change, therefore, is not a characteristic of the *essence* of physical nature, i.e., its idea or concept, but of its existence.[75] Most things, when they are transformed into concepts or essences, shed their existential characteristics: for example, physical quantity and volume have extension in existential reality but their concept is not extended. But in the case of existence itself, as we have shown in the first chapter of this Part, its nature can never be captured by the mind and formed into a concept; hence existence is a unique fact which has no real essence. Now, all physical nature, at the existential level, is a constant flow which cannot be captured by the mind: it can be known only through a direct intuition.[76]

At this point, it may be objected that there must be some recipient of this constantly changing physical nature and these successive bodily forms, since it is not possible to conceive that these forms exist by themselves without a substratum. But if that is so, then Ṣadrā's denial of a permanently identical body, for example, to the heaven stands nullified by the acceptance of a permanent, indeed, eternal matter which is the substratum of successive forms. This question is, in fact, about the identity of the substratum of change which Ṣadrā has already dealt with in the first section of the present chapter and he more or less repeats the same solution here. Since matter is in itself pure potentiality and has no numerical unity—i.e., an existential identity—but only a generic unity, it can be actualized by *any given* form, not by any special, permanent or eternal form. So, at any given point of the flow of existence, the form actually obtaining is the form which actualizes the potentiality of matter: it is not the case that matter first stands actualized by a specially privileged form and *then* other forms supervene upon it successively so that matter must be regarded as eternal. It is, of course, true that successive forms supervene upon earlier ones, and it is their cumulative process which constitutes evolution; but the essential thesis is that *at each point* the *present* form actualizes matter. When animal comes into existence, animal attributes are not *additional* to, say, the attributes of plant but the form of animal *yields* both the attributes of plant and animal. But there is no discontinuity in the succession of forms, which is a continuous, single process. This process, therefore, does not involve the existence of an identical, eternal matter as substratum, although at each point the emergent form has a substratum.[77]

Indeed, as al-Ṭabāṭabā'ī luminously interprets Ṣadrā here,[78] the concept of matter is really needed as bearer of the potentiality which precedes the actual existence of a thing, but this is only with reference to essences or specific forms, or, rather, since the preceding matter is always conjoined with a certain form, the bearer of the potentiality of a thing is the preceding form. Hence there is no matter free from a form, which may be characterized as bearing the potentiality of a thing; or, in other words, there is no free matter at all. But at the level of existence, as opposed to essences or specific forms, an "underlying" matter is not really needed at all, for the meaning of "being material" is simply to be resolved into "process of change." All we have is a continuous spatio-temporal process of forms, which the mind can artificially divide into segments called essences.

Ṣadrā, therefore, says that the question as to why a certain form (or a certain event) occurs at a particular time is to be answered, not on the basis of a continuing, underlying matter which bears its preceding potentiality, but on the basis of the internal structure of the process itself.[79] Every spatio-temporal occurrence is, therefore, *sui generis*. Just as one cannot ask why today is today and not yesterday or tomorrow, since every point of time is *sui generis*, this is also the case with any given point within the world-process; and time is, in fact, something which arises by an analysis (*taḥlīl*) of this process. This process itself is also self-explanatory and does not require an outside temporal cause to explain it.[80] In other words, what the philosophers say about the eternity of the movement of the heavenly body, Ṣadrā says about the eternity of the world-process. To be a process, a continuous succession of forms is the very nature of physical existence. God certainly made or produced the world but he did not cause the world to change or be a process; to change and to be an eternal process is the very nature of the world. We, again, have a case here of "simple causation (*ja'l basīṭ*)", not of "compound causation (*ja'l murakkab*)."

In another sense, of course, there is a *reason*—although not a *cause*—for the world-process. This reason is to be found in the fact that every form of existence in the world "loves" and "yearns for" the higher and wants to be like it and, therefore, *moves* towards it. It is this primordial yearning that makes for a cosmos, i.e., the universe as an orderly whole. Ibn Sīnā had found it diffiicult to affirm that primary matter was capable of such a love and yearning and had characterized this view as talk of Sufis rather than a philosophic argument. He gave as his reasons that a psychic yearning can never be attributed to matter and that so far as a physical propulsion is concerned, that also must be excluded from matter: primary matter, being never devoid of a form, cannot have a yearning for a form and primary matter, being a pure passivity, has forms come upon it from the outside so that matter itself has no movement.[81] This, despite the fact that Ibn Sīnā himself wrote a special treatise on cosmic love where he affirmed that primary matter possesses love.[82]

In order to prove this primordial yearning, Ṣadrā urges the following argument.[83] Primary Matter, although it is a pure potentiality, nevertheless is not mere nothing, since a potentiality is something positive. Matter, therefore, is endowed with some kind of positive being and hence shares some kind of existence. Now, existence is fundamentally the same in all existents although it differs in all existents as well, being systematically ambiguous in terms of "more or less." Since wherever existence is to be found, the consequences or essential attributes—knowledge, power, will—must also be found in varying degrees of intensity, we must attribute some kind of consciousness to matter, hower potential and nebulous. Granted this nebulous consciousness and the *fact* that matter is capable of receiving an infinity of forms in succession, we must conclude that matter has a yearning for forms. As for the intensity of this yearning, although the nebulousness of consciousness of matter argues for a weak degree of yearning, the fact that it is possible for it to receive an infinity of forms, argues for an intense yearning since the intensity of yearning depends not only on the degree of consciousness of the yearner but equally on the degree of the perfection of the object of yearning. Matter, therefore, is characterized by the *greatest* intensity of yearning for the higher in the entire existence since it is the most deficient in all existence.

Ṣadrā corroborates this argument by another derived from a consideration of the idea of contingency or possibility itself.[84] Since contingency or possibility belongs to the very nature of Intelligences—which, as we have seen, are the content of God's mind and His Attributes—everything that flows from them is contingent, this contingency being intensified in proportion to the degree a being is removed from the source of existence, God. Now, the essential or pure possibility or contingency (*imkān dhātī*) which characterizes Intelligences comes to assume the character of the possibility in the sense of potentiality (*imkān isti'dādī*) in matter. All potentiality and its actualization, therefore, are due to the nature of matter which seeks ever higher forms at different levels of existence in the physical world—inorganic matter, plants, animals, and man, including both the body and the soul in the case of the latter two. This upward movement is inconceivable without an innate yearning on the part of matter. It is because yearning is a characteristic of matter that, for example, images, which do not have matter but are pure extension, do not have potentialities to be realized and do not change.[85]

This yearning, then, satisfies itself in two directions. In the vertical direction, matter, after progressively attaining different levels of being, allows material forms to reach a point where they enter the Divine Realm in the form of the Perfect Man who has perfected his moral and intellective powers. He becomes, in a sense, one with the Intelligences or the Attributes of God. These Intelligences themselves have little to attain by way of perfection since all their perfections are already realized, for, as Divine Attributes, they are united with God's existence. They do not, therefore, "yearn" for anything higher except that when they contemplate their own proper being, they are overcome by the negative self-feeling arising from their innate contingency which—as opposed to the pure and authentic existence of God—is non-being, darkness, and imperfection which characterize all essences and are then lost in the contemplation of God's being itself.[86] But all other beings are subject to a genuine yearning simply because their nature needs to be perfected.

In the second, horizontal direction, matter goes through an infinity of successive forms. This direction is characterized by infinity in the sense that it has neither a beginning nor an end. But this does not mean that the endless series is purposeless. As we have seen in our discussion on causation, the endless series has as its purpose that those forms or species which cannot be perpetuated as such should be perpetuated in individual manifestations; each succeeding individual behaving, as it were, as the purpose of the preceding.[87] If matter did not have this kind of potentiality and inherent impulsion for change, it would always be with the same form which would, therefore, be eternal. God, therefore, bestows new forms upon it every moment, since God's creative impulse is ceaseless.[88] Since the temporal series is endless, it is obvious that the "other life" or the "hereafter" cannot take place in this horizontal direction. It is the vertical order which means "hereafter" in the proper sense, although the common man and the theologian conceive of the after-life "after" the end of time![89] This motivation to establish an after-life in some sense certainly plays an important role in Ṣadrā's distinction between the horizontal and the vertical orders of reality. Certain basic currents in the preceding Muslim philosophic and mystic thought—from Ibn Sīnā to Ibn 'Arabī—have undoubtedly facilitated this distinction, which is not really congruent with the idea of evolutionary process *in time,* which Ṣadrā at other times and in a more fundamental sense formulates and expounds.

NOTES

1. *Asfār,* I, 3, p. 31, line 6–p. 32, line 8.
2. *Ibid.,* p. 32, lines 9–15.
3. *Ibid.,* p. 27, lines 23 ff.
4. *Ibid.,* p. 32, line 17 till the end of the chapter, particularly p. 34, lines 2–9.
5. *Ibid.,* p. 32, note 2; p. 33, note 1.
6. See below, notes 12, 21, 22.
7. *Ibid.,* p. 61, lines 7 ff.
8. *Ibid.,* p. 62, lines 5–6.
9. *Ibid.,* p. 62, lines 6–9.
10. *Ibid.,* p. 62, lines 9–10.
11. *Ibid.,* p. 63, lines 5 ff.
12. *Ibid.,* p. 64, line 8–p. 65, line 15.
13. *Ibid.,* p. 65, line 16–p. 66, line 12.
14. *Ibid.,* p. 64, lines 1–4 and note 1 on the same page by al-Ṭabāṭabā'ī; p. 125, lines 15 ff. See the whole chapter beginning on p. 80, particularly p. 83, lines 8 ff., and note 1 on p. 87.
15. *Ibid.,* p. 84, lines 14–18; p. 82, line 19–p. 83, line 5; *ibid.,* Chapter 21, pp. 68–69.
16. See above Chapter II, notes 34, 40, 41, and the references in the preceding note (n. 15).
17. *Ibid.,* p. 64, lines 1–4; p. 8, lines 12 ff.; p. 73, lines 12 ff.; p. 10, lines 19 ff. According to recurrent statements of Ṣadrā, the continuity of movement exists thanks to the "bodily nature" or "physical form" which is continuously changing and receiving new forms every moment.
18. For example, *ibid.,* p. 83, lines 8 ff.
19. For example, his note on p. 83, note 2 on p. 82, and note 1 on p. 84; cf. al-Ṭabāṭabā'ī's note on p. 61.
20. *Ibid.,* p. 80, last line ff. and note 2 (pp. 80–81) by al-Sabzawārī; note 1 by al-Ṭabāṭabā'ī on p. 81; also his note 2 on p. 62.
21. *Ibid.,* p. 81, lines 3 ff.
22. *Ibid.,* p. 82, lines 8 ff.

23. *Ibid.*, p. 89, lines 2 ff. and the important note 3 on the same page by al-Sabzawārī.

24. *Ibid.*, p. 90, line 1–p. 92, line 9.

25. *Ibid.*, p. 92, line 10–p. 93, line 8.

26. *Ibid.*, p. 96, lines 6 ff.

27. *Ibid.*, reference in the preceding note, particularly p. 96, line 9–p. 97, line 5.

28. See above, reference in note 22; *ibid.*, p. 97, lines 5 ff.

29. See references in the preceding note. Ṣadrā then declares, "Movement is like an individual whose soul is natural or bodily form (*al-ṭabīʿa*), just as time is an individual whose soul is eternity (*dahr*)," *ibid.*, p. 97, lines 15–16.

30. References in note 25 above.

31. *Ibid.*, p. 93, line 11–p. 95, line 8; also see the discussion on *differentia* in Chapter II above.

32. *Ibid.*, p. 94, lines 4–12.

33. *Ibid.*, p. 88, line 3–p. 89, line 2; see also *ibid.*, p. 136, lines 1 ff.

34. *Ibid.*, p. 83, lines 12 ff.

35. Van den Bergh, *op. cit.*, Vol. II, note 4 on p. 353 of the text.

36. *Ibid.*, Vol. I, p. 353, line 25–p. 354, line 10.

37. *Asfār*, I, 3, p. 84, lines 11–15.

38. *Ibid.*, p. 85, lines 7–11; p. 88, line 6–p. 89, line 2.

39. *Ibid.*, p. 85, line 12–p. 86, line 1.

40. *Ibid.*, p. 86, line 2–p. 87, line 1; also *ibid.*, p. 105, line 8–p. 107, line 15.

41. *Ibid.*, see pp. 82 and 86, for example, but this looseness of expression is common.

42. See al-Sabzawārī's note 1, *ibid.*, p. 86.

43. *Ibid.*, p. 118, line 6–p. 121, line 1.

44. *Ibid.*, p. 121, line 2–p. 122, line 11.

45. See Part III below, Chapter I, III, and V on the nature of the soul, on Imagination and Eschatology.

46. *Ibid.*, p. 117, lines 1–12; p. 122, lines 11 ff.; for Plotinus on Time, see *Enn.*, VII, 7–13, particularly VII, 7 and 9.

47. *Asfār*, I, 3, p. 108, line 3–p. 109, line 1.

48. *Ibid.*, p. 109, 2–111, 7; this verse occurs in *Qur'ān*, XXVII, 88.

49. *Qur'ān*, I, 15.

50. *Qur'ān*, XIV, 48.

51. *Qur'ān*, LVI, 61.

52. For example, *Asfār*, I, 3, p. 116, line 14; I, 2, p. 314, lines 9–10 (*Qurʿān*, LV, 29).

53. Lahore, 1962, p. 142, line 2. To establish change, however, Iqbāl re-

lies heavily on the frequent Qur'ānic verse concerning the succession of day and night (see *ibid.*, pp. 14–16).

54. Cf. Muḥammad Iqbāl, *Development of Metaphysics in Persia;* this work, however, shows little trace of any serious study of Ṣadrā and the most important of Ṣadrā's thought for Iqbāl is the identity of subject and object. Iqbāl is not even aware of Ṣadrā's doctrine of existence.

55. *Ibid.*, p. 140, lines 4–5 and 6–7.

56. *Ibid.*, p. 141, lines 1–3.

57. *Ibid.*, p. 141, lines 3–11.

58. *Ibid.*, p. 147, lines 3–4.

59. *Ibid.*, note 1 on p. 14.

60. *Ibid.*, p. 124, lines 11 ff.; also p. 148, lines 5 ff., where Aristotle is referred to as having said that whoever believes in the temporal origination of time, unwittingly accepts the eternity of time.

61. *Ibid.*, p. 149, line 5–p. 150, line 5.

62. *Ibid.*, p. 151, lines 11 ff.

63. *Ibid.*, p. 151, lines 19 ff. For Ṣadrā this is equally true of movement and the physical nature which is inherently characterized by movement: *ibid.*, p. 131, lines 5 ff.; indeed, for Ṣadrā, all three are existentially the same. Of the three the "really existential" is the physical nature which, since it is in perpetual change, gives rise to movement which, in turn, is measured by time, movement being "more real" or "less unreal" than time.

64. See above notes 55 and 56; also al-Suhrawārdī's statement referred to *ibid.*, p. 141, lines 12–14 that movement *as measured is* time.

65. *Ibid.*, p. 173, lines 10 ff. This is the second of the two meanings of "moment" (*ān*), i.e., that which "produces time." For the other meaning of *ān* or "now" which is produced by time and as to whether it is real or not, see the discussion on p. 166, lines 10 ff. See also above, note 57.

66. See above, Chapter III, p. 14.

67. See above, Chapter III, note 30. Ṣadrā does not restate here the arguments for and against the infinity of a causal chain given in Chapter III above, the reason being that the present infinity is the temporal or "horizontal" infinity which Ṣadrā with his predecessors, particularly al-Suhrawardī, distinguishes from the causal or "vertical infinity." Whereas he disallows the latter, he defends the former. We have pointed out above in Chapter III, however, that the two cannot be really separated.

68. *Asfār,* I, 3, p. 158, line 9 ff., particularly p. 159, lines 7 ff.

69. *Ibid.*, p. 160, line 4–p. 162, line 2.

70. Van den Bergh, *op. cit.*, Vol. I, p. 38, lines 4 ff.; *ibid.*, p. 19, line 7.

71. See Chapter III above, note 18.

72. *Asfār,* I, 3, p. 164, last line–p. 166, line 3 (quotation, p. 166, lines 1–3).

73. *Ibid.*, p. 128, line 3–p. 129, line 2.

74. *Ibid.*, p. 131, lines 2 ff.; also note 43 and 44 in this chapter.
75. See above, note 63 in this chapter.
76. *Asfār,* I, 3, p. 132, line 9–p. 133, line 14, and al-Ṭabāṭabā'ī's note 3 on p. 135.
77. *Ibid.*, p. 133, line 15–p. 138, line 11; also p. 84, lines 1 ff. and al-Ṭabāṭabā'ī's note 1 on the same page.
78. See al-Ṭabāṭabā'ī's references in the preceding notes; also his important note 2 on p. 69.
79. *Asfār,* I, 3, p. 138, lines 12–15.
80. *Ibid.*, p. 139, lines 13 ff.; p. 151, lines 12 ff.
81. *Asfār,* I, 2, chapter beginning on p. 232; Ibn Sīnā's text, p. 233, lines 14 ff.
82. *Ibid.*, p. 245, line 8—reference to Ibn Sīnā's *Risāla fī'l-'ishq.*
83. *Ibid.*, p. 239, lines 1 ff.
84. *Ibid.*, p. 237, lines 17 ff.
85. *Ibid.*, p. 240, lines 7 ff. and al-Sabzawārī's important corresponding note.
86. *Ibid.*, p. 243, lines 21 ff.; see also note 84 above.
87. *Ibid.*, p. 244, lines 8 ff.; p. 265, line 5–p. 267, line 14.
88. *Ibid.*, p. 243, lines 1–11; *Asfār,* I, 3, p. 149, lines 1–2.
89. Cf. below Part III, Chapter V, Section B.

PART II

Theology

CHAPTER I
GOD'S NATURE

A. *Proof of God's Existence*

Ṣadrā states that proofs given traditionally for God's existence are many, since "ways to God are multiple"; yet all these proofs are limited in their value, for they seek to prove God by something other than God. Now God, being the Ground of all else, cannot strictly be "proved" by all else, but is Himself the proof for all else. God has to be His own proof, or else He cannot be literally "proved." We shall first state Ṣadrā's own proof and then pass on to his criticism of other proofs given by philosophers, theologians, and physicists or natural philosophers.

We have seen in the early chapters of Part I that Existence is the only reality. Hence existence and reality are commensurate and identical. Existence is that unique and all-comprehensive reality outside of which there is nothing. Even essences which in themselves are negative, acquire some sort of semi-reality by being "sucked into" existence. Existence as such, being positive, powerful, titanic in its grasp, is therefore incapable of being negated or denied. Al-Ṭabāṭabā'ī, Ṣadrā's contemporary commentator, rightly points out that if reality were to be altogether denied, this denial would itself have to offer itself as reality and assume existential nature.[1] Therefore, existence, by definition, cannot be negated. It should be borne in mind, first, that we are not talking here of existence as a concept (*mafhūm*) but of being or reality as such. Secondly, as al-Sabzawārī points out, we are not talking of a particular being or existent but of existence as an open nature or reality (*ṭabī'a mursala*). Now this open reality which is existence *is* God in its absolute and "simple" form. God is not, therefore, *to be searched for* beyond the realm of existence but is rather *to be found* in it as its absolute ground: "God is His own Witness," as the Qur'ān puts it.[2]

This proof is, of course, based on the principle of *tashkīk* or systematic ambiguity of existence. We recall from Chapter I of Part I that existence, while being one, is also many. Further, existence does not have two aspects, one by virtue of which it is one and the other by virtue of which it is many, but is one simple reality which *by virtue of its being one is many.* Only existence has this characteristic basically, which is also shared by movement and time derivatively, but the latter are, in a sense, not real. Now, many people deny, since it is difficult for them to conceive, something that is intrinsically and in the same breath one and many, perfect and imperfect, absolute and relative. The trouble is that these people conceive of existence as an essence, i.e., as a concept which uniformly and unequivocally applies to all members of a class or species, e.g., every man is man, no less and no more. But essences are, in their very nature, different from existence. Essences are strictly definable, existence is not; essences are, therefore, divisive of reality into classes and categories like man, animal, plant, substance, accident, etc., while existence unites and holds all these in its simple and all-inclusive grasp and is yet capable of differences. Its contents are the same, yet, by virtue of being the same, diverse—so diverse, in fact, that each entity is unique. The unity of all existents, therefore, is a different kind of unity from that given by essences and so is the case of difference.[3]

Al-Suhrawardī from whom Ṣadrā adopted the idea of a hierarchical order of being, i.e., the idea of "perfect and imperfect" or "more and less" and, by adding to it his principle of substantive movement, constructed his peculiar concept of *tashkīk,* had also answered this question on similar lines. But for the Illuminationist philosopher, only essence was real, not existence, which he declared to be a purely mental abstraction. Within a single essence, al-Suhrawardī had endeavored to find differences; indeed, for him, a man can be more of a man or less of a man. Ṣadrā criticizes him for this, since an essence as such is incapable of such differentiation, being static and closed. Only existence is not static and closed; it moves incessantly and is always open. It is because of this that only existence is capable of *tashkīk* or systematic ambiguity: it is universal, yet unique in each instance. Hence existence can never become a real universal like an essence.[4] Let us now turn to Ṣadrā's criticism of other proofs of God's existence.

The best and most important of these arguments is that based on contingency and the causation of the contingent by the Necessary Being, employed by Ibn Sīnā and other philosophers after him. Ṣadrā discusses and criticizes it at length. The other two arguments, that of the theologians based on temporal causation or origination and that of the natural philosophers based on movement are, in a sense, special forms of the philosophical argument. But these two arguments, while they suffer from the limitations of the philosophical argument, are liable to an additional objection which is fatal. This is because, by treating causation horizontally and not vertically, as does the philosophical argument, they cannot prove that the world-series had a temporal beginning. But Ṣadrā restates them on the basis of his doctrine of substantive movement so that temporal change is interpreted as substantive change and, in fact, Ṣadrā himself has principally used this argument to prove that the world is not eternal, because at no two moments is it the same.[5]

The argument from contingency states that a contingent existent cannot exist by itself—since contingency means "hanging in the balance between existence and non-existence"—and, therefore, needs a cause which should tilt this balance towards existence. But this series of causes cannot regress *ad infinitum* and so we must reach a cause which exists by itself and does not need another cause. Ṣadrā has two criticisms to make of this argument. The first is that it does not proceed from and is not based upon existence as reality but existence as a concept (*mafhūm*): The concept "existence" is inspected and analyzed into two kinds, viz., contingent and necessary. Ṣadrā has launched this attack on the philosophers in different contexts. In his criticism of their logical division of essences, as we have seen in Chapter I of Part I, they are accused of holding that an essence is either necessary-by-itself or possible-by-itself or impossible-by-itself, and that that which is necessary-by-itself is God. But then the philosophers discover that neither God has an essence, nor can an essence require its own existence.[6]

Ṣadrā's second and more basic criticism is that the causal argument simply brings in God to terminate the infinite regress and that, therefore, the value of this argument to prove God's existence is inferential and indirect at best. Starting from the contingent, they find it necessary to come to *some* necessary being which *may* be God! Thus, God, who is the Cause and Ground of all things, becomes, in this argument, their effect or consequence. In order to avoid recourse to an infinite causal regress, some philosophers say that their argument does not necessarily assume a contingent but *some being:* if this being is necessary, well and good, if it is contingent, then the argument from regress applies. But this simply means that there is some being, either necessary or contingent, and this is far from proving the existence of God. Or, they say that part of the concept of existence is necessary existence and hence when we have said "existence," we have implied necessary existence, or God. These people also have to admit that they are not talking about God, the most real existent, but about *some* necessary being, and that this argument (like Descartes' ontological argument, where a transition is also required from the concept to reality) is at best only inferential: whereas in actuality, God implies the world, in this argument the world implies God, and that too in a somewhat dubious manner, since to talk of *some* necessary being is hardly to talk of God.[7]

Al-Suhrawardī attempted to reformulate this argument so as to avoid the idea of an infinite regress. His reformulation states that all contingents, taken together, whether finite or infinite, can be treated as a single contingent. Now, this contingent-as-a-whole can either be self-caused or caused by one of its parts or caused from the outside. Since the first two alternatives are impossible, the third, viz., its causation from the outside—by the Necessary Being—is established. Ṣadrā rejects this argument on the ground that a "whole" of this kind has no reality over and above its individual parts. The argument, therefore, cannot avoid involving infinite regress, as it seeks to do, and ends up by begging the question.[8] For a more detailed discussion of this point, viz., whether a series can be said to cause itself or can be caused by a part thereof and Ṣadrā's refutation of this argument, see his treatment of an infinity of a causal regress in Chapter III of Part I.

B. *God as Pure Existence*

Now that God's existence has been proved by the very nature of existence itself, it remains to be shown that God's nature is pure existence without there being any essence in it. It should be noted at the outset that Ṣadrā's statements on this point, as they appear in *Asfār* I and *Asfār* III, seem at first sight to be inconsistent. In his first treatment of the subject in *Asfār* I, Ṣadrā supports the common philosophic thesis that God cannot have an essence because this would introduce a duality into God's nature, which would mean that God's existence is caused by His essence and is hence contingent. In *Asfār* III, on the other hand, he rejects this argument as inadequate and seems to hold that some manner of essence—i.e., as a "subjective" or derivative idea (*mafhūm*) of divine Attributes—is not incompatible with God being Pure Existence. As we saw in the last section of Chapter IV of Part I, while discussing higher causation, Ṣadrā does contend, following Ibn 'Arabi, that God's Being cannot be denuded of Attributes altogether, even though these latter are to be regarded only as "subjective" and secondary or derivative, like all essences, (see pp. 87–90 above) except that divine Attributes are not contingent as are essences of created things. For contingency characterizes only finite and closed essences, while God's Attributes, being infinite and interpenetrating, cannot be strictly called essences and cannot be contingent (see p. 90 above).

This apparent contradiction in the treatment of this important subject is to be resolved, it seems, on the ground that in the earlier part Ṣadrā is taking essence as something real (as was done generally by philosophers before him) *and hence as co-ordinate with existence.* At this level of discussion, essence has to be rejected since it would endanger the necessity and originality of God's existence. In this earlier part, therefore, Ṣadrā's concern is to show the unreality of essence over against existence, which is the sole objective reality. Having done this, Ṣadrā proceeds in the latter part to reaffirm essence as divine Attributes with some sort of reality as ideas or mental entities (*mafāhīm*)and rejects the argument which was the stock-in-trade of the philosophers for a total denial of divine essence. We shall now follow Ṣadrā's analysis of the subject as he develops it.

There are several arguments to prove that God is pure existence without an additional essence, but the most important is the following. If God had an essence besides existence, His nature would be characterized by a duality. His existence, being an accident, would then be caused either by an outside factor or by His essence. It cannot be caused from the outside because God would then become contingent, and would cease to be necessary. But if His existence is caused by His essence, then two fatal difficulties follow. First, His existence would become an effect and hence would become contingent. Secondly, His essence would have to be assumed to exist (being cause) prior to its existence. Therefore, God must be simple and absolute existence without an essence.[9]

Fakhr al-Dīn al-Rāzī criticized this argument by asking why the essence *as such* cannot cause existence not by a prior existence, just as the essence of a triangle *as such*, e.g., causes certain properties, viz., the being of its angles equivalent to two right angles, and no existence is assumed on the part of triangle. God's existence would thus be a property necessitated by His essence. Ṣadrā quotes Ibn Sīnā and al-Ṭūsī in refutation of al-Rāzī's argument to the effect that existence can never be an effect of an essence or an idea but can only be the effect of an existent cause.[10] Ṣadrā elaborates [11] this by saying that if an essence as such could be the cause of existence, it could cause existence whether it itself existed or not: by being merely conceived it would entail existence. But this is surely not the case since, although an idea can entail another idea (as a triangle entails the sum total of its triangle being equal to two right angles), it cannot entail existence unless it itself existed; only an *existing* triangle can result in the sum total of its angles being equal to two right angles *as an existential reality*. Under no conditions, then, can an essence yield existence.

Or, shall we say that existence itself can be conceived as an essence, as an idea, without entailing real existence? God's essence, then, would be such that when it is conceived, it yields the *idea* of existence and when His essence actually exists His existence also becomes real and ceases to be a mere idea. This cannot be accepted, either. This is because the very idea of existence is impossible without real existence. The idea of existence differs in this respect fundamentally from all other ideas or essences, for no other idea implicates existence except the idea of existence itself. This is why the very idea of existence is said to be the primary and self-evident idea which resists any definition in terms of other ideas.

Indeed, the notion that essence can cause existence is absurd. This is because the relationship between these two, as has been shown in earlier discussions, is that of unity or existential identity, not of *union:* essence and existence are not two things or separate entities which somehow *come* together. Their relationship is that between something general and indeterminate (essence) and its concrete, determinate expression (existence) as is the case with the relationship between a genus and its concrete differentia. Now, far from the general and the vague being the cause of the concrete and the determinate, the truth is exactly the opposite: the differentia is the cause of the genus (i.e., of its concrete existence), existence of essence. But existence is its own cause; it is the original and sole content of reality. Essence is something subjective, mental and derivative and existence is its cause and sole ground. How could it be said, then, that God's essence causes His existence when this is not the case even with contingent beings? [12]

There are other arguments to prove that God has no essence besides His existence, two of them elaborated by al-Suhrawardī and accepted by Ṣadrā. One of these arguments states that since an essence is a universal, there could be potentially any number of necessary beings, even if actually its instance is only one. According to the second argument, God's essence, if He had one, would fall under the category of (secondary) substance and would, therefore, require a differentia which would make it concrete.[13]

But objections can be raised against God being pure existence as well. One objection, stated in various forms, is that if being pure existence is an inherent property of God, all existents, inasmuch as they are existent, should be likewise pure existence since God shares existence with all other beings. It is not proper to set one being apart from others so that it alone is pure and necessary being. The answer to this objection, in the Muslim Peripatetic view, is that God's nature, His existence, differs radically and entirely from all other existents since His existence is original and is the source of all derivative existence, whereas all other existents derive their existence from God's. This fact sets God's existence and its nature entirely apart from all other existents. On the formulation of the "Persian sages," the answer is that since existence is systematically ambiguous, admitting of "more or less" or "perfect and imperfect," God's existence represents its absolute form and below Him are ranged all contingent existents hierarchically. In this view, the existence of God and that of the contingents is basically one and unitary, yet each existent is unique and different and God's is the most perfect, the absolute existence. What God and the contingents share and share equally is the *concept* of existence which is a secondary idea or pure notion (although even this notion cannot be derived from contingents independently of God, who is their source and ground), but what is under discussion here is not the notion of existence but the particular existents (*afrād al-wujūd*), viz., God and particular contingents.[14]

The second serious objection states that if God is pure existence without an essence, then God should be knowable since existence is held to be the most self-evident idea. Yet God is also held to be unknowable. The most common reply is that what is universally and self-evidently known is the *notion* of being, a secondary intelligible, while what is unknowable is the particular being of God (as a *fard*). Ṣadrā's answer is different and is directly related to his proof of God on the basis of his principle of existence. That God's being-in-itself cannot be known through discursive reason is certain and this is why, we recall from the preceding section, Ṣadrā criticized the argument that seeks to bring in God merely in order to terminate the infinite regress of contingents. God cannot be known except through God. It is equally true that God cannot be known totally and exhaustively even by direct intuition, since God, being the source of all existents, cannot be fully "comprehended" by these latter. Yet a direct primordial knowledge of God must be affirmed for all existents "each according to its own measure." Just as God is at the base of all contingent existence, a direct "witnessing" of God must be at the root of all knowledge, whether conscious or unconscious. Indeed, when we know anything at all, and *in* our knowledge of anything at all, a knowledge of God must be inalienably present as the ground both of existence and knowledge. This is the meaning of the Qur'ānic verse that God "is nearer to man than the latter's jugular vein" and of the saying attributed to the Prophet, "If you were to be thrown down to the very bottom of the earth, you would fall upon God."

In this simple, primordial sense, then, everything witnesses God and proclaims the existence of its Maker. The question is, if existence is known directly and if God is nothing but existence, why not admit a full and total knowledge of God on the part of His witness and a complete union of the latter with the former? This is because everything else besides God is finite, determined, and determinate and, no matter how much it develops, it cannot transcend this finitude. It is true that in mystic experience the experient can lose sight of his finite self and fix his gaze entirely upon God and "be lost" in Him, but losing sight of his finitude is not the same as losing his finitude. A drop, as part of the ocean, may enjoy the ocean, but cannot cease to be a drop, as the Persian verses quoted by al-Sabzawārī on the point have it. It was this finitude and its inalienable otherness (or, was it, rather, its *consciousness?*) with which al-Ḥallāj was so impatient when he exclaimed:

Between You and me, my "I am" is in constant struggle with me;
Lift this "I am" from the middle by Your Grace!

On this interpretation of the mystic experience, Ṣadrā's view is close to that of al-Ghazālī and identical with that of his Indian contemporary Shaikh Aḥmad Sirhindī who declared the unity experienced by the mystic to be a unity of perception (*waḥdat al-shuhūd*) rather than unity of being (*waḥdat al-wujūd*). Yet, this immediate knowledge of God vouchsafed to everything in the universe and immune from error is not the basis of religious and moral obligation, says Ṣadrā. For that, a more conscious knowledge is required, which is, by its nature, liable to error, is capable of degree and qualitative differences, and *becomes* immune from error only in rare and exceptional cases which constitute the logical limit of the form of knowledge and where the truth is "revealed" to the human agent.[15]

Having come this far, i.e., (1) having started with the general philosophical position that essence is a reality coordinate with existence, (2) having then shown, with the philosophers, the impossibility of God's having such an essence and finally (3) having proved, contrary to the general philosophical position, that existence, not essence, is the sole reality, let us now review the original argument of the philosophers and criticize it in the light of our own conclusion. This is the task performed in *Safar* III in the renewed discussion on this subject. The philosophical argument was that if God were a composite of essence and existence, existence would be an additional attribute of the essence and thus essence would have to exist before it existed. But why should this be so if existence is the primitive and, indeed, the sole reality and essence a purely mental or derivative phenomenon? When even in the contingent being this is the case, why should it not be all the more true of God? Let us then say that in the contingent, existence is produced (*maj'ūl,* i.e., by God) primarily and directly, while essence is produced indirectly and derivatively; in God both his existence and essence are unproduced and original except that His essence is secondary to His existence.[16] And since the need for a cause arises only out of contingency, it is open to someone to say that the qualification of God's essence by His existence is not a contingent but a necessary fact. The proposition, "God's essence *requires* existence," would not, then, mean that there is an essence without existence which is now being added to essence, but would simply mean, "God's being or nature is such that it cannot be without the ascription of existence to it." [17]

Indeed, if the philosophers' argument is effective, it is so because they regard existence as a general, secondary notion and essence as primary reality. Thus, their statement, "existence is additional (to essence) in contingents, original and self-identical in God" means that a contingent is an essence such that "being existent" cannot be derived from it independently of God, while God is an essence such that "being existent" can be derived from it alone—where "being existent" simply means an essence qualified by a general notion of existence. This is clearly brought out, for example, in the statements of al-Dawwānī to the effect that existence, as a general notion, is equally additional both to God and to contingents except that in the case of the latter its attribution is made possible because of God, their source, while in the case of God, He Himself is the sufficient ground of such attribution.[18]

This shows that when these "latter-day philosophers" talk of the existence of God as self-identical reality, they are only using conventional language without there being any real substance to it: God's self-identity, His being pure existence is more a matter of courtesy with them than literal truth, for they do not recognize that corresponding to this general notion of existence, there is also a reality—indeed, *the* reality—which is existence itself. They believe that essence is *the* reality; only, when they come to God, they find it difficult to hold that God could be an essence to which existence is given as an extrinsic attribute like contingents, so they affirm that He is only existence, i.e., a general notion of existence! The conclusion may appear grotesque, yet it follows directly from their assumptions. Ṣadrā then formulates his own view in stark contrast to theirs. Far from existence being derived from the essences of the contingents, it is their essences that are derived from their various modes of existence which are unique. The proposition, "existence is additional in contingents, identical in God" does *not* mean that it is additional, i.e., extrinsic to the essences of contingents, intrinsic to God's, but means that in contingents it is not original but *produced* by God, while God's existence is original and primordial. So far as essence is concerned, it is derivative from existence in the contingents, i.e., the mind extracts a contingent's essence from its existence. This may well be, indeed must be, the case with regard to God also, since He has real Attributes which are not to be explained away either as mere relations or as negations as philosophers have done—although, so far as we humans are concerned, these Attributes are only a mental subjective notion, since God-in-Himself cannot be fully known by us.[19]

C. *God's Unity*

Unity of God is one of the most fundamental problems of metaphysics, yet most philosophers who are essentialists have failed to solve it since a proper solution can only be given on the basis of existentialism. Some philosophers, like al-Rāzī, have held that God is an essence such that only one being exists of its kind, i.e., God is a being whose existence is identical with its essence. This proof is inadequate, for, why cannot one imagine more than one being whose essence will entail its existence, as in the case of transcendental Intelligences? We, therefore, need another argument to prove God's uniqueness.[20] This argument can be stated as follows. Let us suppose two necessary beings. These beings would equally share the notion of necessary existence and would mutually differ with regard to their natures or essences. Now, if they differ in respect of the totality of their essence, then, necessary existence would become extrinsic to them, which is untenable. If they differ in a part of their essence, they would become composite and cease to be simple, since they would equally share a part of their essence, while they would differ in respect of the other part. Finally, the entirety of their mutual difference may lie outside their essence. This is, again, untenable, for in that case they would be in need of an outside factor for their existence, or else, they would be entirely identical with each other; they would cease to be two and will be numerically only one, which would contradict the assumption of their being two.[21]

But now a formidable difficulty arises in regard to this argument. It is pointed out that by their proposition, "Necessary existence is identical with the essence of the necessary being," philosophers mean that God's essence is such that it manifests *the property of* "being necessary of existence," not that necessary existence is the same as or literally identical with God's essence. Thus "necessary existence" being only a quality or attribute of God, is over and above His essence; hence two (or more) different beings may well share this attribute, while being totally different in their natures.[22] Thus, this argument cannot establish the unity of God. It should be noted that this was the first of the three alternatives given in the preceding paragraph, with a difference. There, "necessary existence" lay outside the essences of the two supposed beings; here, although it lies outside their essences, yet it is caused by those essences as a necessary *property*. For this reason, it has been said that, on this point, the philosophical argument suffers from a veiled fallacy born of a confusion between notion and reality. For, when they say, "God's existence is identical with His nature or being," they are talking or mean to talk about His proper, real being; but when they assert the same proposition while proving His unity, they are talking about a notion, i.e., that in the notion of God's unique being His existence is necessarily given. In the first case, they talk about the real existence of God, but cannot prove His uniqueness; in the second, they talk about His uniqueness, not about His real existence but only about a necessary relationship between two concepts.[23]

It is on the basis of essentialist doctrines concerning God and the world that the situation arose in Islamic philosophy, which made it possible for a philosopher Ibn Kammūna to formulate his notorious doubt about the unity of God: Why is it not possible that there be two (or more) simple beings of unknown nature, differing entirely in their natures or essences, such that each one of them will be a self-necessary existent, the concept "necessary existent" being extractable from each of them and applicable to them as a (necessary) accident or property; thus they will equally share this extracted notion but will differ from each other in the entirety of their essences? [24] Although this difficulty has become generally associated with the name of Ibn Kammūna, says Ṣadrā, it was actually formulated by al-Suhrawardī, summarily in his work *al-Talwiḥāt* but more explicitly in his *al-Muṭāraḥāt*. Ibn Kammūna also commented upon some of al-Suhrawardī's works, whom he followed in his belief that existence is a pure notion and essence is reality. Ibn Kammūna, indeed, states in one of his writings: "The arguments brought forth [by the philosophers—i.e., to prove God's uniqueness] tell against the possibility of more than one necessary being only if their essences are identical, but if their essences are different, one needs some further argument [to disprove a multiplicity of Gods]. However, I have not found one until now." [25]

This dilemma, in fact, arises for all those doctrines which do not assign primacy to existence but hold either that existence is something additional to essence or that existence is only a general mental notion having no counterpart in reality at all. On the former view, existence lies outside essence; in the latter, existence is something entirely notional, as al-Suhrawardī and his followers (including Ibn Kammūna) believe. Ṣadrā repeats his charge, mentioned in the preceding section, that these philosophers, when they talk about the particular, real being of God, are only using conventional philosophical language without any real meaning, since they do not admit that existence has actual particulars (*afrād*) in reality.[26] But on an existentialist basis, Ibn Kammūna's doubt has little force and can be refuted easily as follows. If two or more things do not have a common characteristic, no common proposition can be asserted of them at all. Now, if these two supposed beings are to share the characteristic of "necessary being," they must possess something in common which warrants this common attribute. The abstract general notion of existence can be correctly asserted of all things only because they all really exist; hence this abstract notion "existence" is of the nature of an abstract noun like "humanity" extracted from actual human beings. If these two beings possess an essence which is different from their necessary existence, then they must necessarily become composite and cease to be simple beings. But a composite nature can never be a necessary existent since at least one of the two factors will have to be caused or produced from the outside.[27]

There is, then, no sure proof of God's unity except on the basis of the reality—the sole reality—of existence, which has already served us as the only real proof of God's existence. This is because, on this basis, existence will not be a mere notion but will "stand for (*'unwān*)" the objective reality of existence. Existence as such, however, is unitary, unanlyzable, and indivisible, since its multiplicity arises through its "modes (*anḥā'*)," thanks to essences which are generated by existence itself in the realm of contingency. Existence, taken absolutely, therefore, cannot tolerate duality. For if we suppose another absolute existence, it will be absolutely identical with it —hence no duality is conceivable. That is why al-Suhrawardī declared that even if you were to suppose a second pure and absolute being, it will turn out to be no other than the first, since there can be no distinctions in something which is taken to be pure and absolute.[28]

In other words, "a simple existence must comprehend everything" in its simplicity, for if it did not, it would cease to be simple. This is the most telling reply to Ibn Kammūna's doubts about the unity of God. If one supposes another being besides the simple being, the former would either be included in the latter or would be identical with it.[29] The crux of this argument is that "necessary being" means "absolute being" and that "absolute being" *conceptually* cannot be but one being since "two absolute beings" is an absurd concept. If the question is raised that while it is admitted that an absolute being must necessarily be unique, what is the guarantee that such an absolute being does, in fact, exist?, the answer is that the factual existence of an absolute has been proved in the first section of the present chapter on the basis of the reality of existence.

Jalāl al-Dīn al-Dawwānī had also formulated a proof for the unity of God, which subsequently gained wide acceptance but which Ṣadrā makes the target of a scathing criticism. The starting point of this proof is that common language is but a poor guide for attaining philosophic truth. Common language uses, for example, expressions like *ḥaddād* (from *ḥadīd* = iron) and *mushammas* (from *shams* = sun). Since many derivative forms in common linguistic usage imply that the root-meaning subsists in the derivative forms (for example, the root-meaning *'ilm* = knowledge is held to subsist in the active participle *'ālim* = a person who possesses knowledge), this may suggest that iron subsists in *ḥaddād* and the sun subsists in *mushammas*. *Ḥaddād,* however, means "iron-monger," not a person in whom iron subsists; similarly, *mushammas* means "water heated by the sun," not something wherein the sun subsists. In other words, these two terms refer to a *relationship* of something to what the root means, and do not indicate that what the root means is subsistent in that something. In fact, iron and the sun are independent realities existing in their own right and are not like knowledge, which subsists in a knower. Now, the derivative term "existent (*maujūd*)" is to be construed in the same manner. Its root-meaning "existence (*wujūd*)" does not subsist in an "existent" but exists independently and absolutely, while an existent is *that which comes into relation with it* just as we have seen in the case of ironmonger and sun-heated water. Pure existence itself is God, while contingent beings are "existents" in the sense that existence neither subsists in them nor is their accident or attribute, but their *relationship* to God.[30]

Since, however, pure existence exists, it is also "existent" but in a different sense than contingent "existents." Existence is "existent" in its pure and absolute form, just as whiteness would be "white" and heat would be "hot," if whiteness and heat could exist in their purity and absoluteness. Yet these two may be brought together under a common category of "existent" when by "existent" is meant "that which produces effects" or "that wherein existence subsists," and even though subsistence of existence in the contingent is metaphorical, the application of the term "existent" need not be metaphorical.[31] The term "existent" is thus used in three different senses: a self-subsistent existent, that is, God; a contingent existent whose existence means "being related to God"; and, thirdly, existent in a most general and abstract sense, which is acknowledged to be the most self-evident idea or notion and is, as such, inapplicable to God. This account avoids the common objection that since "existent" is a mere general abstract notion, how can God be its referent?[32]

The self-subsisting existence—God—is, therefore, self-necessary and must be one and unique. For, if there were two such beings, both will be characterized by necessary existence. The characteristic of necessary existence, being common, will, then, have to be additional to their essential nature and will have to be caused by something outside them. Hence, they will be contingent, not necessary. Hence, when we say, "The necessary being exists," we cannot mean that necessary being *happens* to exist, but that necessary existence is its essence. That is why al-Fārābī and Ibn Sīnā said that the application of the term "existent" to the necessary being, as is suggested by the common linguistic usage, is metaphorical, not real, since "existence" is not His extrinsic attribute.[33]

Against this widely accepted proof of God's unity, Ṣadrā urges ten objections, some of which are of doubtful validity and one, at least, contradicts his own principles. He contends that unless the referent or the meaning of the root-term is known, there is no question of "deriving" another form from it, and since existence (i.e., God) is itself unknowable, the derivative form "existent" is out of the question. But, as we have said in the preceding section of this chapter, Ṣadrā admits a universal intuitive knowledge of God, even though at the sub-human level that knowledge is unconscious. As has been pointed out by al-Sabzawārī, this knowledge is sufficient to warrant the term "existence." [34] But Ṣadrā has two objections which seriously tell against al-Dawwānī. The first objection is that a derivative term is either literal, e.g., *'ālim* (a knower = a person in whom knowledge subsists) or relational and metaphorical, e.g., *ḥaddād* (ironmonger = a person who deals in iron to make iron-products), but cannot be both at the same time. In the case of existence (*wujūd*), however, al-Dawwānī invites us to accept both at the same time—i.e., in the case of God, its use is literal while in the case of contingents it is only relational, since a contingent, in his view, is not that wherein existence subsists but that which is related to existence. Al-Dawwānī's attempt to introduce the common category of "existent" covering both God and the contingent cannot succeed because "existent"—whether it means "that which produces effects (*mabda' al-āthār*)" or "that wherein existence subsists"—itself will have a double meaning, the one applicable to God, the other applicable to the contingent.[35]

The second objection is still more serious. Al-Dawwānī is a die-hard essentialist for whom existence is a mere general notion without having a counterpart in objective reality. This being so, he cannot legitimately make a transition from the realm of concepts to the realm of reality and affirm the existence of God as a particular being (as a *fard al-wujūd*), since existence has no particulars (*afrād*) for him. He has labored hard to show how pure existence can be described as "existent" but this is, surely, a case of "side-tracking the issue during the debate" since this is not the point at issue. The question is, rather, what is the warrant for God's objective existence—not to mention unique existence—on the assumption that existence is only a subjective idea while essence is the primordial reality? [36] How can reason allow that a mere notion *have* (as opposed to "stand for") a self-subsistent being? [37] All one can say, on that assumption, is that a self-necessary essence obtains objectively to which "existence" is attributable by the mind; but, then, why can there not be more than one such essence in reality to which existence may be attributable in this manner, since existence itself is not the reality but something added by the mind? [38] The uniqueness of God can, therefore, be established only on the ground that existence is the primary reality, with its systematically ambiguous forms, culminating in absolute existence which, by definition, can be only one.

NOTES

1. *Asfār,* III, 1, note 3 on p. 14; this is, however, based on Ṣadrā's own statement in the *Shawāhid* (p. 10, lines 1–2) that the very denial of existence involves its affirmation.

2. *Ibid.,* p. 13, lines 3 ff.; Qur'ān: III, 18; al-Sabzawārī's note 1 on p. 14 in the interpretation of Ṣadrā's proof; cf. Part I, Chapter IV.

3. *Ibid.,* p. 17, note 2; p. 21, note 1 (both by al-Sabzawārī).

4. *Ibid.,* p. 19, line 10–p. 21, end.

5. *Ibid.,* p. 41, line 11–p. 47, end, particularly p. 47, line 9–end of page.

6. *Asfār,* I, 1, p. 84, lines 11 ff.; III, 1, p. 27, lines 2 ff.

7. *Asfār,* III, 1, p. 27, line 9–p. 28, line 3.

8. *Ibid.,* p. 30, line 1–p. 31, line 1.

9. *Asfār,* I, 1, p. 96, line 7–p. 97, line 6.

10. *Ibid.,* p. 98, lines 2 ff.

11. *Ibid.,* p. 99, lines 4 ff.; p. 102, lines 6 ff.

12. *Ibid.,* p. 100, lines 6 ff.

13. *Ibid.,* p. 103, lines 14 ff.

14. *Ibid.,* p. 108, line 7–p. 109, line 2; p. 110, lines 10–13.

15. *Ibid.,* p. 113, line 1–p. 118, line 2.

16. *Asfār,* III, 1, p. 48, line 3–p. 50, line 5.

17. *Ibid.,* p. 52, lines 1–8.

18. *Ibid.,* p. 53, line 12–p. 54, line 5.

19. *Ibid.,* p. 54, line 5–p. 55, line 7.

20. *Asfār,* I, 1, p. 129, lines 6–13; III, 1, p. 57, lines 7–9.

21. *Ibid.,* I, 1, p. 129, line 14–p. 130, line 9; III, 1, p. 57, lines 10–19.

22. *Ibid.,* I, 1, p. 130, lines 10–14; III, 1, lines 20 ff.

23. *Ibid.,* III, 1, p. 58, lines 3–13.

24. *Ibid.,* III, 1, p. 58, line 5–p. 60, line 3; I, 1, p. 132, line 2–p. 133, line 2.

25. *Ibid.,* III, 1, p. 63, lines 6–12; cf. I, 1, reference in the preceding note.

26. *Ibid.,* III, 1, p. 58, last line–p. 60, line 3.

27. *Ibid.,* III, 1, p. 60, lines 3–17; I, 1, p. 133, line 3–p. 134, line 9.

28. *Ibid.,* I, 1, p. 134, line 10–p. 135, line 6.

29. *Ibid.,* I, 1, p. 135, lines 7 ff.

30. *Ibid.*, III, 1, p. 63, lines 15–p. 65, line 6.
31. *Ibid.*, III, 1, p. 65, line 7–p. 66, line 4.
32. *Ibid.*, III, 1, p. 66, lines 5–14.
33. *Ibid.*, p. 66, line 15-p. 67, line 3.
34. *Ibid.*, p. 68, lines 13 ff.; particularly p. 71, lines 4 ff.; and al-Sabzawārī's note 2 on the same page.
35. *Ibid.*, p. 172, lines 5 ff.
36. *Ibid.*, p. 73, line 5–p. 74, line 13.
37. *Ibid.*, p. 74, lines 13–19 (see also criticism no. 7: p. 74, line 20–p. 75, line 4).
38. *Ibid.*, p. 75, lines 5–12; also see the whole of Chapter I, Part I of the present work, on Existence and God as simple or pure existence.

CHAPTER II

GOD'S ATTRIBUTES—I

A. *God's Being and Attributes*

We saw in Chapter IV of Part I on Causation (and in the preceding chapter of this part) that God had attributes; we also saw that these attributes are identical with God's Existence, are not additional to it, but have the status of notions (*mafāhīm*). These are somewhat analogous to essences in contingent existents but cannot be strictly characterized as essences since essences are finite and are not identical with the existence of contingents. In the following pages Ṣadrā will explain the nature of divine attributes and their relationship to God's being. But before we discuss this in detail, it has to be noted that among the attributes there are those that are pure negations and those that are positive, the latter category being itself divisible into those attributes that are real or substantive (*ḥaqīqī*) and those that are relations and, as such, do not have a substantive being. The negative attributes are all reducible to the negation of contingency and, since contingency itself is negative, being privation of necessity, negative attributes come to mean negation of negation.[1] As for relations, these are also reducible to one single relation—the relation of sustaining all existence (*qayyūmiya*), of which creation, and giving life and sustenance, etc., are all parts. This *qayyūmiya* manifests itself in the first instance in the rise of the Breath of the Merciful (*Nafas al-Raḥmān*) discussed in Chapter IV of Part I, and, through it, in particular contingent beings.[2] But it is the substantive attributes like knowledge and power which are the most important for God's nature-in-itself and which form the subject of the present discussion.

God's attributes are original and essential, whereas these attributes in contingent beings are derivative and accidental; and Ṣadrā quotes from al-Fārābī to the effect that just as in the case of existence there is the original existence which belongs to God and a derivative, contingent existence which belongs to contingents, so with attributes like knowledge and power: there is an original, essential knowledge or power which belongs to God and a derivative, accidental knowledge or power which belongs to contingents.[3] Ṣadrā elaborates this by saying that since all attributes arise out of existence, which is the primordial reality, in the Necessary Existence they are necessary while in contingent existence they are contingent.[4]

Indeed, thanks to the identity of the attributes with existence in the sense that attributes have no existence of their own which may be added externally to existence, the principle of the *tashkīk* (systematic ambiguity) of existence is extended by Ṣadrā to include attributes as well: the nature of attributes in a being is of the same order as its existence. Thus in God, who is the fullness of existence, pure and simple, underived and original, in which there is no composition (*tarkīb*), attributes are identical with His existence; in a contingent, on the other hand, since its existence is derived and non-necessary and is hence subject to the dualism of essence and existence, attributes and existence make up some kind of duality or composition. In God, knowledge, for example, is as self-necessary as His existence; in the Intelligence it is of the order of intellect, while in the soul it is of a psychic order. It also follows that whereas in God knowledge, life, power and will are *existentially* identical with each other (although not *conceptually,* since their meanings or notions—*mafāhīm*—differ from each other), they are existentially different in contingent beings since these latter do not have fully integrated existence.[5]

But the true method of attribution, i.e., the identification of attributes with being, is possible only when the primordiality of existence is admitted, for then existence itself will be found to contain within itself, without the addition of a new factor, all the attributes. Since most Muslim philosophers, particularly of the later period, have not held this view but have regarded existence as a secondary idea (*ma'qūl thānī*), they have believed that in God's case, different attributes are identical with each other in the sense that they *mean* the same—i.e., that the meaning of "knowledge" and "power," for example, is the same—which is manifestly absurd, since each of these terms means something different or else when one has said "knowledge" one has also said "power," "will," etc.; or they have denied all attributes of God and totally denuded Him of positive nature. On the second view, they have held that although God has no *real* attributes, yet all those consequences which flow from and are attendant upon real attributes in other beings, do so, in God's case, from His sheer being.[6] This view is obviously sophistical and has arisen from the non-recognition of the truth that existence by itself creates in itself its attributes or properties, on the analogy of an essence which by itself generates its properties as, for example, it follows from the nature of the number "four" that it is a sum total of four units. But this state of affairs characterizes existence only when it becomes progressively fuller and fuller and simpler and simpler until absolute existence is reached in God. Lower forms of existence, always characterized by contingency and correspondent duality, cannot get rid of their attributes being additional to themselves.

Those among later philosophers who have denied attributes to God (presumably inspired by the Mu'tazilite model) have argued like this. An attribute or quality needs a substance to inhere in the latter; hence, that which inheres cannot be necessary-in-itself for its necessity is derived from that wherein it inheres. This is because the aspect in which a certain thing is "receptive" of a quality is different from the aspect in which it is "productive" of that quality. Hence, if God had qualities, He would be a composite of receptivity and productivity, which is impossible in view of God's simple nature. That receptivity and productivity differ is shown by the fact that productivity sometimes occurs in something other than the agent (as, for example, when fire heats water); if the two were identical, then every agent of a quality would also be receptive of it and *vice versa*.[7] God, therefore, cannot have attributes.

Ṣadrā's reply, taken over from Ibn Sīnā, is that receptivity and productivity differ from each other only in cases which are characterized by potentiality and passivity, as in the case of water being heated by fire. But, whereas water passively receives heat from fire, fire possesses heat inherently in itself and not from the outside. In the case of fire, therefore, productivity and receptivity are identical. Indeed, all necessary attributes of an essence can be said to be both "produced" by the essence and "inherent" in it as well. That is why Ibn Sīnā said that in all simple beings "from" and "in," i.e., activity and receptivity, coalesce. Now, God's attributes can be envisaged on the analogy of essences. Further, in the case of a created being, its necessary attributes are also *indirectly* created (not *directly*, since essences for Ṣadrā are not created *per se*, but only through existents which are directly created), while the attributes of God, who is uncreated and original, are also uncreated.[8]

It may, however, be objected that a simple essence has no necessary attributes which belong only to composite essences; hence, in a composite, reception and production may be different. God, being simple, therefore cannot have attributes. Ṣadrā's reply to this objection is, first, that every composite essence has simple parts, each of which can have attributes. Secondly, and more importantly, even a composite essence has, as a whole, a simple nature and certain attributes pertain to it as such. A triangle, for instance, has the attribute that its angles amount to two right angles. Now, a triangle is a composite of several parts, but this particular attribute does not belong to parts as such but only to the simple whole. A simple nature, therefore, can have attributes. This is why Muslim Peripatetics like Ibn Sīnā have not shied from assigning to God cognitive forms which, according to them, are additional to His essence, without incurring the risk of attributing duality (of reception and production) to Him.[9]

Ṣadrā also urges that if this argument of those who deny attributes to God—viz., that attributes would become something additional to His being —is given validity, then relational attributes of God like creation, sustenance, etc., would either have to cease to be attributes or they cannot be considered additional to His being. Al-Sabzawārī rejects this argument of Ṣadrā on the ground that relations have no real being and, therefore, cannot be considered as *something* that is added to the subject.[10] But, surely, not all relations can be said to be unreal abstractions which do not affect the subject of attribution. While attributes like "being to the right of" or "being to the left of" and even "being a brother of" may be unreal in this sense, it is difficult to believe that causational attributes like "creation" can be unreal and do not affect the being of the agent. If this were true, there would be nothing corresponding in reality to terms like "builder," "writer," etc.

On the question of the attributes of God, then, there are those who deny them altogether, there are those who say that God has attributes but they are additional to His being, like the properties of an essence, and finally, there are those who think that the identity of attributes with God's being means that these attributes have the same *meaning*. All these views are false and their falsity basically arises from the fact that they have not believed in or have not realized the full implications of the fact that existence is the sole reality and that the more perfect eixstence is, the more it has of positive attributes which are not additional to it but *are it*. Having criticized these views, Ṣadrā proceeds[11] to give his own proof for the identity of attributes with the being of God. But the way our philosopher formulates his proof so obviously contradicts his previous statements that al-Sabzawārī, in part, at least, rightly takes him to task. Ṣadrā states that if these attributes of perfection like life, knowledge, and power are not identical with God's being but are something additional, then God's being-in-itself would be denuded of them; this means that God-with-power, for example, would be more perfect than God's being as such. So far, this argument appears sound and I do not think al-Sabzawārī's criticism is quite to the point. For al-Sabzawārī says that this argument is *petitio principii* and that the opponent admits that God's being-in-itself is denuded of attributes. Ṣadrā's point, however, is that *in that case,* God's being plus attributes must be admitted to be more perfect than God's being as such—since these attributes are perfections—which is not *petitio principii.*

But then Ṣadrā goes on to say that if attributes are regarded as something over and above His being, this would mean that God owes His perfections to something *other* than Himself. This, however, blatantly contradicts what he has said in the preceding chapter in the discussion of whether God has an essence or not and what he has been saying here just before stating his own proof, viz., that it is not correct to say that all attributes involve existential plurality in a being since in simple beings and in simple essences, "being from" and "being in" are identical, as these attributes are not caused from without. It seems as though Ṣadrā is running with the hare and hunting with the hound in the same breath. Al-Sabzawārī interprets him correctly in the light of his own real doctrine by saying that something devoid of positive perfections will either have to be an essence—but God has no essence—or a being which has potentialities—and God has no potentialities to be realized. God, indeed, is pure and absolute existence and, as such, must have all attributes of perfection, not additionally to His being, but as being identical with His being; otherwise, God would not be absolute existence.[12]

It is clear, then, that the "identity of attributes with God's being" does not mean either that only God's being is real and His attributes do not exist as those who deny His attributes—like the Mu'tazilites and their followers—insist,[13] or that God's attributes are so like each other and with God's being that their meaning is the same, as we have pointed out earlier, but means that what is real is existence and God's existence, being absolute and most perfect, *is* all these attributes. God's attributes are, therefore, as necessary as His existence.[14] Ṣadrā seeks to clarify this identity of attributes and existence in God on the analogy of the soul and its attributes and operations. This is because the soul has been created in the image of God upon this earth.[15] The soul, therefore, is a unitary, simple being while at the same time it has *conceptually* distinct faculties; but these faculties, while *conceptually* distinct, are *existentially* identical with each other and their identity with each other is due to the fact that they are identical with the existence of the soul. On this analogy is to be understood the unity and the multiplicity of God's being and His attributes. God, as pure existence, "eminently" contains within His absolute simplicity all the attributes but these are not distinguishable either from His being or from each other. This state of absolute simplicity is called the "stage of absolute unity (*martabat al-aḥadīya*)." But it is also true that these attributes *can be regarded* as distinct both from each other and from God's being; this state is called the "stage of Godhead (*martabat al-ilāhiya*)." Yet even when attributes are regarded as distinct, it must be remembered that *existentially speaking,* the only reality is existence; the attributes are real only notionally and conceptually.

This whole question, then, once again, boils down, for Ṣadrā, to the fact that existence is the only original reality (*al-aṣl*), essences or attributes being only secondarily or derivatively or, indeed, notionally real.[16] Existence is all-inclusive and comprehensive, while essences are mutually exclusive. They lack the amplitude which is the basic characteristic of reality and which existence alone can possess. Infinite existence, that is, God, comprehends all, but even a finite existence can, by substantive movement, create a greater amplitude for itself while essences are always static. The reason why God's attributes cannot be called "essences" is that the term "essence" is restricted to the realm of finite existence where it attaches to existents from "the outside," as it were. But in God's case, His attributes are original and do not come from the outside; hence the term "essence" is inappropriate. But both essences and divine attributes agree in this, viz., that both are notional and have a derivative reality. Those philosophers for whom existence is notional and derivative and essence is the reality must concede a plurality of separate attributes for God, since there is no existence to hold them together. But since they are reluctant to admit a plurality of gods, in order to flee from this unpalatable conclusion, they seek refuge in their dictum that all attributes of God mean the same thing, which, as we have pointed out, is absurd.[17]

Even though God's attributes are *notions* (*mafāhīm*), they are nevertheless *necessary* since they belong to the Necessary Existence; thus, God's knowledge, power, and will are as necessary as His existence.[18] This is a necessary corollary of Ṣadrā's argument. It seems to me, therefore, that al-Ṭabāṭabā'ī's remark[19] that this is not proved by the argument is out of place. For, if God's attributes were not necessary, they would have to be contingent and would have the same status as other essences. The tenor of Ṣadrā's whole argument is against it. This is, indeed, the very meaning of his view that God's attributes are *identical* with His existence; it is in contingent beings that attributes are attached to existence as something additional. This view of the "necessity" of divine attributes is apparently different from al-Fārābī's view referred to earlier by Ṣadrā himself, which seems to say that *just as* all existence must end up in a necessary existence, *so must* all knowledge end up in a necessary knowledge, all power in a necessary power, etc. But Ṣadrā wants to say that divine knowledge, power, and will are necessary *because they are identical with His necessary existence.* Al-Ṭabāṭabā'ī seems to confuse the two.

B. *Knowledge*

We now turn to a consideration of the two most important and traditionally most widely discussed attributes of God, viz., His knowledge and His power. On God's knowledge, Ṣadrā enumerates nine or ten views, some of which he accepts after necessary modifications, while rejecting others. He then formulates his own view—once again on the basis of the doctrine that existence alone is real and God is pure existence. Philosophers who have put forward different views on the subject have either held that He has knowledge of things or that He has no knowledge of things other than Himself—as was stated by Aristotle—since this would introduce multiplicity in God (some have even denied all knowledge to God, including self-knowledge, since all knowledge, for them, is a relationship which is inconceivable between a thing and its self). Ṣadrā rejects the latter view on the ground that knowledge, being a perfection, cannot be denied to God.[20] Those who affirm knowledge on the part of God either hold that it is separate from His being or not. Those who hold His knowledge to be separate from Him believe that non-existents subsist (*thābit*) either in external reality—as the Mu'tazila hold—or in God's knowledge—as several statements of certain Sufi thinkers like Ibn 'Arabī appear to indicate—or, if the "separatists" do not believe in the subsistence of non-existents, they either say that God's knowledge is identical with Platonic Forms, which have an indepedent existence, or that God's knowledge actually depends upon things themselves, which, as separate, distinct, and successive existents, are the *objects* of God's knowledge, but insofar as they are present to Him collectively and emanate from Him, constitute His *knowledge*. On this latter view, held by al-Suhrawardī and also accepted by al-Ṭūsī, change, therefore, affects not God's knowledge but the objects of His knowledge. Of those who hold God's knowledge not to be separate from Him, some think that it is, nevertheless, additional to His being itself and is related to His being as properties or necessary attributes are related to an essence. This is the view of Muslim Peripatetics like al-Fārābī and Ibn Sīnā. Those who do not think that knowledge is additional to God's being are of two varieties: some, like Porphyry, are of the belief that in God, as Intellect, there is identity of the knower and the known or the intellect and the intelligible; while some latter-day Muslim philosophers, following certain remarks of Ibn Sīnā about the "simple intellect," believe that God's knowledge is simple and in its simplicity contains—and is further creatively related to—the entire multiplicity of forms and concepts.[21]

The first target of Ṣadrās' criticism is the view that essences subsist before their actual existence and in this state of "subsistence (*thubūt*)" are known by God.[22] This theory of subsistence is held by the Mu'tazila school who believe that all non-existents are, nevertheless, "something" that can be talked about as referent of thought and hence "subsist." This theory, Stoic in origin, was rejected both by the Ash'arī school and by the Muslim philosophers. Ṣadrā also rejects it on the ground that essences have no reality at all unless they are invested with real, external existence and that the non-existent cannot "subsist" by itself whether this subsistence is said to be real or mental. Now, whereas the Mu'tazila believe in real subsistence of non-existents, certain statements emanating, for example, from Ibn 'Arabī regard essences as subsisting in God's mind (as distinguished from God's existence). Ibn 'Arabī's view, therefore, as expressed in these statements, must be rejected also. When we come to these statements, Ibn 'Arabī does, indeed, hold that, prior to their actual existence, essences have a being in God's mind and are objects of His knowledge. All non-existents are said to be "seeing and seen, hearing and heard by a subsistent sight and audition." Some are good, some bad. God does nothing except to give existence to such among them as are capable of existence by His word "be." [23]

Ṣadrā, however, seeks to interpret Ibn 'Arabī's statements on the basis of his own doctrine of simple existence which contains all so that Ibn 'Arabī is saved from the objection that he is committed to the subsistence of non-existents. In sum, Ṣadrā says that these essences, before their spatio-temporal existence, *exist in a simple manner* as necessary consequencs of God's attributes.[24] That is to say, they have a higher existence prior to temporal existence. The trouble, however, with this interpretation is that Ibn 'Arabī does not appear to subscribe to Ṣadrā's doctrine of simple existence and that essences arise out of the reality of this existence as such. But quite apart from this, Ṣadrā's interpretation will not hold since Ibn 'Arabī says explicitly that these subsistent essences (*a'yān thābita*) do not have being just in a *simple manner* but that each essence is distinct with its own consequences except such consequences as flow from positive existence. Nor, further, can the contents of God's attributes and their subdivisions (which Ṣadrā insists are identical with God's simple existence) be called essences for, as Ṣadrā explicitly states in his final treatment of the question of God's knowledge (*Asfār,* III, 1, p. 271, line 6 ff.), essences only belong to contingent beings whose existence is finite; in the case of God, whose attributes are as infinite as His existence (even though His attributes are only notional, not real), there can be no talk of essences. How, then, can finite, strictly defined essences—which are mutually exclusive—be attributed to God's being or His attributes? This interpretation is, therefore, no more than a *tour de force* on Ṣadrā's part, carried out through pious motives.

Ṣadrā also rejects the view of those who identify God's knowledge with Platonic Forms as separate from God's being. This is because, in the traditional view of these Forms, they are posterior to God's existence and His knowledge of them. How could they, in that case, be God's eternal and primordial knowledge? [25] Also, since these Forms are real entities and not mental forms, the question arises with regard to them as to how they are known by God. There is, then, no escape from positing a prior knowledge on God's part of these entities.[26] Ṣadrā, of course, patently accepts Platonic Forms but, as was pointed out in Chapter IV of Part I on Causation, and as will be discussed again presently in relation to his interpretation of Ibn Sīnā's view, he regards these Forms as the content of the first determination (i.e., the First Intelligence) of the first self-manifestation of the Ultimate Reality termed the "Self-unfolding Being" or the "Breath of the Merciful," or the "Universal Intelligible Matter."[27] This first self-manifestation of God's being is existentially identical with God and only conceptually different from it. In Chapter IV of Part I referred to here, Ṣadrā however calls this Universal Substance or Intelligible Matter—the Realm of Forms—a "contingent substance"—a kind of bridge between the Ultimate Reality and the contingent world. But this "contingency" simply means that it is the result of a conceptual analysis; otherwise, it is existentially absolutely identical with God.

When so interpreted, Platonic Forms are identified by Ṣadrā with the transcendental Intelligences of the Peripatetics; both cease to be, then, independent existents, separate from God and, as we shall see below when we discuss the Peripatetic doctrine of God's knowledge, they are described by Ṣadrā as non-posterior concomitants of God's being: they are not "caused" by Him, nor do they "emanate" from Him but "are with" Him, i.e., can be conceptually distinguished from Him as His cognitive forms or attributes.[28]

Nor does Ṣadrā accept the traditional view that God's knowledge, in its "simplicity," ensures knowledge of all things. He, indeed, strongly upholds the doctrine of "simplicity" and has formulated the principle that "a simple being is all things" and he will presently invoke this very principle to give his final solution to the problem of God's knowledge. But his basic objection to Ibn Sīnā, who was the first to formulate the idea of "simple knowledge" (the *Scientia Simplex* of the medieval Latin scholastics), is that he denies the absolute identity of the intellect and the intelligible.[29] The identity of the intellect and the intelligible, in turn, requires, in Ṣadrā's view, that existence be regarded as the original reality from which the attribute of knowledge is derived as a "notional abstraction." Hence, for Ṣadrā, knowledge and existence are co-extensive and just as existence admits of an infinite gradation and is applied with systematic ambiguity, so is knowledge. In his doctrine of the Intellect, Ṣadrā states and rejects the objections of al-Suhrawardī and al-Rāzī against Ibn Sīnā's idea of simple knowledge but here he states those very objections and apparently approves of them.[30] This is because, whereas the idea of simple knowledge is basically regarded as correct by him, the traditional formulation of it—since it is not based on the fundamental idea of the originality of existence and existence alone (and he regards the denial of the identity of the subject and object in intellection as a corollary of the denial of originality of existence)—is strongly disapproved of by him at the same time.

Ṣadrā reports two formulations of the doctrine of God's simple knowledge. According to one version, God knows Himself and is also the principle or source of all things. Hence God knows all things. On this view, God knows all things not just because he knows Himself but because He is the Cause or Source of all things. The holders of this view contend that God's knowledge of all things *means* His being the source of all things. They argue that knowledge is the cause of distinction between the knowables and since God causes distinctions among things by *producing* them as distinct, "knowledge" and "productive cause" are equivalents. Ṣadrā's objection to this reasoning is that it involves the fallacy that a universal, positive proposition can be simply inverted—i.e., that the proposition "all knowledge is the cause of distinction" can be converted into "all that causes distinction is knowledge." [31]

According to the second version of the argument, God *knows all things with their distinctive characteristics* because His knowledge is creative, not receptive as is the case with our knowledge. God possesses this creative knowledge because in His self-knowledge the knowledge of everything is implicitly involved. Ṣadrā says that if these people are asked how a simple knowledge can be conceived as a form which contains all other forms, and in which all forms are "implicitly involved," they can give no answer.[32] For these philosophers, i.e., Peripatetics, have themselves defined knowledge of a thing as a "form equivalent to that thing and constitutive of its essence." Where and how, then, do they find a form that will apply to everything? [33] And if one can speak of such a form at all, how will it do justice to distinct essences, while at this simple stage no essences are forthcoming? [34]

The holders of the first version of the argument reply [35] to this objection by saying that just as distinctions are created by cognitive forms or concepts, so can they be produced by a cause, since a cause requires a specific effect. Now, since God's simple being is the cause of every specific existent, in that being all specific characteristics are given in a simple manner. Ṣadrā replies [36] that this proof illegitimately assimilates a cause to a cognitive form like certain false analogical reasonings of jurists! A cognitive form, for example, constitutes the essence of a thing but not so its cause. Al-Sabzawārī seeks to defend their analogy against Ṣadrā's criticism [37] on the basis of the principle that in the case of separate existents the "what" and the "why" are identical, hence their form and their cause are one and the same. But Ṣadrā's basis of criticism seems to be his view, voiced in the preceding Section of this Chapter, that attributes like power and knowledge, although *existentially* identical, must be *conceptually* distinguished, else power and knowledge would mean the same, which is absurd.

Those who maintain the version of simple knowledge as creative knowledge reply to Ṣadrā's objection that it is the very nature of simple knowledge to create and apply to everything and that distinctions are in the *objects* of knowledge not in knowledge itself. Against this Ṣadrā urges that it is inconceivable that one single idea or concept can apply to all separate and distinct objects even though one knower or subject of knowledge may contain diverse ideas in himself.[38]

As has been indicated at the beginning of this discussion, Ṣadrā is a strong believer in the doctrine of simple knowledge but disagrees with Ibn Sīnā's statement of it which has made it vulnerable to the kind of objections stated here and which were urged by al-Suhrawardī and al-Rāzī. In his view the only satisfactory way to formulate the idea of God's simple, creative knowledge is to regard existence and knowledge as coextensive and to view existence as the original reality and knowledge as an "abstracted notion." For it is existence alone which in its all-comprehensiveness can contain everything in a simple manner. Once knowledge is disengaged from existence and is viewed *per se,* then one must talk of so many essences, concepts and ideas as mutually exclusive units that it is impossible to reduce them to any simple unity. The only principle of unity-in-diversity is the principle of existence as it is the only veritable reality, while attributes like knowledge, power, and will are derivative realities or notions.

We now come to a consideration of the most important and most widely discussed of the historical views about God's knowledge, viz., that of Ibn Sīnā, who held that God's knowledge cannot derive from things since this would make Him dependent upon something other than Himself and, since there is a succession in temporal things, His knowledge would change from moment to moment. God's knowledge, therefore, is not produced by things; on the contrary, things are created by His knowledge. This instantaneous knowledge, however, is an *ordered* knowledge in accordance with the order of causes and effects. Thanks to this order, God knows everything—all particulars to their last details and including temporal priorities and posteriorities—even though He does not possess sense-perception. God knows, for example, that a certain solar eclipse will occur so many years, months, and days after a certain other sun-eclipse, thanks to the order of causes and effects.

The question as to how this knowledge and the forms it consists of are related to God is discussed by Ibn Sīnā at length. If one made these forms a part of His very being, His being would become a composite and the simplicity of His being would be destroyed. If one conceived of these forms as independently existing, they would become Platonic Forms and would be liable to the same objections as are urged against these Forms. If one held these forms not to be separate from Him as Platonic Forms but related to Him as extrinsic accidents, He would not be absolutely necessary. Finally, one may hold that forms are in some other being, either a soul or an intellect, in such a manner that when God thinks them they come to exist in such an intellect or soul. But one must not say that the existence of these forms in this other being is one thing and their emanation from God another, for in that case, their existence, being a fact in its own right, will again require another intellect to think it and this process would go on *ad infinitum*. Hence, their existence in a being and their intellection by God *must be one and the same fact*. To say, therefore, that "these forms were intellected [i.e., by God] and *therefore* came into existence [i.e., in another being]" is to say that "they were intellected and were therefore intellected" or to say that "they became existent and therefore became existent." This is because, as we have argued, their intellection and their existence are one and the same thing. Hence these forms cannot exist in a being other than God. There is, therefore, no escape from the consequence that these forms must be accepted, not as part of God's being, nor yet as His accidents, but as the necessary consequences or properties (*lawāzim*) of His being.[39] The argument is, of course, explicitly based on the premise that God's knowledge of His cognitive forms must precede actual existents, of which they are forms, and not follow these existents, for in that case God's knowledge, being derivative from things, would become contingent.[40]

This theory of Ibn Sīnā was severely criticized and rejected by several philosophers after him, but Ṣadrā defends Ibn Sīnā against all these critics, although he himself criticizes the theory, not perhaps so much as formulated by Ibn Sīnā but as elaborated by his disciples like Bahmanyār, who declared these forms to be "accidents inhering in God" and as "properties posterior to God's being (*lawāzim muta'akhkhira*)." Ṣadrā essentially refers to three criticisms of Ibn Sīnā's theory by Abū 'l-Barakāt, al-Suhrawardī, and al-Ṭūsī, all of whom hold that God's knowledge is directly related to things and not through prior cognitive forms. Abū 'l-Barakāt urges that if the function of prior cognitive forms is to save God from being directly related to contingents or to prevent contingents from becoming eternal, then the same difficulty arises with regard to God's power as with regard to His knowledge, for God's power is also related to that over which it is power as His knowledge is related to that of which it is knowledge. In other words, just as God needs other things besides Himself to be a knower, even so He needs other things besides Himself to be a doer. But if one saves the eternity of God's knowledge by positing eternal cognitive forms, how can the eternity of His power be saved, since one apparently cannot insert forms in this case between God's power and its objects? Some people have tried to differentiate between objects of knowledge and objects of power by saying that whereas power need not have an object, knowledge must, i.e., whereas knowledge requires a *real* relation to its object, power does not. Ṣadrā rejects this distinction by saying that relations in both cases are real. However, he says that what is required in both cases is not an actual, existential relation but its principle and possibility and that this requirement is satisfied by forms which are at the same time both cognitive and action-oriented and an existential object is not needed. That is to say, it is sufficient for God's knowledge and power to have a form through which He both knows what will be and intends what He will do but the existential counterpart of this form is not necessary.[41]

But the most relentless critic of Ibn Sīnā and the Peripatetic tradition on this question is al-Suhrawardī, who has urged against this position several considerations, viz., that it renders God into a subject characterized by a variety of qualities or accidents that inhere in it and that it is inconceivable that a substratum is not "affected [i.e., changed]" by such qualities; that whether or not the first form contemplated by God precedes or follows or is simultaneous with the first external effect, God, in His own being, will not be complete cause since He needs a form to cause the first external effect; and finally, that the first form will have a dual role in giving a form to God's being and helping cause the external effect and in its former role, at least, will be an agent of God's perfection. Ṣadrā replies to these objections point by point that qualities or attributes change or affect a subject only when the former are extrinsic to the latter, not when they necessarily arise from it as in the case of the necessary attributes of a simple essence (that is why Ibn Sīnā insists that in a simple being "being caused by it (*'anhu*)" and "being inherent in it (*fīhi*)," i.e., the causational and attributional aspects, are one and the same.[42] The reply to the second question is that the first form necessarily precedes the first external effect, otherwise God's providence (*'ināya*) will be set at naught, as we shall see below; however, these forms being related to different contingents—non-material and material—have to be different and Ibn Sīnā has accepted this as the least objectionable of all the alternative modes of God's knowledge cited earlier.[43] Finally, there is no surprise nor harm in the dual nature of the first form since the Peripatetics themselves insist that these forms, as necessary consequences (*lawāzim*) of God's knowledge do not constitute His perfections which is rather the principle and source of these forms, which is God's being itself.[44]

Indeed, the ultimate basis of such objections is that when an attribute is attached to a subject as a necessary but posterior consequence, it must be related to the subject as a contingent. But this is surely not true of necessary attributes which are inherently caused by the subject. The reason is that that subject possesses in itself that whereby it causes such an attribute.[45] Thus, when, for example, fire actually burns, this is an attribute which arises from the very nature of fire, which is prior to its actual burning operation. It is indeed the natural perfection of fire to be possessed of a nature from which actual burning flows as a necessary consequence, and this consequence itself does not constitute its primary perfection. That is why Ibn Sīnā recurrently stated that the perfection of God consists in His *being such that forms flow from Him,* not in the actual forms themselves. As we have repeatedly pointed out, "God's causing something" and "something being in God" have the same meaning. That is also why he unfailingly attests that the existence of these forms is not something additional to His intellection of them, nor His intellection of them something additional to their existence; both are absolutely identical.[46] These forms are, therefore, self-intelligible, which is very different from such contingents as display a duality of nature so that their being is only *capable* of being intellected and is not constituted by self-intellection. This latter kind of being has its essence as additional to its existence; and, at least through a conceptual analysis, possesses a duality which prevents it from being self-intelligible and, therefore, in such a case "being from it [i.e., its causation]" and "being in it [i.e., its reception]" are two different things.[47]

Similar considerations are also urged against Ibn Sīnā by al Ṭūsī, which are, according to Ṣadrā, taken from al-Suhrawardī, about the relationship of these forms to the being of God; and Ṣadrā replies in the same vein as he does against al-Suhrawardī on the basis of Ibn Sīnā's theory of the self-intelligibility of these forms. The question as to whether al-Ṭūsī actually borrowed from al-Suhrawardī we shall consider below. But Ṣadrā once again criticizes Ibn Sīnā for his inconsistency in holding, on the one hand, that the being and intelligibility of these forms is one and the same and, on the other, in denying the identity of the intellect and the intelligible attributed to Porphyry in his theory of knowledge. On the same basis must be understood Ṣadrā's reply to al-Ṭūsī's objection that these forms would produce multiplicity in God. Ṣadrā quotes from Ibn Sīnā to the effect that since these forms have an order of causal priority and posteriority, although temporal extension is eliminated, this argues for a multiplicity-in-unity. *From this point of view,* this doctrine resembles Bergson's idea of "pure duration" from which serial time is eliminated but where pure order remains. I do not think, therefore, that al-Sabzawārī's objection that this does not get rid of multiplicity is justified.[48] For pure order does not produce malignant multiplicity but either temporal sequence or logical disorder.

For Ṣadrā, then, the real objection to Ibn Sīnā's theory of God's knowledge is not on the ground of there being forms or of the multiplicity of cognitive forms, nor on the ground that these forms are necessary consequences of God's being itself, but on the ground that they are described as posterior "accidents" of and as "imprinted" upon God's mind,[49] just as ideas are "imprinted" upon our minds when we conceive of things. The objection, then, is two-fold, viz., that these forms are mental, not existenial, and that they constitute "necessary accidents" of God's mind, posterior to the mind itself. To disprove this, Ṣadrā brings three arguments. The first argument states that necessary attributes may be divided into three types: (1) purely subjective as e.g., "being a class" is an attribute of men; (2) existential attributes, as, e.g., being hot is an attribute of fire; (3) properties of essences, as, e.g., "being equal to two right angles" is an attribute of a triangle. Divine forms obviously cannot be of the first type. The second type is existential and even the third type becomes existential when the essence comes to exist. God's attributes or cognitive forms, therefore, must be existential realities, veritable entities, and not mental affairs.[50]

It is probable that the term "attribute of God" used in this context does not strictly refer to conventional attributes like knowledge, power, etc., since these, as we have seen, are only conceptual (*mafāhīm*). Ṣadrā is here talking of the *content* of God's knowledge (which is, of course, also the content of His power and will) i.e., cognitive forms which are related to God on the one hand and to the created things on the other. But it must be admitted that even on this point his thought is not at all clear. For Ṣadrā has already—as in Chapter IV of Part I and in the present chapter as well—identified God's cognitive forms with Platonic Forms, with the "Breath of the Merciful," etc., and declared them to be notional (*ma'ānī; mafhūmāt,* etc.). Ṣadrā himself raises the question as to how it is possible to conceive of these forms both as veritable entities and yet in the same breath as inseparable properties of God.[51] The final answer he gives, as we shall see presently, is that since God is pure existence, His attributes, inasmuch as they share this absolute existence, are also existential. However, when these are regarded as separate from His being, by a kind of mental analysis, and are viewed as pure attributes, they are of the mental order of existence. On the whole, therefore, it is not really possible to distinguish between divine attributes and their contents, thanks essentially to the mutual identity of the attributes themselves.

Ṣadrā's second argument against the theory of these forms as "imprinted" in God's mind is that the Peripatetics' own principle that perfect knowledge of an effect can only be obtained through its cause goes against this theory. Ṣadrā insists that this principle does not mean that an effect can be *conceived* (as an essence, that is) only when its cause is conceived, but that it has to do with an *existential* cause and effect. That is to say, this principle does not say, e.g., "whenever there is fire, it burns" but "*this* is fire, hence it burns." In other words, the principle is talking of direct existential entities, not of indirect inferential essences. Hence, these forms, as caused by God directly, are directly known as existential realities, not as mere concepts.[52] Al-Ṭabāṭabā'ī has criticized this argument on the ground that this principle does not talk about direct knowledge but only about indirect knowledge, since Peripatetics do not admit any direct knowledge except in the case of self-knowledge.[53] But the principle, which comes from Aristotle, says that those things which have causes, can be known with scientific certainty or perfection only through a knowledge of these causes. This would hold good for both indirect and direct knowledge, since in the latter, the cause—the self—is directly present. Now, these cognitive forms have a cause, viz., God's being. From the human standpoint, this knowledge would be "indirect" but from God's point of view would be direct, since He Himself has caused these Forms. In either case, the knowledge of cause is essential for a perfect knowledge of these forms or attributes.

Ṣadrā's third argument on which he lays great emphasis rests on a principle which he took directly from al-Suhrawardī. According to this principle, called "the principle of the higher possibility," everything that exists at a lower level of being is sure proof that it exists *a fortiori* at a higher level, which is its cause. On this principle, it is inconceivable that what exists at a higher level as cause of the lower level shall be inferior to the latter. It is, therefore, absurd, says Ṣadrā, that divine cognitive forms, which are the cause of the contingent world, should be only conceptual while the contingent world itself is existential, existence being perfection—indeed, the highest form of perfection.[54]

Ṣadrā then proceeds to amend both the Islamic Peripatetic and Islamic Platonic traditions in the light of his own thought. The former are wrong in viewing God's cognitive forms as accidents, for these are veritable existential entities, while the latter are wrong in declaring these entities to be separate from God for these, although they are existential entities, are part of God since they are, after all, His cognitive forms. If these are regarded as separate from God, a prior knowledge will be required on God's part in order to know them and this would involve a vicious regress.[55] Being part of God and yet being self-subsistent entities, these forms cannot be viewed as being related to God in the sense of emanating (*ṣudūr*) from Him as Ibn Sīnā's language suggests. They are rather to be seen as simple entities systematically differentiated among themselves in terms of the degree of existence they possess and free from contingency.[56] Their being systematically differentiated in terms of the degree of existence apparently means that the forms of the higher beings like the Peripatetics' Intelligences have an existential priority over other contingent beings. But, strictly speaking, according to Ṣadrā, these cognitive forms are identical with the Platonic Forms and with the Peripatetics' Intelligences; how, then, can they exhibit differences in terms of the degree of existence? Again, Platonic Forms are numerous while the Peripatetics' Intelligences are ten in number.

Next, Ṣadrā passes on to a consideration of al-Suhrawardī's theory—taken over, according to him, also by al-Ṭūsī, otherwise a Peripatetic—viz., that God's knowledge (for al-Suhrawardī, indeed, *all* knowledge) occurs by a special illuminational relationship between God and things. This "illuminational" relationship is radically different from all other relationships which imply a difference between related things. The prototype of this illuminational cognition in the field of perceptual knowledge for al-Suhrawardī is vision which does not occur, according to him, by rays of light emitted by the eye, as Platonists hold, or by the transmission, through light, of the form of the external object to the eye, as Aristotelians hold, but by a direct, illuminational relationship between the perceiving subject and the seen object. This relationship is explained by al-Suhrawardī as that of creation (*fāi'liya*) and lordship (*qahr*) which exist between every higher and lower form of being. This relationship of illumination and lordship exists between the soul and all its objects of knowledge, be they perceptible or imaginative and, indeed, between the soul and its own body, which is the soul's artifact. Every knower, therefore, knows its object thanks to this relationship of *ishrāq* (illumination) and to the extent that this relationship subsists between the two. God, therefore, knows things directly because of this relationship of *ishrāq* and does not need any intermediate cognitive forms.[57] We have already seen al-Suhrawardī's detailed objections to the Peripatetics' doctrine of forms and Ṣadrā's refutation of these objections. Here it only needs to be reiterated that for al-Suhrawardī, cognitive forms involve a receptivity which is unbecoming of God, or, indeed, of every higher being vis-à-vis the lower. Hence al-Suhrawardī opposes to this idea of receptivity his idea of creativity, "illuminational lordship."

For al-Suhrawardī, therefore, knowledge *is* this *ishrāq* (which also *is* the existence of the effect) and not any preceding cognitive forms from which the effect might come into existence. As we saw above, al-Ṭūsī also rejects Ibn Sīnā's doctrine of forms in God's mind and attributes God's knowledge to, or, rather, interprets it *as being the same as,* God's causation of external effects. External effects, for example, the First Intelligence *et al.,* therefore are known to God directly because He is their immediate cause or creator. Just as the soul knows such imaginative and intellective forms as it itself creates directly, not through any preceding forms, but because it is their creator, so does God know things directly because they flow from Him as His creations, not through any preceding cognitive forms. The affinity of this view with that of al-Suhrawardī in certain essential respects is obvious: both deny Ibn Sīnā's cognitive forms and identify God's knowledge of things with the fact that things flow from God, i.e., a direct knowledge based upon God's creative activity. This view gives priority to God's creativity over His knowledge and, in a sense, reduces the latter to the former. Ṣadrā's statement, however, that al-Ṭūsī simply borrowed this view from al-Suhrawardī is doubtful.[58] To begin with, al-Ṭūsī does not use the key-term of the illuminationist philosopher, *ishrāq.* All he says is that God's knowledge of things *is* His creation of them and thus is direct and not mediated by forms.

This is, in a good sense, a legitimate or at least understandable development from Ibn Sīnā himself, particularly under the influence of al-Suhrawardī's criticism of the latter. For Ibn Sīnā had repeatedly said about the forms themselves, that their being contemplated by God and their existence are one and the same—thereby giving a certain priority to the knowledge aspect over the existential aspect of these forms. Al-Ṭūsī, who is worried about forms themselves because they threaten to become *accidents* of God, now transfers this same view about knowledge-existence identity from forms to external effects of God and transforms knowledge-existence identity to existence-knowledge identity, thus giving a certain priority to existence over knowledge. This is not at all surprising since many other thinkers had also criticized Ibn Sīnā for attributing accidents to God.

Al-Ṭūsī and al-Suhrawardī agree, then, that God's knowledge of things is the things themselves. They further agree that this direct knowledge of God is not only of universals but also of particulars and, indeed, material objects. But they disagree in the manner of God's knowledge of this latter category. For al-Suhrawardī, God's knowledge of material objects is also by way of *ishrāq* or direct illumination. This is in conscious contradiction to Ibn Sīnā's view that God knows all things, even particulars, but His knowledge is by a simultaneous but ordered cognition of all the causes and their effects. Thus, for example, God knows that an eclipse of the sun A will occur so many years after an eclipse B; but this knowledge of the particular eclipses is through a general "universal" knowledge of the causal process; since God does not have sense-perception, He does not know, *i.e., see* these eclipses when they actually occur. This ingenious theory was devised by Ibn Sīnā to meet the religious demand that God know particulars as well as universals. Nevertheless, this theory still denied God a direct knowledge of particulars as particulars i.e., as objects of sense perception, since, based as it was on the causal process, it was indirect. For al-Suhrawardī, God knows all particulars thanks to direct illumination.

But here al-Ṭūsī's view differs widely from al-Suhrawardī's. God, for him, gives rise to the First Intelligence, which is separate from Him but which He knows directly, being its creator. Further, He also knows the content of this Intelligence directly. Now, part of that content is the forms of the material world, both in its spatial and temporal dimensions. The content of the material world is divided into "here" and "there"—spatially—and present, past and future—temporally—only for a space-time bound being, e.g., man. But for the First Intelligence this cannot be the case, since for it all is "here," no "there," and all is "is," no "was" or "will be." It is just as when a reader reads a book word by word, these words exist separately for him, both spatially and temporally, but when he has the whole book "with him," all words exist for him simultaneously and together. By the book al-Ṭūsī appears to mean the First Intelligence. Now God, when He knows the Active Intelligence directly, being its cause, also knows directly these forms of the material objects.[59] There is, therefore, no need of postulating cognitive forms on God's part.

Ṣadrā, who previously had defended Ibn Sīnā or, rather, his interpretation of Ibn Sīnā, against these two philosophers point by point, now urges several considerations against their own doctrines as outlined above. His first and most important objection is that, in their view, God, at the level of pure unity, is denied all knowledge—since these philosophers do not recognize prior cognitive forms on God's part—and that His knowledge is derived from things rather than things being derived from His prior knowledge. It is this prior knowledge that is called *'ināya* (i.e., purposive plan.) [60] It is this plan, which has a cause-effect order, that ensures the perfection of the well-knit world system as we know it; otherwise, it will not be a system but a haphazard flow of things. Whereas most philosophers have asserted purposiveness and a sort of unconscious knowledge even of physical movements and processes, how strange that these philosophers should deny this to God! [61] Al-Suhrawardī claims that the relational system in this world is a replica of the system in the higher realm, but the question is whence does *that* system come unless it is posited in God's own nature? [62] Again, as we shall see in the discussion of knowledge and particularly intellective knowledge in Chapter IV of Part III, knowledge cannot be reduced to pure relation, whether this relation is described as *ishrāq* or not.[63] But even supposing we accept the nature of knowledge as *ishrāq*, i.e., as creation and consequent lordship (*qahr*), how can this relationship subsist between the perceiver and the perceived, since a perceiver does not create his object of perception in al-Suhrawardī's view? Nor does imagination create an image which, according to him, it simply perceives in the World of Images.[64]

Further, if God knows perceptibles as perceptibles, which is claimed by al-Suhrawardī and al-Ṭūsī (we have seen, however, that al-Ṭūsī differs here from al-Suhrawardī for he posits *forms* of material things in the First Intelligence which is the object of God's knowledge in turn; but it must be admitted that sometimes he speaks as though God knows perceptibles *qua* perceptibles directly, cf. *Asfār*, I, 3, pp. 410–11, referred to in note 58 above), then God must have sense perception.[65] But, as we shall see in the account of sense perception in Chapter III of Part III, material objects as such cannot even become objects of sense perception for humans, let alone for God. This is because these objects—their parts being mutually exclusive—are not even present to themselves, let alone present to a percipient. The soul, therefore, when confronted with a material object, creates a form from within itself which corresponds to but is not identical with the material object. It is this form which is known directly and the material object only indirectly and accidentally. If such be the case with us, what about God? [66] It is, therefore, worse than futile to attempt to compromise with the orthodox demand to an extent that would betray philosophic principles. God certainly knows all particulars, including material objects, as Ibn Sīnā held, but only through forms and not directly.

As we have said before, these forms, as metaphysical realities, are part of God's being and only when regarded *in abstracto* do they differ and become distinguishable from Him. When so regarded, they are posterior to His being as His necessary consequents. They then become mutually different and exhibit an order of priority and posteriority among themselves, as we have seen. But existentially, they are not different from Him: thus, the Intelligences of the Muslim Peripatetics, the Forms of Plato, and the Attributes of the theologians are identical with God's being—*existentially,* that is to say. It is this Divine Realm which is best described as "truth-in-itself (*nafs al-amr*)." [67] Truths that are seen only as being *applicable* in this material world but are not regarded as existential realities here—for example, two and two equal four,—are existential realities in the Divine Realm which contains, in the simplicity and totality of existence, all truths. We must now turn to Ṣadrā's final account of this existence-truth equation in the simple being of God.

Cognitive forms are, in a sense, real and in a sense they are identical with God's existence, as we have seen. They belong to that level of Godhead which is called "Divinity (*martaba ulūhiya*)," where God's attributes appear. But the appearance of this level of self-manifestation itself shows that they are latent in the level of God as Absolute Existent which is called "the level of absolute unity (*aḥadiya*)" or "absolute unseen (*ghaib al-ghaib*)." There are two ways to prove this, a philosophic way and a Sufi way. The philosophic proof is premised on four principles. First, a simple existential reality, as we have seen, can be the subject of attribution of multiple qualities or attributes, and this is particularly true of the final differentia as has been noted in our discussion of Essence in Chapter II of Part I. This is because the differentiae are simple existents.[68] Secondly, the more an existent is developed and strong, the more capable it is of giving rise to multiple attributes and ideas (*mafāhīm, ma'ānī*). This is the meaning of the principle "a simple nature in everything." [69] This apparently contradicts what Ṣadrā had said in Chapter I of Part I on Existence, viz., that essence is dysfunctionally related to existence and that the more of essence something has the less of existence it has. But "essence" strictly speaking means such notions as limit a thing and mark it off from other things by definition. The more of existence something has, the less of such limitations it can accept, for existence by itself is the principle of inclusiveness, not of exclusiveness; hence "essences" weaken when existence increases until we reach God or the Perfect Man whose nature is all-inclusive. Although even in this case attributes are only mental abstracts or notions extracted from existence, yet the capacity to yield notions in such a being is limitless. It is this unlimitedness of existence, giving rise to unlimited attributes, that lifts such a being from the realm of essences.[70]

But thirdly, as we saw in Section C, Chapter I of this Part while discussing the principle that a simple nature must be all-inclusive, although a higher form of existence contains the lower ones, these latter do not *exist* in it distinctly and severally but only analytically or notionally. Hence, one cannot predicate lower forms of existence of the higher. Although animal functions exist in man as part of his nature and vegetative functions exist in the animal, one cannot say "man is animal" or "animal is plant." Therefore, although all existence is *notionally* contained in God, forms or modes of existence do not exist in Him distinctly so that lower forms of existence might be predicated of Him.[71] Finally, every cause contains its effects eminently in itself in accordance with the principle of "the Higher Possibility" mentioned earlier.[72]

Now, since all existence is present in God's simple being, it follows that when He contemplate Himself, without any duality between the subject and the object, He knows everything both simply and in detail—with all particulars—since His being is *existentially* simple but *notionally* involves an infinite multiplicity.[73] This notional multiplicity does not create an essence in God as it does in other beings since, as we have pointed out above, God's existence being infinite, these notions are also infinite. The mark of an essence is its finitude which marks it out from other essences, a finitude which is due to the conjunction of an essence with finite existence. It is this finitude of existence resulting in essences that is the clear sign of contingency. God, on the other hand, being absolutely infinite and all-inclusive cannot be infected with contingency or essences.[74]

Lest this proposition about essences appear a mere play of words, we shall elaborate it further to make it more intelligible. According to our third principle stated above, a lower-form function may be exhibited by a higher form of being without the corresponding essence being attributable to the higher form. Thus, man has animal functions but is not animal; animal has vegetative functions but is not plant. This is because man's *existence* is that of man, not of animal and animal's *existence* is that of animal, not of plant. An essence, properly speaking, then, belongs to a proper level of existence where it has its being. Animality may be manifested by man but man's *existence* does not constitute the proper being of animality as an essence whose proper being is animal alone. There is, thus, a capital difference between where an essence has its proper being and where it is simply manifested. Hence, whereas God, the most perfect and concrete existent, contains and "manifests" essences, His being is not the being of those essences.[75]

God, then, has no essences at the level of His absolute being. But the question now is: if God possesses all forms of existence in His utter simplicity, what is the need for additionally positing so many different forms which Ibn Sīnā and his followers had affirmed to be His accidents (and whereby they mean Intelligences) and which Ṣadrā has striven so hard to lift from the realm of pure contingency and make part of the Divine Realm? Ṣadrā's answer is that, besides that simple knowledge which God possesses in His very being of all forms of existence, He must also know them *in an order, i.e., as His effects.* Merely to know something is not the same as knowing it as the cause of an effect or effect of a cause.[76] This answer seems highly dubious for, surely, if God possesses all forms, He must already possess them in an order; for it is the principle of existence which, for Ṣadrā, orders the entire realm of being, and God, being pure existence, must possess this order in Himself as the paragon of all existence. In Section B of Chapter IV of Part I we had criticized Ṣadrā for positing separate ideas or attributes in God's mind and we expressed there the suspicion that his motivation for doing this was to bring together diverse elements in Islamic philosophical, mystical, and theological thought. This suspicion is now further confirmed since, after positing all forms in God's being in a simple manner, there seems little need for attributing duplicate explicit forms. It appears certain that he wants to combine in one stroke the Intelligences of the philosophers, the "Essences of Contingents" of Ibn 'Arabī, the Platonic Forms of the Platonists, and the angelology of the theologians. This *genre* of thought was much too widespread and much too firmly rooted in the diverse currents of the Islamic tradition to be simply ignored or contradicted. But it is apparently not easily compatible with Ṣadrā's doctrine of existence and its movement through various hierarchical forms of existential reality.

But among the various Islamic thought-currents, probably the most important source of inspiration for Ṣadrā on this subject is Ibn 'Arabī. From Ibn 'Arabī he takes the idea of the "descents (*tanazzulāt*)" of the Absolute, that at the first stage of descent—the stage of Godhead (*ulūhīya*)—attributes and essences appear and that these essences, although they have effects and can be spoken of (*lahā aḥkām*), *have absolutely no share of existence.* Inspired with this doctrine, Ṣadrā then goes back to the philosophic tradition of Islam, notably to Ibn Sīnā and his critic, al-Suhrawardī, and interprets this whole tradition under the impact of this inspiration. This is, of course, not to say that our philosopher lacks originality—on the contrary, his doctrine of existence and constant movement of existential forms is uniquely his own, even though his source of inspiration remains Ibn 'Arabī, and to a lesser extent al-Suhrawardī among post-Ibn Sīnā thinkers.

The second method of proving God's knowledge—the Sufi method—is in essence the same as we have seen in another context in Section B, Chapter IV of Part I. God's being, while simple and unitary existence, is nevertheless characterizable by certain attributes.[77] This multiplicity of attributes, their consequents, and their attendant relationships and permutations do not interfere with this simple unity since these are mere abstractions, mental in character and "have never even smelt of existence," as Ibn 'Arabī's famous dictum has it. They are neither existent nor non-existent; existence is not their attribute nor are they attributes of existence. They simply "are there (*thābit*)" as by-products of divine existence. They cannot even be said to "follow upon" existence since the phrase "follow upon" also smacks of some kind of existence.[78]

Now, when God knows Himself, He necessarily also knows these notional beings or essences. Hence, He knows, by the same unitary and simple act of knowledge, all the multiplicity of the world, all causes with their effects. Ṣadrā here distinguishes three stages of God's knowledge (and indeed, His being). The first stage is that of absolute unity, of pure existence, which he calls the "stage of absolute unity" or "absolute Absence"; the second that of Godhead (*ulūhīya*) where distinct attributes appear and which he calls the "stage of unity" (since all attributes and essences, though distinct, share the same divine existence); the third that of Platonic Forms where every Form exists by itself and which he calls the "stage of distinction." Here the Divine Realm ends and the material realm begins; but we must remember that these three stages or "descents" for Ṣadrā are logical, i.e., are abstractions, for in reality there is nothing but the simple existence of God. After the last stage of the Divine Realm, we have the material world with increasingly "absolute difference." [79]

NOTES

1. *Asfār,* III, 1, lines 6–10; p. 121, line 14–p. 122, end, particularly p. 122, line 2.

2. *Ibid.,* p. 119, line 2–p. 130, line 1; p. 130, line 12–p. 131, line 1.

3. *Ibid.,* p. 124, lines 9–12; cf. p. 121, lines 4–5.

4. *Ibid.,* p. 124, line 13–p. 125, line 13; p. 144, lines 8–17.

5. See references in the preceding note.

6. *Ibid.,* p. 125, lines 10–13.

7. *Ibid.,* p. 126, line 1–p. 128, line 1.

8. *Ibid.,* p. 128, lines 3–9; p. 131, lines 10–19; cf. the preceding Chapter of this Part, Section B; cf. also *ibid.,* I, 2, p. 177, lines 2 ff.

9. *Ibid.,* p. 131, line 20–p. 132, end.

10. *Ibid.,* p. 128, line 10–p. 129, line 2; al-Sabzawārī's note 3 on p. 128.

11. *Ibid.,* p. 133, line 3–p. 134, line 4; al-Sabzawārī's note 1 on p. 133.

12. *Ibid.,* p. 133, al-Sabzawārī's note 3.

13. *Ibid.,* p. 142, lines 11–p. 143, line 1; pp. 144, line 1–p. 145, line 10; p. 145, lines 13 ff.

14. *Ibid.,* p. 135, lines 3–6; p. 144, lines 1–7.

15. *Ibid.,* p. 147, line 10–p. 149, line 2; p. 145, lines 2–10.

16. *Ibid.,* p. 148, line 11–p. 149, line 2; *ibid.,* p. 271, line 6–p. 272, line 3; cf. preceding chapter, Section B.

17. *Ibid.,* p. 148, lines 5–10.

18. *Ibid.,* p. 135, lines 3 ff.

19. *Ibid.,* al-Ṭabāṭabā'ī's note 1 on p. 135.

20. *Ibid.,* p. 176, lines 2–10; p. 180, lines 2 ff.

21. *Ibid.,* p. 180, line 14–p. 182, line 10.

22. *Ibid.,* p. 182, lines 15–18.

23. *Ibid.,* p. 184, line 1–p. 185, last line.

24. *Ibid.,* p. 186, lines 5 ff.

25. *Ibid.,* p. 188, lines 5–10.

26. *Ibid.,* p. 188, lines 11 ff.

27. See Part I, Chapter IV, Section C; also *Asfār,* III, 1, p. 227, lines 19–23; p. 234, lines 8 ff.

28. See *Asfār,* III, 1, p. 211, lines 15–18; p. 233, lines 18 ff., also notes 45, 46.
29. See below, Chapter IV of Part III.
30. Compare the reference in the preceding note with *Asfār,* III, 1, p. 243, lines 18 ff.
31. *Asfār,* III, 1, p. 238, lines 4–14; p. 240, lines 5–13.
32. *Ibid.,* p. 243, lines 1 ff.; p. 238, last line.
33. *Ibid.,* p. 239, last line–p. 240, line 2.
34. *Ibid.,* p. 240, lines 3–4.
35. *Ibid.,* p. 240, lines 5–16.
36. *Ibid.,* p. 241, lines 1–6.
37. *Ibid.,* p. 241, comments 1 and 2.
38. *Ibid.,* p. 241, lines 7–10.
39. *Ibid.,* p. 189, lines 10–20; p. 190, line 18–p. 191, line 8; p. 195, lines 3-8; p. 195, line 16– p. 198, line 5; p. 198, lines 10–11.
40. See the first two references in the preceding note.
41. *Asfār,* p. 191, line 9–p. 193, line 3; p. 199 lines 2–12.
42. *Ibid.,* p. 199, line 13–p. 201, line 3; p. 201, line 4–p. 202, line 5.
43. *Ibid.,* p. 202, lines 6–11; p. 256, lines 11 ff.
44. *Ibid.,* p. 203, line 8–p. 205, line 14.
45. *Ibid.,* p. 200, lines 1–10; cf. references in note 8 above.
46. *Ibid.,* quotations from Ibn Sīnā, p. 207, line 1–p. 208, line 4; p. 210, line 10–p. 211, line 10.
47. References in the two preceding notes.
48. *Ibid.,* p. 214, line 11–p. 217, line 2.
49. *Ibid.,* p. 198, lines 6–15; p. 227, lines 19–22.
50. *Ibid.,* p. 228, line 4–p. 232, line 10.
51. *Ibid.,* p. 229, lines 2–3; p. 230, line 10–p. 231, line 8.
52. *Ibid.,* p. 229, lines 4 ff.
53. *Ibid.,* al-Ṭabāṭabā'ī's note 1 on p. 229.
54. *Ibid.,* p. 232, lines 1–10; p. 234, lines 11–13.
55. *Ibid.,* p. 234, lines 8–20.
56. *Ibid.,* p. 261, lines 8 ff.
57. *Ibid.,* p. 249, line 6–p. 253, line 9.
58. Ṣadrā has repeatedly stated that al-Ṭūsī *followed* al-Suhrawardī: *ibid.,* p. 181, line 2; p. 209, line 6; p. 233, lines 10–15 (where a distinction between the two is made); p. 253, line 10.
59. *Ibid.,* p. 254, line 12–p. 256, line 5; for the analogy of the book, see below, al-Ṭūsī's account of Divine knowledge of particulars in Chapter IV, Part III.
60. *Ibid.,* p. 256, line 10–p. 257, line 4.
61. *Ibid.,* p. 261, lines 3–7.

62. *Ibid.*, p. 256, line 12–p. 257, line 2.
63. *Ibid.*, p. 257, lines 5 ff.
64. *Ibid.*, p. 260, lines 5–16.
65. *Ibid.*, p. 259, lines 10–p. 260, line 4.
66. *Ibid.*, p. 260, lines 7–10; cf. p. 259, lines 3–7.
67. *Ibid.*, p. 261, line 12–p. 262, line 7.
68. *Ibid.*, p. 263, lines 13 ff.; particularly, p. 264, line 11–p. 267, line 1.
69. *Ibid.*, p. 267, lines 2–7.
70. *Ibid.*, p. 271, lines 6 ff.
71. *Ibid.*, p. 267, line 8–p. 269, line 1.
72. *Ibid.*, p. 269, lines 2–8.
73. *Ibid.*, p. 269, last line–p. 271, line 5.
74. References in note 70 above.
75. Reference in note 71 above; *ibid.*, p. 272, line 4–p. 273, line 18.
76. *Ibid.*, p. 273, line 19–p. 275, line 5.
77. *Ibid.*, p. 280, line 18–p. 281, line 9.
78. *Ibid.*, p. 281, line 10–p. 283, line 4.
79. *Ibid.*, p. 283, lines 5 ff.—particularly, p. 284, lines 9–21.

CHAPTER III

GOD'S ATTRIBUTES—II

A. *Power and Will*

1. *A Survey of Alternative Views*

Since for Ṣadrā, like the philosophers, creation flows from God's foreknowledge, God's power and will are identical with His knowledge; otherwise, a multiplicity will arise in God's being. God's power and will are, therefore, radically different from man's power and will which are over and above his being and also additional to his knowledge. Ṣadrā opens the discussion of God's power with a general historical review. Historically, two definitions of power have been given. Most theologians define volitional power as "the possibility of an agent's doing an act or not doing it," while for philosophers power means that "if the agent wills, he will do the act; if he does not will it, he will not do it." Fakhr al-Dīn al-Rāzī thought that the two definitions are the same in essence since the philosophers also appear to concede that power itself—if we discount the will—hangs in the balance between the doing of an act and not doing it and that it is only the will that makes one side preponderate.[1]

Ṣadrā rejects this equation of the two definitions *in the case of God,* since "hanging in the balance between an act and its absence" is a clear sign of native contingency (*al-imkān al-dhātī*) which affects only contingents—in *some* of their actions—and not God. The theologians' definition, therefore, cannot hold with respect to God. But the philosophical definition is correct, since the conditional proposition, "If he wills the act, he will do it," is fully satisfied also in a being like God who is eternally willing and so is the conditional "If he does not will the act, he will not do it," fully satisfied in God's case even if He never stops willing. Yet, this does not imply that God's acts are determined and not free, because in the case of a being whose acts are necessary and determined, this conditional proposition is not satisfied, for one cannot say of fire, for example, "If it wills to burn, it will burn, otherwise not." [2]

Al-Rāzī, in fact, goes on to say that there is no disagreement between theologians and philosophers on the meaning of the terms "cause" and "will" for, on their part, the theologians also admit that *if* the world were eternal, it would have an eternal *cause*. But they reject the idea of an eternal cause because such a cause could not be a *free will,* since a will can at least delay its effect, whereas a cause cannot. For their part, philosophers also agree that an eternal act cannot be the result of a free will and yet they hold the world to be eternal. Al-Ṭūsī characterizes al-Rāzī's statement as "an agreement without the parties' consent," for, to begin with, the theologians seek to prove the temporal creation of the world without even talking of God's free will and, secondly, many theologians reject the notion of cause-effect altogether. Ṣadrā declares al-Ṭūsī's statement to be "excellent" [3] but it is clear that it is not at all fair to the theologians. It is not correct that theologians *only* approach the question taking the world as their point of departure and certainly since al-Ghazālī they discuss the question of the nature of God's will as well, accusing the philosophers of positing a God who has no free will worthy of the name. Besides, those theologians who deny cause-effect, deny it *within the world* and this they do in order to give the entire field to one Supreme Cause, viz., the Will of God.

Now Ṣadrā, along with philosophers like Ibn Sīnā and al-Ṭūsī, holds, and we shall elaborate this further below, that in the case of God and to an extent in some—perhaps even most—human actions as well, knowledge, power, and will are identical, and that the "will" is not a unique and specific act as it is generally supposed to be, but is rather part of a total cognitive-conative process. We shall also see that Ṣadrā differs from these philosophers in that for him, knowledge, power, and will are factually reducible to existence and are hence universally present in *everything,* but in a systematically ambiguous sense like existence itself. This enables him also to differ from these philosophers' conclusions that man is not really free in his will but only has the appearance of the freedom of the will. Apart from these two crucial points, however, in his views on the nature of the will and power and the consequent view of the eternity of the world, Ṣadrā closely follows the philosophers. But before we come to Ṣadrā's own view, we have to follow his critical analysis of various other opinions held on the matter.

The three main adversaries in the field are the Mu'tazila, the Ash'arīs, and the philosophers. The first two schools distinguish between God's power and will: since both believe that God's power being equally related to doing a thing and not doing it, will is required to tip the scale to one side. These two groups differ mutually, however, on two points. For the Ash'arīs, God's will is the sole determinant of His acts, whose *raison d'être* does not go beyond that will: the question, that is to say, as to why God does or ordains something is an absurd one, since the only answer can be, "Because He so willed." The Mu'tazila, on the other hand, think that God has always a purpose in His actions and the purpose is always the well-being (*maṣlaḥa*) of the creation. Secondly, and closely allied to the first point, while most Mu'tazilites, particularly the later ones, believe that God's will, for its formation, needs an *absolute* determinant so that, given that determinant (e.g., a particular moment of time for the creation of the world rather than another moment of time), the will must be irrevocably formed, the Ash'arites say that since there are always alternatives open to God (of which some may be better than others)—of doing one thing rather than another—the reasons for the irrevocability of God's will do not lie outside that will but within it and that God's will itself is the closure of other alternatives.[4]

The philosophers differ from the Mu'tazila in rejecting the view that God acts out of purposes beyond Himself, for example, for the sake of the world, since such a concept of purpose implies a certain imperfection in God, who thus seeks to perfect Himself by being conditioned by something outside Himself. Such a concept of purpose applies to man, not to God. Indeed, a basic principle of the philosophers is that nothing higher acts *for the sake of the lower* and that the perfection of the lower comes about *as a by-product* of the action of the higher. The purpose of God's action is, therefore, nothing but God Himself, i.e., His action is a necessary part of His nature which is goodness and perfection. From this point of view, therefore, the philosophers are, to some extent, in agreement with the Ash'arites. Yet their disagreements with the Ash'arites are of far greater dimensions. They sternly reject the Ash'arite view that there are no absolute determinants for God's will, to which alternatives are always open and that cause and effect are really meaningless. While the philosophers say that God works within the framework of the causal process and, for example, He needs a seed and other necessary conditions to produce a mature plant, the Ash'arites hold that, if God so willed, He could produce a plant without any causes and prior conditions.[5] The gist of the philosophers' view of God's will and power is that these are distinguishable only in the case of man, where "power" means only something potential and is then actualized by will. In God's case, however, since there is no potentiality in Him awaiting realization, power and will are identical. They explain the production of the world by God, not on the ground that it is in the best interest of the world (although this interest is real, it is a by-product)—as the Mu'tazilites say, nor on the ground of a *liberum arbitrium* on God's part—as the Ash'arites hold—but on the basis of their doctrine of divine Providence (*al-'ināya,* literally: attention, care). As we have seen in the preceding chapter, *'ināya* means that in God's self-knowledge, the knowledge of the world is given.

This knowledge, since it is perfect like God's being, reveals the entire cause-effect structure which then takes on external existence exactly on the pattern according to which it existed in God's mind. Now, the perfectness (*al-atammīya*) of this knowledge ensures that there will be no *alternatives* to the actual course existence takes; to falter, deliberate, and hence to *choose* and to intend (*qaṣd*) belongs to the human will, which cannot work by *'ināya* but by deliberate choice, conflict, and decision. Yet, even in the human sphere there are certain indications of the *'ināya*-type will; for example, when we normally work by routine or through an already settled purpose, we certainly work voluntarily, yet we work almost automatically as it were, not through deliberation and choice.[6]

There follows the definition of will on the principles of the philosophers. Will *par excellence* is a process *originating in knowledge and ending in an action which is not disagreeable to the agent.* It must be noted that their definition leaves out "will" altogether and makes suffice with a cognitive-conative process; there is, therefore, no need to postulate a specific *act of will* clearly marked out and distinguishable from the knowledge-action complex. This is also applicable *mutatis mutandis* to the human will although one does speak of things like "decision," "resolve," etc., in the human case, since human beings, having only partial knowledge, are often exposed to the "making of choices." [7] Al-Ṭabāṭabā'ī criticizes this view by urging that since the idea of will is different from that of knowledge, the former cannot be reduced to the latter, neither in us nor in God—if, that is, there does exist a clearly discernible mental state expressed by the term "will." [8] But, surely, the whole point of Ṣadrā and other philosophers is that there *is no* such unique and clearly discernible mental act called "will." We shall resume this discussion further when we analyze Ṣadrā's concept of the *human* will in particular. Here we note that Ṣadrā simply states that a "willer is he who knows what he is doing and what he is doing is agreeable to him, i.e., he is not doing it under constraint." [9]

Finally, the philosophers hold that since the place of everything is unalterably fixed in the entire order, nothing is really free. The human will *appears* to be free, but, viewed in the entire context of God's will, it is predetermined. This is explicitly stated by Ibn Sīnā and other Muslim Peripatetics. Al-Ṭūsī, however, states that when a person looks at his own direct consciousness of freedom, he thinks he is free, but when he puts his actions in the general context of past causes and conditions over which he had no control, he thinks all his actions are pre-determined. The truth, however, is that man "is neither absolutely pre-determined nor totally free but shares a part of both." [10] What this really means is not clear, since philosophers hold that in case of the human will, when a certain motivation (*dā'ī*) comes to hold sway, free will disappears.[11] Further, this statement is somewhat confused. The point at issue here is not so much freedom versus *causal* determinism, but freedom versus *theistic* determinism, i.e., the determinism produced by the all-pervasive Will of God. Of course, the causal chain determines the content of the process, but God's will, or rather the knowledge-action complex that has produced this causal chain, has unalterably fixed the place of everything. Indeed, on this point, the language of the philosophers closely approaches that of the Ash'arites, who deny causation but affirm the omnipotent and all-pervasive Will of God. We shall see below how Ṣadrā grapples with this problem of human determinism.

2. *Ṣadrā's Criticism of These Views and His Position*

Ṣadrā rejects Ash'arism for several reasons. First, to define will in terms of "the possibility of the agent's doing a thing or its opposite," when applied to God, introduces into Him possibilities which may or may not be realized. This is untenable because it goes against the very notion of God's perfection which implies that everything in God is *actual,* not just *possible.*[12] The Ash'arites object that with the elimination of the notion of possibility and choice from God's will, God would become necessarily determined in His action and would not remain free since the world will become eternal, and both these propositions are unacceptable on *religious* grounds.

Ṣadrā meets the second objection by saying that the world *as a process* is eternal but that since nothing in the world remains the same any two moments—as he has proved in his theory of substantive movement in Chapter V, Part I—the world ceases to be eternal in its contents and even the world's eternity *as a process* is not an independent one but derivative from God's being: the derivative cannot become a rival to the original particularly when the latter is stable and self-same, while the former is continually subject to change.[13] So far as the first objection is concerned, viz., that "God will act through necessity and will not be free," Ṣadrā says that the opposite of "freedom" is not "necessity," as is commonly believed, but "constraint" i.e., lack of freedom.[14] God acts by necessity in the sense that He follows the best course of action which forecloses other less desirable alternatives, thanks to His Providence (*'ināya*), but He does not work under constraint and is, therefore, free and the counterfactual hypothetical is true of Him: "If He so willed, He would act otherwise"—which is the hallmark of freedom.[15] Ṣadrā also criticizes his teacher, Mīr Bāqir Dāmād, for accepting the theologians' definition of free will in terms of the "possibility of doing or not-doing an action" and then seeking to defend himself against the introduction of the notion of possibility in God by saying that what is possible is not the subject, i.e., God's will, but the object, i.e., the action and hence while the world is only possible (i.e., not necessary) when regarded in itself, it is necessary when related to God's will. Ṣadrā rejects this reply on the ground that if an effect is possible-in-itself (and necessary-by-its-cause), this does not render the cause necessarily a *volitional* cause (as distinguished from a *natural* cause); else all causes would become volitional. The best course, concludes Ṣadrā, for those who prefer this definition of power and will, is to say that power is related to will as the imperfect is related to the perfect, but, of course, this too is obviously unsatisfactory, since it introduces at least a conceptual imperfection in God.[16]

Ṣadrā's second reason for rejecting the theologians' view of will as "attaching itself to one of the two sides of a possible act (i.e., of doing or not doing or doing one thing rather than another) by itself without any reason that would tip the balance on one side" is that this would do away with all notion of rational necessity and all certainty: "one could not even draw a necessary conclusion from premises." [17] Further, if will were inherently characterized by "possibility," then one would have to seek for another act of will to tip the balance and so on *ad infinitum.* For it is certain that when will does translate itself into a particular actual action, other possibilities must be foreclosed at this point and will must become necessary; it then behaves like any other natural cause which necessarily produces its effect.[18] It has, therefore, to be reiterated that the inherent difference between a volitional cause and a natural cause does not lie in the fact that the one is "open" and the other "closed," i.e., necessary, but in the fact that the one is volitional and the other is not.[19] That is, the one is a cognitive-conative type while the other is of a natural cause-effect type, or, in other words, the action of an actor who acts through rational necessity is not describable by any linguistic usage as "constrained" or "involuntary." [20] Indeed, the highest and most perfect form of volitional action is this type of action, for this necessity of volition, far from detracting from its volitional character, strengthens it.[21]

In the case of a human being, conation is often a complex process. A person knows something and may either have an appetition or desire (*shawq*) towards it or an aversion (*karāha*) for it. This desire may intensify and result in a pursuit of action. Or, a person may be presented with several alternatives and he will make a *decision* (*'azm*) in favor of one course; under favorable conditions, this may result in action. Now, which part of this process is to be characterized as being uniquely an act of will? (It is to be noted that in God's case, this process as such cannot exist, for in His case there is a simple cognition-conation.) In the face of these difficulties, many [i.e., later] Mu'tazilites defined will as belief in utility (*i'tiqād al-naf'*), which tips the balance towards the side of positive action. The difficulty, however, is that we often believe in the goodness or utility of something and yet do the contrary. Some Mu'tazilites say that will is the maximal point of desire and that when that fruition point is reached, it is called will and results in action. But the trouble is that we often have a strong desire for some things but we do not will them—for instance, such things as are forbidden by law. It is also true that we sometimes do things without any express will (but not involuntarily), as in the case of such habits as cracking one's fingers or stroking one's beard; or, we may will certain things against our desire, as when we take distasteful medicine.[22]

Ṣadrā's final answer to the theologians, to the difficulties in the foregoing Mu'tazilite views, as well as those of the philosophers (who deny that man is *really* free) is that all these people are talking about will in terms of straight jacket concepts: they are talking about a will-in-general which can be found anywhere as little as existence-in-general. Ṣadrā insists that will and knowledge are all grounded in and are concomitants (*rafīq*) of existence, to which they are finally reducible.[23] Hence, will is as systematically ambiguous (*mushakkak*) as is existence itself.[24] Will in God is something basically different from will in man and will in man is similarly different from will in animals. This is because existence itself differs fundamentally at different levels of being. Indeed, will is in some sense present, just as knowledge is present, even in inanimate objects—in the form of a physical "tendency (*mayl*)"—although it may not be called by that name in linguistic usage (since will is always said to be possessed only by conscious beings). Thus, in inanimate objects it appears as a physical tendency, in animals as pure appetition, in man as rational appetition, and in God as pure rational providence:

"It is, therefore, clear that what is termed will, or love or desire or tendency, etc., exactly corresponds to [the nature of] existence in everything but in some cases it is not called by these terms in pure convention or linguistic usage. . . . It is just like a material form which, according to us, is *one of the levels* of knowledge but the term 'knowledge' is not applied to it but only to that form which is free from matter and any admixture of [material] non-being." [25]

Because will is a concomitant of existence like knowledge, its relation to its objects is absolutely specific and unique. A will's relation to its object and a cognition's relation to its object parallels the relation of existence to an existent. One can, therefore, as little talk of a will's attachment to an object and its contrary at the same time (as theologians say) as one can talk of an existence becoming equally attachable to A or not-A.[26] Indeed, there is no such thing as will-in-general, or knowledge-in-general, or existence-in-general: all are absolutely particular and specific.[27] The question, however, is whether this contention does not contradict our expressly stated view that God's unitary will is creatively related to all contingents just as His own unitary and simple knowledge is so related to the entire diversity of existence. The answer is that when we speak of "one simple and unitary will or knowledge," we do not mean by that unity a numerical but a true creative unity which comprehends everything.[28] We must, therefore, state categorically that there is an absolute unity of subject and object in knowledge and complete identity of all will with the willed object, even as existent and existence are uniquely identical. It is, therefore, inconceivable that one will can be attached to more than one object.[29]

Now, in the case of humans and animals, there is a continuous stream of consciousness in which all mental phenomena like cognition, volition, pleasure, and pain are *immediately experienced.* Further, in this continuous stream of experience (which *as experience* is essentially private and incommunicable), usually all mental phenomena are present together. There is no such thing as pure cognition or pure volition or even pure desire or aversion although in any given experience one or more of these elements may be prominent. It is because of this immediately experienced quality of mental phenomena (*al-ḥuḍūr bi'l-huwīyat al-wijdānīya li'l-kaifīyāt al-nafsānīya*) and their co-presence that we cannot distill their general essences or definitions (if they have definitions at all) from particular experiences, although one can point to certain general areas of conscious mental life by constructing ideas of a will-in-general or a knowledge-in-general.[30] It has to be pointed out here that Ṣadrā will give us in Chapter II of Part III of the present work, devoted to his theory of knowledge, a definition of knowledge, viz., that it is pure, self-intellective, and self-intelligible form, although he will affirm there again the identity of thought and existence. But he has also insisted throughout that there are other forms of unconscious knowledge pressent in lower forms of existence and there is a supra-conscious form of knowledge that belongs to God. The essence of what he is saying here, therefore, is that, like existence, will and knowledge do not have the same meaning everywhere because they are systematically ambiguous. Difficulties and dilemmas arise for all sorts of thinkers—philosophers, the Mu'tazilite and the Ash'arite theologians—when they try to illegitimately extend the meaning, for example, of will, obtaining at one level of existence, to another. In some ways they are all correct, in others they are all wrong and for different reasons.

3. *Relationship of God's Will to Man*

The most important point at issue is the relationship of the divine Will to the human will. The Mu'tazila, although they rejected all substantive attributes of God in the interests of a pure monotheism, nevertheless affirmed that God acted for the benefit and "in the best interests (*al-aṣlaḥ*)" of His creation and, further, that God allowed man a totally free will so that man might be entirely responsible for his own actions and God might be free from the blame of determining men's behavior and then rewarding or punishing him. This view was untenable on two grounds. First, because it portrayed God as willing and acting for purposes extrinsic to His own absolute being and, secondly, because it postulated two original and absoulte actors —God in the physical universe and man in the sphere of human actions. The Mu'tazila were rightly accused of being dualists or even polytheists.[31] The Ash'arite theologians, reacting to this, went to the other extreme and held that God, being omnipotent, *directly* created everything—including man, his will and his actions; they denied all power to man, saying that man can be said to "act" only in a metaphorical, not a real sense, and they equally rejected the notion of causation altogether, saying that what we call causes are only *seeming* causes, since the only real and effective cause of everything is the Will of God. Since God wills and creates everything, He is equally "pleased" with everything, whether it be good or bad, since good and bad are human categories which cannot be projected to God. In fact, in a pure state of nature there is nothing intrinsically good or bad; it becomes so only by God's declaration through revelations vouchsafed to prophets.[32]

The third group, that of philosophers (like Ibn Sīnā) and "our top Shi'ite thinkers" (like al-Ṭūsī) hold that existence flows from God *in an order* and not haphazardly; hence, although all existence comes from God, it comes through a mediating *causal chain* and due efficacy must be assigned to a cause. It is absurd to say that God can, for example, produce a tree without a seed. This is not because of a lack of sufficient efficacy on the part of God, but because it is inherent in the nature of the physical world that things should come into existence on the basis of proper conditions, antecedents, and causes. It is because of this fact, viz., that things in this world exist only piecemeal and seriatim, that evil enters into it, God's will and knowledge being absolutely free from it, since it is total and absolute, not piecemeal and seriatim. Evil is, therefore, of an accidental, secondary, and negative nature. It may, therefore, be said that "God intends, but is not pleased with, evil," since evil is, *at this level of existence,* a necessary concomitant of God's maximal production of good.[33] This school of thought seeks to mediate between the absolute freedom of will granted to man by the Mu'tazila and the complete negation of freedom to man characteristic of Ash'arism and is, as such, better than the previous two views,[34] although sometimes representatives of this school—like Ibn Sīnā—also say that man is actually predetermined and only formally free.[35]

There is, however, a fourth group of "inspired" philosophers and rare

Sufis who hold that there is a *real* multiplicity of things which still contains and points to a unity, and a *real* unity which in its simplicity contains all multiplicity (*waḥda fi'l-kathra* and *kathra fi'l waḥda,* as Ṣadrā usually puts it); this is nothing else but Ṣadrā's principle of *tashkīk* or systematic ambiguity of existence which maintains that existence *by the very fact* of its being the principle of unity is the principle of diversity—yet, the two must not be simply identified with one another nor confused with one another, nor substituted for one another, nor yet must one be negated in the interests of the other. Diversity-in-unity does not mean that God is a numerical composite of diverse parts, nor does unity-in-diversity mean that God is any and everything: it means that God is *present* in or "with" everything but not in the form of a mixture of two co-ordinate elements, and He transcends everything not in a way so that He is "removed" from it.[36]

This means that when A acts, he produces his action in a real, not metaphorical, sense; yet the same act is also due to the omnipresence and omnipotence of God. But we must not say that this act is in part A's product and in part God's product, for the same act is exactly and in its *sameness* attributable to both—to A as his action and to God as His creation. This also shows the falsity of the philosophers' view according to which either man's freedom and will are only formal and apparent, the real determinant being God's eternal will, or man's action is *in part* free and *in part* predetermined as al-Ṭūsī held. Man is literally and truly said to be free in his action, for this is what freedom and will *in man's case* mean, i.e., when man is said to be free, this does not mean or imply that man has no other determinants except his will and that his will is born *ex nihilo* and without any context. To demand this sort of freedom for man is simply absurd:

> The saying attributed to the foremost monotheist, 'Ali, "There is neither total determinism [of human acts] nor total freedom," does not mean that a given human action is a sort of composite of determinism and freedom; nor does it mean that it neutralizes both [by becoming a compound of them]; nor does it mean that from one point of view [*min jiha*] it is by constraint while from another point of view it is free; nor yet does it mean that man is really determined and is free only in form —as the chief of the philosophers [Ibn Sīnā and indeed al-Fārābī] has expressed it; nor, finally, does it mean that man has a partial and deficient freedom and a similarly partial and deficient determinism. What this saying means is that in man's [voluntary actions] . . . freedom and determinism *are the same.* The adage, "In everything the golden mean is the best," is truly realized in this view; [only we must make its meaning precise in this context]. For, the mean between extremes is sometimes produced by a compounding of the two extremes in such a way

> that both sides lose their extremeness; for example, water may achieve such a balance between hot and cold that it is no longer either hot or cold actually, and yet it cannot go outside these two categories. In such a mean, it is said, the mean "cancels out" both sides. But there is another sense of "mean" [which is more appropriate in our case]; this means that in a simpler and higher level or mode of existence, both sides are actually present [and neither of them is removed], but they become identical with one another in such a way that they do not contradict each other [nor do they cancel each other out]. "Mean" in this sense is better than the "mean" in the earlier sense.[37]

This must also, then, be Ṣadrā's answer to those theologians and philosophers who believe in psychological determinism. According to this view, when a certain motivation comes to hold sway over the human mind, the will and action become absolutely determined, and man "has no freedom any longer." This view is expressed (although it ill accords with the Ash'arite view that will remains open and never reaches a point of closure of alternatives, as does a cause) by several theologians like al-Rāzī, the philosophers like Ibn Sīnā and his school. The answer, then, is that that determining motivation is part of what we call freedom of the human will; indeed, such motivations *are* the human will and to demand that human action be free from motivation in order to be "really free" is simply to demand the absurd. It should be noted, although this is not the place to go into details, that this attitude is common to and is expressed in various ways by many Muslim thinkers—theologians like Ibn Taimīya, philosophers like Ṣadrā, Sufīs like Sirhindī, and other thinkers like Shāh Walīy Allāh of Delhi—in the post-Mu'tazila, Ash'arite and philosophical periods of Islam. That is to say, they all seek to combine the notion of a real and efficacious human will with the idea of an omnipotent and all-pervasive divine will. Their approaches are different, in accordance with their thought-systems, yet the result is basically the same. So far as Ṣadrā is concerned, it is obvious that he bases his solution of this perennial problem of Islamic theology on his most characteristic principle of the simplicity and systematic ambiguity of existence and by extending it to knowledge and will, which for him are concomitants of all existence and like it, subject to *tashkīk:* "Be not like those who are committed to the effeminacy of pure immanence (or anthropomorphism, i.e., of God's will) or the virility of absolute transcendence or the eunuchism of mechanically combining both, like a Janus-faced object, but be in your belief like the inhabitants of the sanctuaries of the Divine Realm, the lofty ones [i.e., those who believe that existence by its very nature is both unitary and diverse, and both in a real sense]." [38]

Ṣadrā also considers certain fresh problems arising out of this account, viz., those of the entry of evil into the divine scheme (which we have already referred to above), of how man's will can be free in face of an omnipotent Divine Will and the characteristically Shi'ite doctrine of *badā'* or God changing His mind on certain things. The first question is: If God has an over-arching eternal Decree (*Qaḍā'*), how can evil come into existence and how can we say that God's Decree is "good"? The Ash'arite theologians al-Ghazālī and al-Rāzī reply that one must make a distinction between decreeing and the object of a decree. While the first is always good, because it occurs at the level of divine providence, which is free from evil, the latter may or may not be good. Thus, whereas God's foreknowledge of a man's disbelief cannot be bad, disbelief itself is bad.[39] This view was attacked by al-Ṭūsī and, following him, by Mīr Dāmād on the ground that the distinction between decree and its object is illegitimate: thus, when we speak of a judge's decreeing something, the term decree applies equally to the judge's act as well as the object of that act.[40] Ṣadrā supports the two Ash'arites on this point by saying that whereas "decreeing" as a relational concept cannot tolerate this distinction, "decree" in the sense of God's simple foreknowledge is capable of such a distinction. His contention is, as we have seen earlier, that at the level of the absolute simplicity of God's knowledge, there is no place for evil; evil, as a secondary, accidental, or negative factor, does enter and infect the level of multiplicity.[41]

The difficulty is then raised at the level of God's fore-knowledge: If God knew in eternity that, for example, A would do an evil act, then it is difficult to save either God from the imputation of evil or man from determinism. Al-Ṭūsī replies, in conformity with his views on God's knowledge in the preceding chapter, that things do not follow upon God's knowledge but God's knowledge follows upon things. Ṣadrā, equally in conformity with his rejection of al-Ṭūsī's views in the preceding chapter, holds that God has fore-knowledge of A's evil act but He also has the fore-knowledge that A's act will proceed from A's free will, since A, *at his level,* is a free agent and hence is responsible for his act, even though his evil act is necessary when the reality as a whole is considered.[42] Ṣadrā then gives a lengthy quotation from al-Rāzī's *K. al-Mabāḥith al-Mashriqīya* in his own support, praises al-Rāzī for departing for once from his usual Ash'arite stand of negating the necessary connection between cause and effect,[43] and ends by affirming that there is a real difference between saying that there exists nothing without God's working and saying that it is only God's working that directly produces everything—the first statement being correct, the second erroneous because it rejects intermediary causes.[44]

The second important question raised is closely allied to the previous one but has as its object determinism of the human will rather than the existence of evil. If man's will, it is asked, is a necessary consequence of certain antecedents ending up in the eternal will of God, how can one say that man's will is free in view of the fact that *his will is not the result of his own will* but of factors outside his control? The answer given by Ṣadrā seems to be correct: a free agent is one whose action is the result of his own free will, not one whose will is the result of his own free will because this would involve a vicious regress.[45] Having given this sound answer, however, Ṣadrā appears to go wrong by giving another answer to the effect that "willing a will" is like "knowing that one knows," for in the latter case one can go on *ad infinitum* to higher-order acts of self-knowledge (one knows that one knows and one knows that one knows that one knows, etc.).[46] First, if "willing one's will" were analogous to "knowing that one knows," then why should it involve a *vicious* regress, for in the case of self-knowledge, there is no *vicious* regress; it can stop at any point a person wishes to cut off this series of self-knowledge, as Ṣadrā himself has said recurrently. But will to will is a different story altogether, because, if there is any such thing at all, this involves not just a subjective but a *causal* regress. Ṣadrā's criticism, however, of the view expressed by his teacher Mīr Dāmād on the point is correct. Dāmād says that when a desire reaches a point where it becomes will and results in action, then we can analyze this will into any number of continuous prior and posterior parts, such that every one of them will be a will and yet all these parts will be comprehended by the same unitary act of will which immediately resulted in the action.[47] Ṣadrā rejects this by saying that such mental analysis into parts is possible only in a case which affords some *real* basis for such analysis even though *existentially* the parts are indistinguishable: "black color," for example, might be analyzed conceptually into a genus "color" and a differentia "black" even though what exists is just "black color," not "black" *and* "color." But this condition is not available in our alleged analysis of "will" into parts.[48] It is strange, however, that the same consideration did not prevent Ṣadrā from drawing a false analogy between "knowledge of knowledge" and "the will to will." For, when one knows that one knows, a higher-order act of knowledge does come into existence *in the mind* which permits us to speak of such higher-order acts of knowledge, while "will to will" is a meaningless phrase to which nothing in reality corresponds either in the external world or in the mind for, as said, this would be made impossible by a vicious regress as Ṣadrā himself admits. Nobody can ever meaningfully say, for example, "I wanted to want to write, or I wanted to want to want to write," etc.

4. *Doctrines of Badā' (Change of Mind in God), Naskh (Abrogation of Laws) and Taraddud (Reluctant Decision)*

Ṣadrā discusses this theologico-juristic question both in connection with God's will and God's speech or Prophetic Revelation, which we will deal with in the next section of this chapter. But since this question is more importantly related to God's will than to His speech, we will discuss it here as Ṣadrā's own treatment of it also appears in greater detail in relation to God's will than to His speech. *Badā'* is a Shī'ī theological doctrine and the term literally means "change of mind—either arbitrarily or on the basis of a better reason or a new truth," and some primitive and "extremist" Shī'ī theologians are reported to have held this literal view. While the Sunnīs reject this doctrine, among the Shī'ā, the term has had several definitions and certainly the philosophic theologians have quite different and highly refined interpretations of it. It appears to this writer that, for example, al-Ṭūsī's view of God's knowledge, which made that knowledge dependent on the object of that knowledge and his refutation of Ibn Sīnā's opposite view (as we saw in the preceding chapter) was at least partly related to the doctrine of *Badā'* even though he may have been influenced in his theory of God's knowledge by al-Suhrawardī, as Ṣadrā alleges. There is another doctrine called *naskh* or abrogation of old laws by God and their replacement by new ones which is more juristic than theological and which probably originated early among Sunnī circles but which the Shī'ā jurists had also adopted. In Ṣadrā's treatment as well as that of his teacher, Mīr Dāmād, *Badā'* and *naskh* became more or less equivalent.

But the concept of "abrogation" cannot exhaust the whole problem, difficult though it is in itself. There are a number of Qur'ānic verses [49] which speak of God as having a kind of "suspended decision" or "a wait-and-see attitude" until man takes a certain initiative in a certain direction. In the Qur'ānic context itself, which has a practical psychological attitude and is anxious to maximize human moral action and initiative, such verses would appear to fit naturally. They are also in essential agreement with the Mu'tazilite doctrine of human free will and action. The Ash'arite reply is simple: God, being absolute, can do whatever He likes and in His absoluteness He may even curtail, by self-imposition, His absoluteness and make it dependent on certain extrinsic factors. This reply may not be entirely out of line with the general Ash'arite doctrine of Divine Absolutism except that, in view of God's absolute will, it is difficult to see what these "extrinsic factors" (e.g., human will and action) might be. But in the context of the system of the Muslim philosophers, with its emphasis on rational, necessary, and eternal Divine Will, such Qur'ānic verses are extremely difficult to explain. According to Ibn Sīnā, the affairs of the changing material world are under the direct management of some heavenly soul, not of God, for such soul is in contact, on the one hand, with God or the Active Intelligence (whence it derives universal principles) and, on the other, with earthly events and, as such, is subject to a succession of images.[50] Ṣadrā himself seeks to draw support from such passages from Ibn Sīnā, as we shall see presently.

Ṣadrā first states and rejects his master's view[51] that such "hesitation" or "reluctance" on God's part really means that there is sometimes a kind of conflict between a lesser and greater good. Ṣadrā rightly points out that there can be no conflict here for a lesser good cannot stand in the way of a greater good prevailing in God's wisdom. Ṣadrā then proceeds to outline his own view, which may be clearly divided into two parts. The first part states that God has an eternal, unalterable will and knowledge which is termed "absolute decision (*qaḍā'*). It is this which the Qur'ān portrays by terms like "the Pen," "the Preserved Tablet," "the Root of all Books," etc. This level of knowledge and will—*qaḍā'*—is simple, unitary, and unchangeable. But, as we have shown in detail in our discussion of movement (Part I, Chapter V), everything outside God's being and His Attributes is subject to constant substantive change, both the material world and the heavens with their souls. The heavenly souls, therefore, represent another kind of "writing" or "book" whose texts are constantly changing, thanks to substantive change. It is this sort of writing called "*qadar* (something which is 'measured out', limited and not absolute or eternal)" which the Qur'ān is talking about when it refers to a book where "God erases things and replaces them with others."[52] While the Realm of *Qaḍā'* is constituted of Higher Angels or Intelligences or God's Attributes, the Realm of *Qadar* is identical with the Lower Angels or souls of the heavenly bodies, which are not pure intellects but are subject to a succession of images as well. In the *Qaḍā'* Realm, since it is simple, all contradictions are unified and all contrarieties are resolved, but the world of change is the home of contradictions and contrarieties.[53]

Since the real basis of change lies in the possibility or potentiality (in a seed lies the possibility of a tree) and the basis of unchangeability is absolute necessity and since the material realm and souls—whether human or heavenly—are the home of possibilities and potentialities, at any given point in the world-process, one may view the future as a *number* of possibilities, not just a single-track possibility, although with a view to the *entirety* of the antecedents, the future may be said to be determined. But even this determination is the *determination of a possibility,* not an absolute determination excluding the notion of possibility altogether, as is the case with the Divine Realm of *Qaḍā'*. The indeterminacy of God's will, therefore, is an indirect way of expressing the fact that the *Qadar* Realm is the realm of possibility, not necessity.[54] Quite apart from the difficulty, in this view, of how possibility in things can be interpreted as "God's hesitancy," it does not answer the original question: for that question was about God's "reluctance" or "wait-and-see" attitude *in certain* cases, more especially cases of human moral action, whereas according to this explanation the entire world-process will be covered by this "hesitancy" of God and "abrogation" of His laws, including natural laws!

If someone asks, why the world of change at all? and why could not God be content with the Realm of Necessity?, the answer is that much good would have been lost without the world of change. For, this substantive change, being always from the lower to the higher, from the imperfect to the perfect, and from the self-alienated to the self-integrated, ensures the redemption of the world, finally resulting, as we shall see further in the chapter on eschatology, in Part III of this work, in a state of affairs where every intellectually developed human being will, in the afterlife, become a species unto himself and will pass the stage where, as in this life, all humans are members of the same species. In other words, like the Intelligences, such human beings will share the Divine Realm. This would not be possible without the substantive movement from the lower to the higher which is the essence of this world.[55]

This is the first part of Ṣadrā's argument for change and abrogation. This account appears sound or at least consistent enough with his general theory of substantive change in which it is rooted. It is also coherent with his belief that this change governs not only the material world but the heavenly souls themselves: indeed, this change first appears in the heavenly souls and then results in change in this world of matter according to its potentialities. (That events in this world follow upon events in the heavenly bodies and their souls is a belief shared by all medieval Muslim philosophers as inherited from Hellenism, but is rejected by the Islamic orthodoxy.) But the second part of this account, which appears to be designed to cover miracles and "arbitrary" happenings in nature and where *naskh* and *badā'* seem to take on a supernatural meaning, does not seem to be congruous with Ṣadrā's naturalistic account of substantive movement.

According to this account, the souls of the heavenly bodies—the Lower Angels—not only act as agencies of change in the material world, but also as agencies of counter-change, i.e., they not only act as catalysts for the realization of potentialities in matter but even produce phenomena *opposed* to these potentialities. The proof Ṣadrā gives for this is essentially borrowed from Ibn Sīnā who, in order to prove the possibility of "certain miracles" starts out by showing the dominance of the soul over the body: by sheer will-power, for example, a sick person can become well and by being obsessed with the thought of being ill a healthy person can really, physically become ill. Ibn Sīnā then asserts, through a series of examples, that a pure soul transcends its own body and, by becoming identified with the World Soul, as it were, can produce strange phenomena in nature and in men.[56] After a similar statement of the soul's effects upon its body,[57] Ṣadrā goes on to say that the heavenly soul (or souls) can exert a similar effect on the World-body.[58] No, when a Prophet's (or an Infallible Imam-Waliy's) mind contacts the heavenly soul or souls—strictly speaking, it should be the soul of the lowest heaven, which is directly in contact with the sublunary world—and witnesses a certain writing there, he announces it to the world exactly and with certainty, not like a soothsayer or an astrologer whose pronouncements are mere guesswork. When he contacts it again, he sees a different writing which might be either due to the changed conditions of the world [59] (i.e., due to the substantive change) or due to a new idea or image that arises in the world-soul *ab initio, and without any basis in the world conditions—indeed, against the sum total of the world potentialities at that time.* As a result, an entirely new species of being may arise by spontaneous generation, not through procreation or emergence, for example, as Ibn Sīnā puts it.[60] When the Prophet sees this new writing, this constitutes *badā'* or *naskh* and is attributable to God as well, since the heavenly souls are absolutely obedient servants of God.[61]

Ṣadrā quotes [62] at length from Ibn Sīnā to confirm his view. But to begin with, Ibn Sīnā never says that these new happenings or "miracles" are *contrary to* the course of nature, as Ṣadrā has it. Ibn Sīnā believes only in such miracles as are explicable psychologically or parapsychologically. Secondly, for Ibn Sīnā, it is the Prophet who "performs" these "miracles," not the world soul. Thirdly, this doctrine is apparently irreconcilably contrary to Ṣadrā's teaching on the world movement, particularly with its emphasis on the *continuity of the world-order,* thanks to this substantive movement (*ittiṣāl al-ḥaraka al-jawhariya*). How can one reconcile this supernatural notion of the rise of images and ideas in the heavenly soul *de novo* and without any preconditioning and their intervention in the world process with Ṣadrā's otherwise highly naturalistic doctrine of world movement?

Al-Sabzawārī has also criticized [63] Ṣadrā, but his criticism is not addressed to this point, on which he apparently endorses Ṣadrā's view, but is directed against Ṣadrā's attribution to the philosophers the belief that in the heavenly souls changes can occur. This criticism seems strange to me, since even in the text of Ibn Sīnā quoted here by Ṣadrā it is explicitly stated that such heavenly souls must know *particulars,*[64] and even otherwise it is the standard Ibn-Sīnāian doctrine that images come to the souls of the heavenly bodies *in succession.* That is why they are called "souls" and not "intellects." What Ibn Sīnā and other philosophers say is that the heavenly souls do not employ bodily organs as do human souls, and they differ from human souls in various other respects—for example, their bodies are indestructible, etc. As for Ṣadrā himself, not only are heavenly bodies not eternal—since they are subject to the law of substantive mutation—neither are their souls in which there is an incessant stream of images and, strictly speaking, these souls are the world of Images (*'Ālam al-Mithāl*) and, indeed, they are the World of Measurement (*'Ālam el-Qadar*) as well.

B. *Divine Speech and Revelation*

Ṣadrā's teaching on Divine Speech and Revelation is heavily dependent on Ibn 'Arabī's doctrine, on the basis of which he draws a close parallel or analogy between the ontological structure (in terms of the Logos doctrine reminiscent of the Christian school of Alexandria) and the Prophetic Revelation and is materially different from the theory of Prophethood constructed by Muslim Peripatetics like al-Fārābī and Ibn Sīnā. This analogy enables him to seek to mediate in the controversy between the Mu'tazila and the Ash'arites, the one holding that the Qur'ān is created while the other insisting that the Qur'ān represents the unchangeable and Eternal Speech of God: in the Mu'tazila view, says Ṣadrā, God brings the Qur'ān into existence (*awjada*), while according to the Ash'arites, it is an eternal act of God inhering in Him.[65]

The purpose of speech is simply "to make something known to someone (*i'lām*)." Now, the highest level of speech is that where this "making known" is an end in itself. The fact that this "making known" may also entail certain other subsidiary purposes—like a command or a prohibition—is secondary. Within this secondary category, again, we may distinguish two levels, one where the secondary purposes are automatically carried out without any possibility of disobedience, and two where the purposes may or may not be carried out—in this second subdivision, even where obedience occurs, the possibility of disobedience always exists unless an Infallible Imam (*'āṣim*) is available. Now, when we apply this three-tiered structure of Divine Speech to the ontological structure of reality, we find that they exactly correspond to each other. The highest grade of contingent (or, rather, necessary contingent) or created reality is the Intellect called the "World of Command (*'Ālam al-Amr*)," where the Intellect emerges through the sheer command of God "Be." Now, although other levels of existence also come into existence by this command to be, the difference is that whereas at this level the command to "be" is an end in itself, at the other two levels this is not the case. After the realm of the Intellect, identified by Ṣadrā with the realm of *Qaḍā'* or God's eternal Decree, comes the level of the heavens and heavenly souls which, as we have seen already, contitute the "world of *Qadar* or 'measured out' entities." The existence of this realm is not an end in itself but beings therein have to obey and carry out other commands of God: namely, to perform revolutions and thus to worship God and to supervise and direct the day-to-day happenings in this world down below. But the Angels of *Qadar,* the heavenly souls, obey God perfectly and without the possibility of disobedience. Last comes the world of matter where, besides the command to "be," certain other orders and prohibitions are also issued by God for man—through the intermediacy of the heavenly souls and the Prophets. In this realm, since it is subject to conflict (not just change, which also characterizes the heavens) between contradictions and self-alienation—thanks to matter—not only do commands have to change according to times and climes through *naskh,* as we have seen, but both obedience and disobedience are to be found: men may obey or disobey these commands. It should be noted that this disobedience is limited to humans and does not extend to material objects. This realm, constituted by the Sharī'a commands, is by its very nature the lowest form of Divine Speech.[66]

This entire creative propulsion expressed through the word "be" is thanks to the "Breath of the Merciful (*Nafas al-Raḥmān*)" which we discussed briefly towards the end of Chapter IV of Part I, and which Ṣadrā borrows from Ibn 'Arabī. The "Breath of the Merciful" is the first substance which God emits when He says "Be" (and the two are existentially identical), analogous to our own breath which we emit when we speak. This is why the entire universe is the Speech of God, since the Breath of the Merciful is a kind of Intelligible Matter, as it were, which constitues the existence of all things, whether eternal or temporal, intellective, psychic, or material: it is called "The [Second] God through which all is created." [67]

This creative ontological process is the "descent (*tanazzul*)" of God. The Prophet comes into the picture in the "ascent (*ṣu'-ūd*)" or return-process when the material world is redeemed and goes back to God. This occurs due to the substantive movement of the material realm (*'Ālam al-Khalq*), through the "measured out" realm or the realm of determination (*Alam al-Qadar*), to the Realm of the Intellect (*Ālam al-Aql*)—which is united with God but is not identical with His being—via and in the form of the Perfect Man (i.e., the person of Muḥammad), who combines in himself all the three realms.[68] Thus, the process which starts with God or rather with the issuance of "the Breath of the Merciful" from His absolute Being ends, upon its return journey, with the Perfect Man: the Breath of the Merciful and the Perfect Man parallel each other.[69] The manner in which the Perfect Man performs this function of identifying himself with the ontological structure of reality is as follows. Through his divine election, the Prophet contacts or is united with the Active Intellect or the High Angelic Being from whom he receives the unchangeable, divine intellective knowledge. This intellective knowledge is both a Speech and a Book: at this level the inner being of the Prophet is illumined not only intellectually but also in terms of sensory knowledge and he "sees" and "hears" the Angel in an intellective form. This knowledge then descends from the Prophet's intellect to his other faculties and he actually sees and hears the Angel, not just in an intellective mode, but also in a sensory mode—not with physical senses, since these are ever subject to change, but through an imaginative mode. This is because at the level of pure imagination (as in a dream), one equally hears and sees things. One must not think, however, that this "sensory" appearance of the Angel is only subjective, as many Muslim Peripatetics like Ibn Sīnā have held: it is absolutely objective and real.[70]

This is because the Angel himself does not move down from the upper intellective level to the lower, sensitive-imaginative level: the truth is that the Angel has an absolute being-in-himself and a being relative to the lower level. Thus, the same Angel who appeared to the Prophet as pure intellect, in his absolute being in the realm of *Qaḍā'* or eternal knowledge, will also appear in the Realm of Determination or *Qadar* as heavenly soul or the World Soul. It is the Prophet who moves down from the eternal Intellective Realm, through the Realm of Determination, to the World of material creation.[71]

Whereas at the intellective level, the Prophet receives eternal knowledge, both as Speech and as Book (which the Qur'ān calls the "Mother of all Books," or their unchanging "Model"), but both are spiritual (*ma'nawi*), his reception of Speech and Book at the level of Determination is in the form of a Book, for this Speech is not like the Speech of the intellective level; and, finally, at the sensory-imaginative level, he again receives both as a Book, which is nothing else than the Qur'ān, which people see, read and touch. The last two stages are characterized by the Sharī'a-law or legal determinations. On the Night of the Ascension (*lailat al-Mi'rāj*), for example, the Prophet had all the three experiences—intellective, purely imaginative, and sensory (or rather, sensory-imaginative).[72] This is how Ṣadrā interprets the famous Qur'ānic verse concerning the three modes of Revelation: "It is not up to a human that God should speak to him [directly, i.e., by His Essence] except through inspiration [i.e., at the intellective level, as Ṣadrā would say], or from behind a veil [i.e., a spiritual veil which, for Ṣadrā, occurs at the level of Determination] or that He send a Messenger who inspires him by God's permission [i.e., at the level of Sharī'a-ordinances, as Ṣadrā would have it]" Qur'ān VIIIL, 51).[73]

Ṣadrā, however, emphatically adds, "But you must not imagine that the

Prophet's reception of God's Speech through the intermediacy of Gabriel and his hearing from the Angel is like your hearing from the Prophet, nor must you say that the Prophet is a blind follower (*muqallid*) of Gabriel as the Muslim community is the blind follower of the Prophet. Far be it from being so, for these two are utterly different kinds [of hearing]. . . . Blind following can never constitute knowledge at all, nor can it ever be called 'true hearing.' "[74] This means that the Prophet, thanks to his contact with the Intellective level of the Angel, does not simply follow the Angel's words or the "Book," but knows the very objectives of these words, since he knows the *mind* of the Angel. In other words, as Ibn Sīnā says, the Prophet has a *reasoned* knowledge, not just an imitative one. The Prophet, thus, correctly, *interprets* the verbal message and, therefore, cannot err either in thought or in action. But those who read and hear the Prophet's words, i.e., the physical Qur'ān, are no longer in this position of immunity from error, since at this level there is not just a "spiritual veil (*ḥijāb ma'nawī*)" but a physical veil (*ḥijāb ṣūrī*), due to the Prophet's physical intermediacy. Hence, to interpret this physical Qur'ān, which is read and written by people, an Infallible Imam is necessary. But since the Infallible Imam must also be a person *who cannot blindly follow the Angel's words*, the question arises, but cannot be answered on the basis of Ṣadrā's doctrine itself, whether such a personage can abrogate the Sharī'a commandments of the Qur'ān; or, it may simply mean that since the Infalliable Imam can go behind the words to the Mind of the Intellect, he can correctly understand the Qur'ān, even though he cannot abrogate the Sharī'a law and substitute them with new laws.

Ṣadrā sometimes differentiates between the Speech and the Book of God, the former emanating from the high source, while the latter originates from the lower or "relative" being of the Angel, as we have seen.[75] Sometimes he distinguishes between a "heard Speech," which belongs to the lower level and a "directly understood Speech," which belongs to the higher.[76] But in general he thinks that the Speech and the Book are not two different things, but the same thing viewed differently and that at all the three above described levels both the Speech and the Book are present.[77] Even at the human level, someone's book can be called his speech and vice versa (although this latter usage is not conventionally correct).[78] Let us illustrate this by an example. When a man speaks, he emits breath from his interior, this breath being the human counterpart of the "Breath of the Merciful," and at the same time forms and imprints words, which also emanate from his interior, i.e., the rational soul. Now, if one views this breath and the words imprinted upon it by themselves, this represents a book which is a writing-material on which words are imprinted. In such a situation, there must be assumed a *separate* "writer" who has inscribed these words on this material. There is, therefore, a kind of separation or duality between the writer and the book. But if the same breath emitted by the soul and the words produced by it are viewed not as a *separate entity* from the producer but as *his action,* then, being inseparable from the actor, it becomes his speech, since speech cannot be conceived to exist apart from the speaker.[79] This is what, for Ṣadrā, the entire controversy between the Mu'tazila and the Ash'arites essentially boils down to; for the former viewed the Qur'ān as separate from God (or the Intellect) and thus called it a "creation (*makhlūq*)," like a book, while the latter viewed it as God's action and hence eternal and inseparable from Him.[80]

In a sense, therefore, both parties were right, but in another both were wrong, since the Qur'ān is different from other Revealed Books, for they are, strictly speaking, only Books, not the Speech of God. This is why also the Qur'ān calls itself both *Qur'ān* (inseparable speech) and *Furqān* (separable, i.e., as a Book), while all other Revealed Books are only *Furqān* and not *Qur'ān.*[81] One must never say, however, that other Books are *not* God's Speech since, as we have indicated, all Books are, *in a sense,* also God's speech. But the Qur'ān is most truly both. It is because the Qur'ān is both part of God and, as such, Uncreated and part of creation and, as such, created, that it, in numerous passages where it mentions the Revelation of the Qur'ān, also talks about the creation of the Universe by God. This is, in fact, so consistently and palpably done by the Qur'ān that it cannot be regarded as fortuitous. Ṣadrā then refers to numerous passages of the Qur'ān where Revelation of the Qur'ān and the Creation are mentioned together.[82] This is because the Creation itself, as we said earlier on in this discussion, is also both the Speech and the Book of God, thanks to the rise from God's mind of the "Breath of the Merciful," which is nothing but the principle of existence, or "the Intelligible Matter," upon which or through which God "inscribes" all creation or emits existential *logoi* in an order and with all the systematic ambiguity implied by the term "existence." The Qur'ān and the Universe, or rather "the Breath of the Merciful," therefore, run parallel and, indeed, are in a definite sense identical. The entire drama begins with God as the "Merciful" and ends with the "Perfect Man." This is why when the Qur'ān talks about its revelation, it also almost invariably talks about the creation of the Universe as well and Ṣadrā once more cites a host of Qur'ānic verses to prove his thesis that the frequent mention of the two together cannot be accidental.[83]

NOTES

1. *Asfār*, III, 1, p. 307, line 5–p. 308, line 5.
2. *Ibid.*, p. 309, line 1–p. 310, line 3; cf. Chapter III, Part I, p. 103 ff., Chapter IV, p. 128 ff.
3. *Ibid.*, p. 310, lines 6–14; Ṣadrā's quotation from al-Ṭūsī p. 310, line 16–p. 312, line 1.
4. *Ibid.*, p. 325, lines 3–16; p. 337, lines 5–15.
5. On God's purpose, see Chapter IV, Part I; *Asfār*, III, 1, p. 369, line 19–p. 371, last line.
6. P. 313, lines 6 ff. (quotation from Ibn Sīnā); see preceding chapter on God's fore-knowledge; also Chapter IV, Part I, on purpose.
7. *Asfār*, III, 1, p. 315, last line–p. 316, line 3; p. 318, lines 3–6.
8. *Ibid.*, p. 315, note 3.
9. References in note 7 above and al-Ṭabāṭabā'ī's note 1 on p. 318.
10. *Ibid.*, p. 312, line 6–p. 313, line 11. It should be noted that Ṣadrā himself varies his language, if not his substance, greatly on the question of human freedom. Sometimes he says, as here, that man is pre-determined really but has the *appearance* of freedom; at other times he quotes al-Ṭūsī with approval that man is *partly* free and *partly* determined. But when he expounds his own views later in this chapter, he will say that the meaning of *human* freedom is just this, and that it would be meaningless to demand any other kind of freedom for him.
11. See reference in the previous note.
12. See Chapters III and IV, Part I, on refutation of the Ash'arite views; *Asfār*, III, 1, p. 315, line 7–p. 320, line 6; *ibid.*, p. 320, line 17–p. 324, end; p. 325, line 9–p. 328, line 2; p. 332, line 6–p. 333, line 9; p. 346, lines 13–18, etc.
13. *Ibid.*, IV, 1, p. 314, line 17–p. 315, line 7.
14. *Ibid.*, p. 318, lines 5–6; p. 320, lines 3–6; p. 332, lines 9–11.
15. *Ibid.*, p. 332, line 11–p. 333, line 1; see references in note 2 above.
16. *Ibid.*, p. 328, line 13–p. 331, line 1.
17. *Ibid.*, p. 321, lines 1–8; cf. Chapters III and IV of Part 1 on the refutation of the Ash'arite doctrine of free will.

18. *Ibid.*, p. 317, line 5–p. 318, line 3; cf. Chapters III and IV of Part I referred to in the preceding note.
19. *Ibid.*, p. 318, lines 3–6; line 12 ff.
20. *Ibid.*, p. 332, lines 9–11.
21. *Ibid.*, p. 332, lines 14–15.
22. *Ibid.*, p. 337, line 12–p. 338, line 4.
23. *Ibid.*, p. 339, line 11–p. 340, line 8; cf. note 26 below.
24. *Ibid.*, p. 339, lines 13–14.
25. *Ibid.*, p. 340, lines 13–18.
26. *Ibid.*, p. 323, lines 6–14.
27. *Ibid.*, p. 323, lines 6–7; p. 335, line 13–p. 336, line 3.
28. *Ibid.*, p. 324, lines 3–11.
29. *Ibid.*, p. 324, lines 11–16.
30. *Ibid.*, p. 336, line 4–p. 337, line 4.
31. *Ibid.*, p. 369, line 21–p. 370, line 9.
32. *Ibid.*, p. 370, line 10–p. 371, line 8.
33. *Ibid.*, p. 371, line 13–p. 372, line 9.
34. *Ibid.*, p. 372, lines 9–11.
35. See references in note 10 above.
36. *Ibid.*, p. 372, last line–p. 373, line 7.
37. *Ibid.*, p. 373, last line ff.; quotation, p. 375, line 18–p. 376, line 9.
38. *Ibid.*, p. 376, lines 13–15.
39. *Ibid.*, p. 380, lines 16–22.
40. *Ibid.*, p. 381, line 1–last line.
41. *Ibid.*, p. 381, last line–p. 382, last line; see also last Section of Chapter IV, Part I.
42. *Ibid.*, p. 384, line 15–p. 385, line 7.
43. *Ibid.*, p. 386, line 1–p. 387, line 14.
44. *Ibid.*, p. 387, lines 15–18.
45. *Ibid.*, p. 388, lines 5–12.
46. *Ibid.*, p. 388, lines 12–15.
47. *Ibid.*, p. 388, last line–p. 389, line 15.
48. *Ibid.*, p. 389, lines 16–30.
49. *Ibid.*, p. 389, lines 16–30.
50. *Ibid.*, p. 399, line 11–p. 401, line 9; see also a series of quotations from Ibn Sīnā beginning p. 404, line 6. The entire discussion begins in *Asfār,* III, 1, p. 392, line 4. The problem for philosophers like Ṣadrā and Ibn Sīnā is, of course, to find a middle-term between the absolute and unchanging knowledge of God and the world of day-to-day change in the material world. The first is termed by Ṣadrā (and Mīr Dāmād) *Qaḍā',* and the other, which mediates between eternity and change, *Qadar.*
51. *Ibid.*, p. 392, line 9–p. 393, line 5.

52. *Ibid.,* p. 393, line 5–p. 394, line 14; p. 395, line 9–p. 396, line 13; p. 397, line 2–p. 399, line 4.
53. *Ibid.,* p. 397, lines 3–9.
54. *Ibid.,* p. 393, lines 15–16.
55. *Ibid.,* p. 397, line 15–p. 398, line 4.
56. For Ibn Sīnā's doctrine, see my *Prophecy in Islam,* London, 1958, Chapter 2, Section 2, on "Imaginative or Technical Revelation."
57. *Asfār,* III, 1, p. 396, line 14–p. 398, line 1.
58. *Ibid.,* p. 396, lines 22–23.
59. *Ibid.,* p. 398, line 7–p. 399, line 2.
60. *Ibid.,* p. 399, lines 1–4.
61. *Ibid.,* p. 395, line 12–p. 396, line 13.
62. See references in note 50 above.
63. See his note on *ibid.,* p. 398.
64. *Ibid.,* p. 400, lines 3–5.
65. (This and the following references in this chapter are not to the recent edition of *Asfār* used in the book, since the remainder of Book III of the *Asfār* is not published as part of this edition; following references to *Asfār,* III are, therefore, to the edition of 1282 A.H.): p. 100, lines 2–4; cf. *ibid.,* p. 97, lines 28–29.
66. *Ibid.,* p. 97, last line–p. 98, line 18.
67. *Ibid.,* p. 97, lines 30–35; p. 99, lines 11 ff. The expression comes from Ibn 'Arabī.
68. *Ibid.,* p. 98, lines 18 ff.
69. *Ibid.,* p. 102, lines 5 ff.
70. *Ibid.,* p. 102, lines 27–p. 103, line 10.
71. *Ibid.,* p. 103, lines 10–32.
72. *Ibid.*
73. *Ibid.,* p. 99, lines 4–5.
74. *Ibid.,* p. 99, lines 9–11; see also Chapter IV of Part IV below, note 28.
75. *Ibid.,* p. 102, lines 16–17.
76. *Ibid.,* p. 103, lines 16–18 and lines 26–27; cf. p. 99, lines 1–2.
77. *Ibid.,* p. 99, lines 11 ff.
78. *Ibid.,* p. 99, lines 16–27.
79. *Ibid.*
80. *Ibid.,* p. 100, line 4.
81. *Ibid.,* p. 103, lines 15–19.
82. *Ibid.,* p. 103, line 18.
83. *Ibid.,* p. 104, lines 1 ff.

PART III

Psychology:

Man and His Destiny

CHAPTER I

NATURE OF THE SOUL

In his work, "On the Soul," Aristotle defines the soul as "the first entelechy (or perfection) of a natural organized body possessing the capacity of life." [1] This definition clearly means that the soul is a form or function of an organized body and is incapable of independent, separate existence. But in the same work Aristotle poses the question as to whether the soul may not be the entelechy of the body in the sense in which a pilot is the entelechy of a ship.[2] This question reflects Aristotle's hesitation as to whether the human intellect may not be separable after physical death, while the rest of the soul perishes, and it is probable that he believed in the survival of the human intellect after it is developed by purely intellectual operations. His great commentator and systematizer, Alexander of Aphrodisias, explicitly holds this view, i.e., that the human mind achieves immortality by contemplating eternal objects.[3] Plotinus, who believes in the existence of the World Soul (of which individual souls are modifications), rejects the Aristotelian definition of the soul as entelechy of the body.[4] In the amalgamation of Aristotelianism and neo-Platonism created by later Hellenic philosophy, particularly as expressed in the neo-Platonizing commentators of Aristotle, the human soul was credited with indestructibility, although the Aristotelian definition of soul as entelechy was also subscribed to.[5]

Among the Muslim philosophers who were heirs to this philosophic tradition of later Hellenism, al-Fārābī explicitly identifies the human soul at the beginning of its career as a faculty or power inherent in the body and not as a spiritual substance capable of existing independently of the body. When, however, the human soul—the material intellect—develops into an actualized intellect and can think immaterial forms, al-Fārābī designates it as "acquired" intellect. The "acquired" intellect emerges as a part of the intelligible universe and survives physical death. According to al-Fārābī, therefore, human souls which have not developed into actualized intellect cannot survive bodily death, since they are mere "powers" in the body. This doctrine of the *transformation* of the human soul into an immaterial, immortal entity appears to be similar to the doctrine of Alexander of Aphrodisias. In other words, for al-Fārābī, whereas the human soul in its initial stage is the entelechy of the body in the first of the two Aristotelian senses, it *becomes* entelechy of the body in the second Aristotelian sense (i.e., in the sense in which a pilot is the entelechy of a ship) at the end of its developmental career.[6] The souls of the heavenly bodies are, however, eternally entelechies of their bodies in the second sense, since they never were mere powers or potentialities immersed in their bodies.[7]

For Ibn Sīnā, the human soul, although it is only a potential intellect at the beginning of its career, is nevertheless an immaterial spiritual substance capable of existing independently of the body.[8] The body is there to serve the purpose of its realization as actual intellect, but after that it becomes a positive hindrance. Ibn Sīnā, therefore, holds that it is better to define the soul as entelechy of the body than to define it as form of the body; this is because 'entelechy' comprises both types of soul, that which is the form of the body and hence inseparable from it—as in the case of the vegetative and animal souls—and that which is separate (or separable) from it, as the human soul. But this means that the term "entelechy" is ambiguous; therefore, when we say that something is an entelechy, we do not know thereby what kind of soul it is—whether it is capable of existence by itself or not.

Again, according to Ibn Sīnā, the definition of the soul as "entelechy" (although he thinks that this is the best possible and most comprehensive definition of the souls "in this world of ours") besides being ambiguous, does not include all the souls, e.g., the souls of the heavenly spheres, which neither work through a physical organ—since they are eternally immaterial substances—nor do they possess sense-perception, while their intellect is also eternally actual and not potential and passive as the human intellect.[9] It is obvious that, basically, these objections arise against Aristotle himself, who was the author of the soul's definition as entelechy of the body, but who at the same time regarded the souls of the heavens as eternally actual and movers of the heavenly bodies.[10] When we have defined the soul as entelechy of the body, Ibn Sīnā goes on, we have only defined the soul *as a relation,* for entelechy, actuality or perfection is entelechy, actuality or perfection *of* something viz., of the body, possessing organs. This definition, therefore, does not yield the nature of the soul-in-itself, i.e., whether it is a separate substance or not. In order to prove that the human soul is an immaterial spiritual substance, Ibn Sīnā has, therefore, recourse to his famous argument whereby a person, under certain suppositions, can affirm his own ego without affirming the existence of his body.[11]

Ibn Sīnā's conception of the human soul as an immaterial substance *ab initio* (most probably motivated by religious considerations) raised fresh objections against him to which an Aristotle or an al-Fārābī was not subject. One of his contemporaries asked him: if the human soul is a separate substance from the start, why is it not an actual intellect and only a potential one, since the only condition of something being an intellect and intelligible in actuality is that it be separate from matter? To this Ibn Sīnā replied that for something to be an actual intellect, it is not sufficient to be separate from matter but to be *absolutely* separate from it, i.e., that matter should neither be the occasion of its coming-into-existence nor the vehicle of its subsistence.[12] The unsatisfactoriness of this reply continued to be a target of criticism and Mullā Ṣadrā rejects Ibn Sīnā's view in various contexts.

Mulla Ṣadrā, who is highly neo-Platonic in his theory of knowledge, as will become clear in the following chapters, nevertheless accepts Aristotle's definition of the soul as entelechy of the body. According to him, since the soul is not eternal but originated (a proposition in whose acceptance he is at one with the entire Aristotelian tradition), it cannot be separate and independent of matter, for to say that the soul is separate and independent of matter is only compatible with belief in the pre-existence of the soul, as Platonists and neo-Platonists believe. Ibn Sīnā is, therefore, self-contradictory when he accepts the one but rejects the other. At the same time, Ṣadrā also rejects Ibn Sīnā's view that the soul is a relational concept and not a substantive one. Since the soul, at its birth, is *in matter,* its soul-ness cannot be construed as a relation as though it had an independent existence of its own and *then came* into a relationship with matter. Again, if the human soul were an independent substance, it would be impossible to integrate the soul and body, so as to form a natural physical species as the concept of "perfection" requires, and therefore the analogy of the pilot and the ship falls to the ground.[13]

However, the relationship of the soul to the body is not like that of any ordinary physical form to its matter. All physical forms *inhere* in their matters in such a way that the two do not constitute a *composite* (*murakkab*) of two existentially distinguishable elements, but are totally fused together to form a complete unity (*ittiḥād*) in existence, and as a result, the form works simply and directly in matter. As opposed to purely material forms, however, the soul works on its matter through the intermediacy of other lower forms or powers. This phenomenon, viz, where one power or form works on matter not directly but through other forms, is called "soul." Ṣadrā, therefore, says that the soul is the entelechy of a material body insofar as it *operates through faculties,* and he insists that the word "organs" as it appears in the Stagirite's definition of the soul cannot mean "physical organs" like hands, liver or stomach, for example, but faculties or powers through which the soul works, as, for example, appetition, nutrition, and digestion.[14]

It is obvious that this novel interpretation constitutes a grave violence against Aristotle, since his language clearly attributes the quality of "being organized" or "possessing organs" to "the natural body," which makes the soul, strictly speaking, a *function* of such a body, while Ṣadrā attributes the quality of having "organs" or "faculties" to the soul. This position is, indeed, a radical departure from Aristotle and should be regarded as a first step toward the final idealization of Ṣadrā's account of the soul. Ṣadrā claims that this interpretation of the word "organs" removes the difficulties experienced by the definition of the soul as entelechy in covering all the cases—from plants to heavenly spheres—since all souls work on their bodies not directly but through faculties. Further, it raises the soul from the status of a purely physical form to a form which, although *in* matter, is capable of transcending it, for the extent of its immanence in matter is less than that of a simple physical form. These considerations should not lead us to think, however, that Ṣadrā has produced this definition for extraneous reasons for, as will become apparent soon, this way of looking upon the soul is intimately related to his doctrine of "emergence" or "substantive change" which lies at the root of his system.

Indeed, the ability of Ṣadrā's definition to comprehend the souls of the heavens is a by-product and is relevant only from the point of view of the Peripatetic philosophy. Otherwise, whereas according to the Peripatetics, the souls of the heavens are eternally actual and, therefore, are not in need of a bodily organ to actualize them and hence are not entelechies of their bodies except insofar as their bodies occupy different positions in their revolutions, according to Ṣadrā, these souls are only potential like earthly souls even though the degree of their potentiality is less than that of earthly souls.[15] Indeed, as we have shown in Chapter V of Part I, the heavenly souls, together with their bodies, are *ḥādith* or originated according to Ṣadrā, and subject to continuous movement and change.[16] Concerning Ibn Sīnā's doctrine on the heavens, Ṣadrā says:

> Among (the failures of Ibn Sīnā) is his assertion that the heavenly souls have no perfection waiting to be realized except in certain extraneous matters and non-essentials, viz (different) relations of positions for their bodies. For a man of insight who has grasped the truth, this is a baseless opinion and a false belief. This is because the soul, so long as its psychic being remains deficient and not perfectly realized in point of its proper individual (level of) existence, is in need of the body to serve as its instrument for the attainment of its existential perfection,

and it must cling to it. . . . How can a man of perception and insight believe that a (pure) intellective substance can allow itself to be imprisoned in a bodily relationship, deserting its abode of light for (this) tenebral world merely for the sake of acquiring extraneous relationships with physical positions—and this despite their (the philosophers') doctrine that the higher does not occupy itself with the lower? [17]

Thus, for Ṣadrā, celestial souls are, in principle, as much entelechies of their bodies as earthly souls.

Ṣadrā's own account of the soul rests on his fundamental principle of "emergence" or "substantive change" (*istiḥāla jauharīya*). He, therefore, holds that the soul is bodily in its origin but spiritual in its survival (*jismānīyat al-ḥudūth, yūḥānīyat al-baqā'*).[18] The same principle demands that, since the soul *emerges* on the basis of matter, it cannot be absolutely material, for "emergence" requires that the "emergent" be of a higher level than that which it emerges out of or on the basis of. Consequently, even the lowest forms of life—like plants, although they are attached to and dependent upon matter, cannot be themselves entirely material. On the contrary, they *use* their matter or body as their instrument and constitute the first step away from the material to the spiritual realm (*malakūt*).[19]

Being entelechy of the body means that the soul renders the genus "body" into a species, i.e., a living body. This means that "body" must enter into the definition of plant, animal, and man, as Aristotle and Ibn Sīnā say. However, since, for Ibn Sīnā, the term "soul" applies only to a relation and not to a substance, he thought that the body was extrinsic to the soul *when considered as a substance*. He, therefore, denied physical resurrection.[20] But certain later Muslim philosophers, like al-Suhrawardī, went farther off the track. They did not see that the "body" in this context had to be taken in the sense of a genus and not in the sense of a material substratum—as Ibn Sīnā had insisted—and when they saw the material substratum to be perishable, they declared body to be dead-in-itself and devoid of life which, they thought, was merely accidental to it—i.e., they did not consider "body" as part of the definition of a living being.[21]

Again, being entelechy of a special type of body means that the soul falls into the category of substance, since such a body cannot be constituted without the soul. This argument comes from Ibn Sīnā. Ibn Sīnā, however, had given another proof, referred to above, based on direct consciousness of the self, to establish that the human soul is a spiritual substance, independent of the body. Yet, in strange contradiction to this proof, when Ibn Sīnā was asked if substantiality is a constitutive factor of the soul, why are we not able to affirm its substantiality as self-evident, without inference, he replied, "About the soul we know nothing except that it governs the body:

in its essence, it remains unknown. Now substantiality is constitutive of that essence . . . but what is constituted by substantiality is unknown to us and what is known to us is not constituted by substantiality." [22] It is obvious that Ibn Sīnā is thinking here of the general definition of the soul as entelechy of the body and does not refer to his special proof which is based on direct experience of the self.

After Ibn Sīnā, the question was raised and discussed whether the substantiality of the soul is given in direct self-consciousness. Al-Suhrawardī, since he believed Aristotelian categories to be purely subjective, asserted that in the direct experience of the self all that was given was a self-aware or self-luminous being to which all other concepts like substance, differentia, etc. were extrinsic.[23] He, therefore, describes the self only as a self-luminous being, of the nature of light. Ṣadrā approaches this question from his principle of the primordiality of existence (*aṣālat al-wujūd*) discussed in Chapter I of Part I, according to which the only reality is existence and essences are constructed by the mind.[24] According to him, whenever soul is conceived as a concept and is defined, it will be found to be an essence. In direct self-experience, however, soul is only given as pure existence, and since existence has no genus, it is not given in experience either as a substance or non-substance. Direct, intuitive experience is the only way, for Ṣadrā, to know reality, for discursive inferential reasoning can only know essences in an adequate manner (*bi'l-iktināh*), and not existences, which are unique.

According to Ṣadrā, both human and animal souls are free from matter and hence capable of existence independently of the body. We shall discuss the question of the human soul later, but the doctrine that the animal soul is capable of independent existence is not found even in al-Suhrawardī and appears to have come from Ibn 'Arabī, to whom, as our previous discussions have shown, Ṣadrā's debt is immense. The reason for this doctrine, in part, is to prove that simple human souls which possess hardly any intellective activity, but simply work with imagination also survive, as we will elaborate in Chapter V of the present Part on eschatology.[25] But Ṣadrā absolutely holds that a being endowed with imagination is independent of natural matter even though it is not independent of a certain kind of extension and quantity (*miqdār*) which, however, is not material. This view, in turn, rests on his doctrine of the *'Ālam al-Mithāl* (World of Images), according to which, an image, although not spiritual, is not material either, is not directly subject to substantive mutation as the world of physical forms and, therefore, exists by itself independent of matter. Ibn Sīnā himself, although he gave an elaborate argument in his *al-Najāt* and *al-Shifā'* to show that an image requires a material organ to be imprinted in and that therefore imagination could not survive physical death, said in *al-Mubāḥa-*

thāt that "If the percipient (faculty or organ) of perceived forms and images were a body or a bodily power, then either that body will suffer separation (*tafarruq,* i.e., discontinuity) of parts when nutrition enters upon it or it will not. The second alternative is false because our bodies are subject to ceaseless corrosion (by fatigue) and augmentation through nutrition."[26] His conclusion was that such a faculty must be non-material.

But after Ibn Sīnā a whole new development takes place, whose terms go back to al-Ghazālī, but which explicitly starts with al-Suhrawardī, according to which images had an independent existence and life of their own in the World of Images (*'Ālam al-Mithāl*) situated ontologically between the spiritual (intelligible) world of pure ideas and the world of coarse matter and material bodies.[27] This development made it easier for Ṣadrā to believe that imagination—the World of extended figures—was not part of the material realm. Ṣadrā, therefore, holds that self-consciousness is not restricted to the rational soul, i.e., man—as philosophers had held—but was a concomitant of imagination as well. Ibn Sīnā was puzzled when asked whether animals have self-consciousness and whether an animal being has a principle in it which preserves that being's identity throughout life even though its body was in constant change. He replied that perhaps animals are not conscious of themselves but only of the objects they perceived and reacted to, or maybe they have a vague awareness of themselves through perception of external objects. On the second question, he was extremely hesitant and pointed to several alternatives among which he did suggest that animals (and perhaps plants) may have an irreducible original factor.[28]

Be that as it may, Ṣadrā categorically affirms that animal souls are capable of survival, because they are separate from matter—thanks to the fact that they have imagination—and that their separateness is not inconsistent with attachment to the quality of extension (or "pure body") which is necessary for an image. Ṣadrā uses the age-old argument for the identity and persistence of the human soul, according to which human bodies are in perpetual change while the inner psyche remains the same, to prove the identity and persistence of the animal soul, since animal bodies are also in perpetual flux while their inner psyche remains the same. It is obvious, says Ṣadrā, that this argument applies to animals as it applies to man.[29]

Similarly, the philosophers' argument from self-knowledge to prove that the human soul is separate from the body, is applied by Ṣadrā to the animals—those higher forms of animal life where sense-perception, some kind of memory-image, and voluntary movement are found. Since animals flee from things causing pain and pursue things giving pleasure, they must have an adequate idea of these things in terms of their images. In doing so, animals must necessarily perceive themselves.[30] Following the neo-Platonic model, Ṣadrā asserts that in sense-perception itself, it is not the external object which is directly perceived; the external object is rather the occasion for the creation by the soul of a perceptible form from within itself. This is much more so in the case of unperceived forms or images which the soul creates by itself.[31] Hence the animal soul is independent of the material body. Again, the animal's self-knowledge is direct, continuous, and independent of its knowledge of the external objects, exactly as is the case with man.[32] Ṣadrā even goes so far as to apply Ibn Sīnā's argument about the immateriality of the human self on the basis of direct self-consciousness to the animal soul. The only difference between man and animal is that the former is capable of intellection which the latter is incapable of; but then even many men are equally devoid of intellectual capacity and work by sheer imagination.[33]

Ṣadrā's view that animal souls are capable of detachment from their bodies—indeed, he insists, they *are* in some sense detached from their bodies because they are of the order of "actual imagination (*khayāl bi'l-fi'l*)," as distinguished from developed human souls, which are "actual intellect (*'aql bi'l-fi'l*)"—is based on the important doctrine of the "World of Images (*'Ālam al-Mithāl*)," developed after al-Ghazālī by al-Suhrawardī, Ibn Arabi, and others. According to this doctrine, the ontological structure of reality comprises three worlds—that of pure ideas or intellectual entities on top, of pure images or figures in the middle, and of material bodies at the lowest rung. Developed animals and undeveloped humans are of the order of the middle world of pure figures: although they cannot rise to the status of pure intellects, they nevertheless belong to the "other world (*al-ākhira*)" compared to this material world which is subject to that perpetual flux to which even the human and heavenly souls are subject so long as they have any intercourse with the physical and are not developed and transformed into pure imagination. But at the same time it is difficult to see how imaginative souls can be completely freed from matter and cease to be subject to perpetual material flux if they have not become pure intellects—a condition stated recurrently by Ṣadrā—and have found final repose in the eternal realm and being of God.

The development of the soul, according to Ṣadrā, is marked by successive stages of increasing unity and simplicity—an application of his principle of substantive motion. Whereas the faculties of plants are diffused throughout their body, the sensitive soul of animals achieves a higher grade of unity, since the sensitive soul, at the level of *sensus communis,* is able to combine all sense perceptions. However, the sensitive soul operates through bodily organs which are diverse and spatially localized even though the subject of perception are not these organs but is the soul itself. Imagination is the first "separate" faculty and does not work through any bodily organ. Imagination, however, entails the extension of the image (although the image does not occupy real space and is not material); and hence not being totally free from some notion of spatiality, it does not possess unity and simplicity proper.[34]

This doctrine of the progressive simplicity and unity of the soul clearly belongs to the neo-Platonic type of thought, although it is not foreign to Aristotelianism. At the level of the human conceptual thought, the soul achieves an adequate measure of unity, for a concept is neither localized anywhere in the body, nor is its object material or in matter; it is pure form without matter and in its intention it denotes an infinity of objects to which it is applicable. A concept is, therefore, truly spiritual. However, concepts as such are mutually exclusive and are therefore plural. Although concepts emerge from the soul (as we shall see in the following chapter), nevertheless a knowledge of external, physical objects—which are the paradigm of the absence of unity—is necessary for their emergence. Concepts are therefore connected in some sense with physical objects. It is only when the soul truly becomes "mind" or "acquired intellect," i.e., when it becomes creative of concepts independently of knowledge through the instrumentality of the body, that it becomes genuine unity and achieves a "simple" level of being which belongs originally to separate intellects.[35]

At this point Ṣadrā attacks Ibn Sīnā's doctrine of the "simple intellect" and its relationship to the psychic or conceptual intellect and says that, according to Ibn Sīnā, the only difference between these two levels of intellect is that what the simple intellect has as a unity—without a temporal succession of concepts but with a logical and causal order—the conceptual intellect possesses in inferential and temporal order and, further, that the simple intellect creates these concepts whereas the conceptual or psychic intellect only receives them. Ṣadrā accuses Ibn Sīnā of not having properly understood the nature of the simple. For Ibn Sīnā, the simple principle creates concepts but these latter do not actually *exist in it* but outside it; whereas, for Ṣadrā, the more simple a principle is, the more it is able to *contain,* in a simple form, all the things below it.[36]

The consequences of this difference appear both on the question of God's knowledge (which, according to Ibn Sīnā, is accidental and external to the Divine Essence, while, according to Ṣadrā, divine knowledge is inherent in God's essence in a simple manner, as we have seen in Chapter II of Part II), and on the question of the relationship of the soul to its faculties. That the soul operates through different faculties is undeniable. The "latter-day" philosophers like Abū'l-Barakāt, Fakhr al-Dīn al Rāzī, al-Ījī, and others, however, misunderstood the basis on which earlier philosophers affirmed the different faculties of the soul and thought that their basis was that every faculty, being simple, produces only one type of act.[37] This is not true; the real principle for the differentiation of faculties is either the fact that one type of action can exist—e.g., nutrition—without the other—e.g., growth, or the fact that two types of action are positive but contradictory as, e.g., assimilation of food and its expulsion.[38] Otherwise, different acts can be performed by the same faculty as, for example, nature, although simple, creates motion in a body when it is out of its natural place but produces rest in it when it is in its natural place. Starting from this misunderstanding, these philosophers and theologians came to deny multiplicity of faculties and powers in natural objects.[39]

Faculties, however, are not independent or quasi-independent *entities* possessing essential differentiae, as vegetative or animal species do. Their differentiation is merely through accidents of the human soul in the sense that some of them function in time prior to others and also through localization of different functions through different organs. Faculties, as such, do not *exist;* yet Ṣadrā does not say that they are distinguishable only conceptually, and thinks that they are, in a sense, real.[40] How, then, are we to conceive of their relationship to the soul?

Ṣadrā says, "The soul *is* all of the faculties." [41] This is not to be understood to mean that the soul is the collection or aggregate of the faculties, since an aggregate for Ṣadrā has no existence apart from the particulars which make it up. It is rather to be understood on the basis of Ṣadrā's general principle, discussed several times earlier in this work, that "a simple nature *is* everything." [42] That is to say, what the multipilicity is *at one level of existence,* unity is precisely that at a simpler, higher level of existence. Faculties are the "modes (*shu'ūn*)" or "manifestations (*maẓāhir*)" of the soul: at their own level, the faculties are real, at the higher, simpler level, they are swallowed up by the soul, whose creations they are at the lower level but wherein they exist as a unity at the higher level. They are related to the soul as servants are related to the king or as angelic beings and cosmic intelligences are related to God.[43]

That the soul, as the true spiritual self, is a unity in all experience is affirmed by philosophers and the attacks of Fakhr al-Dīn al-Rāzī upon them that they regard faculties as subjects of experience as though "in a single human person there exists a host of cognizers" are simply puerile.[44] What is true is that philosophers, including Ibn Sīnā himself, have sometimes talked as though these faculties were independent existents and hence misunderstandings arose about the proper relationship between the soul and its faculties. The fact is that the soul does not emerge as a genuine and complete unity until it reaches the status of the acquired intellect. Two difficulties prevented Ibn Sīnā from the achievement of this insight. First, as has been pointed out earlier, he did not quite understand the nature of a simple principle. Secondly, Ibn Sīnā did not accept the principle of substantive change (*ḥaraka fī'l-jauhar*), which could have led him to hold that at the level of acquired intellect the soul achieves a new order of existence and *emerges* as a pure intellect.[45] Al-Suhrawardī, although he enunciated the principle of "more perfect" and "less perfect," did not come to the idea of substantive change and hence he experienced the same difficulty in defending the unity of the soul. In fact, he believed that vegetative functions, since they are physical (and everything physical is, for him, dead-in-itself), are not due to inherent powers or faculties of the soul, but emanate directly from the "Giver of Forms," i.e., the Intellect or Pure Light, and that faculties only prepared the subject for the reception of these forms. Now, there is an obvious difference between that which prepares and that which causes or necessitates (i.e., between the receptive and the productive principles), the heating power of fire, for example, is not just preparatory for the heating operation but necessitates or causes it.[46]

The truth is that, in accordance with the principle of substantive change or transformation, which is also expressed by the doctrine of the systematic ambiguity (*tashkīk*) [47] of existence, the soul first emerges as vegetative, then as perceptive and locomotive at the animal level, then as potential intellect, and finally as pure intellect when the *term* soul is no longer applicable to it. The soul has its being at all these levels and at each of these levels it is the same in a sense and yet different in a sense because the same being can pass through different levels of development.[48]

Ibn Sīnā had given an excellent example of the relationship between the soul and its faculties from the physical realm when he said that a body may be so related to fire that the former may be only heated by the latter, or it may be so related to the fire that the latter both heats and illuminates that body—in which case, the higher state, the illumination, becomes the cause of the former state, the heating—or, finally, it may be so related to the fire that the sun not only heats and illuminates that body but sets it aflame—in which case, the flame becomes the cause (together with the original fire) of both heat and illumination. Nevertheless, Ibn Sīnā himself, while describing the relationship of the soul to the body, had used contradictory language: on the one hand, he describes the faculties as *emanating from* (*faiḍ*) the soul, which is regarded as their source (*manba'*), while on the other he described the soul as a mere link (*ribāṭ*) integrating the faculties and their activity and called it the meeting point (*majma'*) of the latter. Now this latter conception is against the idea of the soul as a genuine, transcendent simple entity.[49]

Indeed, when the soul achieves its highest form as true unity, it contains all the lower faculties and forms within its simple nature. The commonly held view that when the soul becomes fully developed and separate, it negates and excludes the lower forms, is a cardinal error; many philosophers misconstrue the meaning of "abstraction" as "removal" or "negation" of something.[50] True unity and simplicity does not negate but comprehends everything. That is why the soul, at the highest stage of its development, resembles God, for God, in His absolute simplicity, comprehends everything.[51] Such a soul begins to function like God and creates forms from within itself: indeed, at this stage, the Perfect Man becomes the ruler of all the worlds—physical, psychic, and intelligible—as Ibn Arabī has it. The Perfect Man, according to Ibn 'Arabī, must function directly through the simplicity and unity of his mind, and not through instruments, in order for his will to be obeyed by the entire creation. Such a Perfect Man is the Perfect Saint. But should this Perfect Man choose to work through external instruments—i.e., as a prophet—and enunciate external laws and commands, he may be obeyed by a segment of the creation and disobeyed by another segment. This is nothing surprising and does not detract from the perfection of the Perfect Man, since this is the very nature of functioning through external instruments as distinguished from functioning through the unity of the inner mind. For God Himself, when He decided to work externally through commands and instruments, was disobeyed by a part of His creation, viz., Satan. But at the level of His Divine Unity, where instruments are non-existent, God's obedience is assured by definition, as it were, for there, since his Unity includes all, Satan himself is part of it.[52]

According to Ṣadrā, just as the soul comes into existence as an individual as a power *in* matter—although not as a power *of* matter—so it retains its individual character even when it is severed from the body and becomes a member of the Divine Realm. As we shall see later in his doctrine of eschatology, he rejects the transmigration of souls as well as the view that, after death, the individual souls dissolve themselves in the ocean of Eternal Being.

NOTES

1. *De Anima,* II, 1, 412 a 27; 412 b, line 5.
2. *Ibid.,* 413 a, lines 8–9.
3. *De Anima,* ed. Bruns (Berlin, 1887), p. 108, lines 19 ff.
4. *Enneads,* IV, 7, 85, IV, 3, 21 (cf. I, 1, 8; I, 6, 5; IV, 6, 3, etc.).
5. See particularly the commentaries of Themistius, Simplicius and Philoponus on Aristotle's *De Anima* (cf. my *Avicenna's Psychology,* Oxford, 1952, Introduction).
6. See my *Prophecy in Islam,* London, 1958, Ch. I, Section 1.
7. Al-Fārābī, *al-Madīna al-Fāḍila,* Beirut, 1959, p. 53, line 1 ff.
8. See my *Prophecy in Islam,* London, 1958, Chapter I, Section 2.
9. See *Avicenna's De Anima* (ed. F. Rahman), Oxford, 1959, p. 12, lines 9 ff.
10. Aristotle, for example, *Physics,* 259 b 20 ff. on the continuous motion of the heavens.
11. *Avicenna's De Anima,* p. 16, lines 2 ff.
12. *Asfār,* I, 3, p. 458, lines 7 ff.
13. *Asfār,* IV, 1, p. 12, lines 4–13.
14. *Ibid.,* p. 16, line 4–p. 18, line 7.
15. For example, *Asfār,* III, 1, p. 17, lines 8–13; *ibid.,* I, 3, p. 120, lines 1 ff., and the discussion of substantive movement in Chapter V of Part I above.
16. Section A, Chapter V, Part I.
17. *Asfār,* IV, 1, p. 348, line 16; *ibid.,* IV, 2, p. 116, lines 2–10.
18. *Ibid.,* IV, 1, p. 4, lines 3 ff.; p. 35, last line ff.; p. 121, lines 4 ff.; p. 123, lines 16–22; *ibid.,* p. 326, line 6–p. 327, line 3.
19. *Ibid.,* p. 16, line 14–p. 17, line 1.
20. *Avicenna's De Anima,* p. 16, lines 2 ff.; p. 255, lines 1 ff.; for his denial of physical resurrection, see his *R. Adḥawiya* (Cairo, 1949).
21. *Ibid.,* p. 26, lines 3 ff.
22. *Ibid.,* p. 46, lines 12–15.
23. *Ibid.,* p. 46, line 16–p. 47, line 4; al-Suhrawardī, *Opera Metaphysica,* I, p. 115, lines 6 ff.; *ibid.,* II, p. 112, line 13; p. 114, lines 5 ff. The difference

between the statements of *Opera* I and II is obvious, for in the one, self-consciousness is not constitutive of, but lies outside of, the self, but in the latter this duality is denied. See my *Selected Letters of Shaikh Aḥmad Sirhindi* (Karachi, 1968), *Introduction,* p. 14, lines 9 ff.

24. References in the preceding note to al-Suhrawardī.

25. See Chapter V, Section C of this Part, below.

26. *Asfār,* IV, 1, p. 228, lines 6–9.

27. See my *Sirhindi, Introduction, op. cit.,* p. 62, lines 10 ff.; see also my article, "Dream, Imagination, and *'Ālam al-Mithāl,"* *Islamic Studies* (Karachi-Islamabad), Vol. IV, No. 2, pp. 167–80.

28. *Asfār,* IV, 1, p. 111, lines 2 ff.; p. 113, lines 5 ff.

29. *Ibid.,* p. 42, line 9–p. 44, line 15. This, however, contradicts his own and more basic view that both body and soul are in constant flux.

30. *Ibid.,* p. 43, lines 1 ff.

31. See Chapters II and III below—according to Ṣadrā, all cognitive forms, perceptive, imaginative, and intellective, are created by the soul and yet there is also a World of Imagination and a Realm of Ideas with which the human mind comes into contact.

32. *Asfār,* IV, 1, p. 43, lines 8 ff.

33. *Ibid.,* p. 44, lines 8 ff.; see *ibid.,* p. 48, lines 4–7, where animals are credited with "actual imagination (*khayāl; bi'l-fi'l*)."

34. See references in the three preceding notes, and Chapter III below on Imagination.

35. On the development of the Intellect, see Chapter IV below.

36. *Asfār,* III, 2, p. 117, lines 3 ff.; *ibid.,* I, 1, p. 369, last line ff.; see also Chapter IV of this Part below, and Chapter II of Part II above on God's knowledge.

37. *Asfār,* IV, 1, p. 60, lines 3 ff.

38. *Ibid.,* p. 60, lines 12 ff.; *ibid.,* p. 64, lines 11–15.

39. *Ibid.,* p. 63, lines 1 ff.

40. *Ibid.,* p. 65, lines 13 ff.; p. 68, lines 1 ff.

41. *Ibid.,* p. 51, line 6; p. 121, lines 4 ff.; p. 123, lines 16 ff.; p. 221, lines 5 ff.; p. 135, line 1–p. 136, line 5.

42. *Ibid.,* p. 121, lines 8–9; see also Chapter I, Section C, Part I.

43. *Ibid.,* p. 137, lines 16 ff.; *ibid.,* p. 139, lines 13 ff., and reference to the "Epistles of the Brethren of Purity."

44. *Ibid.,* p. 65, lines 19 ff.

45. *Asfār,* IV, 2, p. 116, lines 11 ff.

46. *Asfar,* IV, 1, p. 108, lines 16–18.

47. See Chapter I, Section 3 of Part I; also references in note 41 above; *Asfār,* IV, 2, p. 21, lines 12 ff.; *ibid.* p. 61, lines 7 ff.–p. 63, line 6, etc.

48. References in the preceding note.

49. *Asfār,* IV, 1, p. 148, line 2 ff. (cf. p. 35, line 4 ff.); see *Avicenna's De Anima,* p. 261, lines 7 ff.

50. On the meaning of "abstraction" see the following three chapters.

51. *Asfār,* IV, 1, p. 121, lines 8–11; *ibid.,* I, 3, p. 277, lines 16 ff., particularly p. 379, lines 11–16.

52. *Ibid.,* IV, 1, p. 140, line 1–p. 142, line 6.

CHAPTER II *

THEORY OF KNOWLEDGE—I

A. *General Considerations*

Ṣadrā affirms the identity of the knower and the known, i.e., of thought and being, in all knowledge. But the nature of this identity must be defined carefully. It is not the case that external objects, as they are, become objects of knowledge. Indeed, the forms of external objects, immersed as they are in matter and material concomitants, cannot move into the mind and become known, since mental forms and material forms are different in several essential respects.[1] It will be shown presently that the status of mental existence is radically different from the status of external existence.[2] When something becomes an object of knowledge, therefore, it acquires an altogether new *genre* of existence (*nash'a 'ilmīya*) where several of its characteristics of external existence are removed and it acquires certain new characteristics. For example, a mental form ceases to be material and becomes a universal—a genus or a species, etc. Ṣadrā, therefore, declares absolutely that neither of the external and mental existences can change into (*lā tanqalib*) each other [3] and thereby moves away from the position of naive realism adopted by Aristotle into a form of idealism with Plotinus.

This position is supported by a consideration of sense perception. It is not true that in sense perception the object of knowledge is the quality coming to inhere in the sense organ (through the external object) and producing a qualitative change in that organ. If that were the case, then, when my hand becomes warm or my tongue sweet, someone else could equally feel the same heat by touching my hand or coming into suitable contact with my tongue. But this is manifestly absurd. Again, if the perceptible form were to inhere in a bodily organ—and the organ, being physical, has a form of

* This chapter was first published in *The Philosophical Forum*, Boston University, Vol. 6, no. 1 (New Series), Fall, 1973, pp. 141–152.

its own—then one physical organ will have two forms, which is also absurd. Indeed, when the soul perceives warmth or cold, it does not become warm or cold.[4]

These considerations show that perceptible forms are not externally existent forms; nor are they forms present in the sense organs at the time of perception. Perceptible forms are, therefore, operations of or emanations from the soul itself and the presentation of an object to a sense organ only provides the occasion for the projection of the form from the soul. All forms in knowledge are produced by the soul in this way and Ṣadrā says that the relationship of cognitive forms to the soul is analogous to the relationship of the contingent to the Necessary Being, God.[5] If this is so with regard to sense perception, how much more true it will be of imagination and still more of intellection? For in sense-perception at least the sense organ mediates between the external object and the act of perception, but in imagination and intellection there is no bodily organ employed.

As for the definition of knowledge, philosophers have given several views about it. Although each of these views is open to serious objections, it is, nevertheless, possible to arrive at a satisfactory definition, using them together as a basis; but it will be found at the same time that some of these views are so far from truth that they cannot be corrected. The first view to be considered is that which defines knowledge—particularly intellectual knowledge—in terms of abstraction or separation from matter. Abstraction is taken to mean abstraction from matter and elimination of material attachments. That is to say, abstraction is taken as something *negative*. Now, whenever we know something, we are aware that knowledge is something positive and we are not aware of any negations. Again, when we know animal or man, we do not negate matter from them; indeed, the concept animal or man includes material dimensions.[6] This shows that abstraction does not occur in the negation of anything. Secondly, whenever it is possible to say, "A knows B," it would be absurd to say, "A is abstract to B," or "B is abstract to A." For if B is abstract, it must be so to everyone else as well as to A. Finally, "to be abstract" can never be a translation of "to be knowledge"; that is why *it requires a proof to show* that all knowledge *includes* abstraction.[7]

The second approach to the definition of knowledge is to say that knowledge consists in the imprinting of the form of the object in the subject. It is obvious that this is not true of self-knowledge, since it is admitted by all that self-knowledge does not come about by the imprinting of one's form into oneself. Secondly, the imprinting of forms in matter does not become knowledge for material bodies. Nor is it true to say that, in matter, the presence of quantity, space, position, etc. prevents it from knowing, for when the soul knows things, it knows them along with quantity, quality, position, etc. And to say that knowledge consists in the imprinting of forms in something whose function it is to know begs the question and is, therefore, not an answer. Certain philosophers, in order to avoid the difficulties that beset the theory of imprinting of forms, have defined knowledge as a unique relationship between the subject and the object. Apart from the fact that this view still does not cover the phenomenon of self-knowledge (since it is difficult to construe self-knowledge as a *relation* between the self and itself), it necessitates the conclusion that those things which do not actually exist cannot be known in any sense, for there can be no relationship between the mind and the non-existent. It is also difficult on this view to explain ignorance in the sense of mis-knowledge, since, if this relationship is present, there is true knowledge; and if it is absent, there is no knowledge at all. If one holds with Fakhr al-Dīn al-Rāzī that knowledge is not a mere relation but a relational quality (*kaifīya dhāt iḍāfa*), one is vulnerable to similar objections. It would also follow that God's knowledge is an extrinsic quality to His being and not essential to Him.[8]

Indeed, the view that knowledge is an accidental quality of the mind was also held by Ibn Sīnā in certain contexts. But Ibn Sīnā notes the well-known difficulty as to how, if the mental form is to correspond to the external reality, a substance in external reality can become an accident in the mind. Ibn Sīnā's answer is that this mental form, which is an accident to the mind, is of such a nature that, if it were to exist externally, it would be a substance and not an accident. That this is not a genuine solution of the difficulty is obvious, since this explanation commits the same mistake as the doctrine of abstraction. For it is meaningless to say that something which is a substance-in-itself turns into an accident in the mind. It is the same thing as if someone were to say that animal, when it exists in a mind, is neither a substance, nor a body, nor growing, nor sentient, etc., which is manifestly absurd. This view, when logically pressed, would make the mental forms exactly like paintings or engravings of an animal on a wall, for it is also true of these that if they were to exist in the external reality, they would be substances, physical, growing, sentient, etc. This fatal mistake arises because "abstraction by the mind" is held to *denude* objects of their essential characteristics and turn them into mere engravings on the mind.[9]

Al-Suhrawardī sought to translate the phenomenon of cognition into the terminology of Light. He posited the categories of Light as that which is Light to itself, and that which is Light to something else. The first is the self-existing, self-knowing substance, which is correct insofar as it identifies true being with knowledge. He was inconsistent, however, in the rest of his theory of knowledge. For even those things which are, according to him, pure Darkness (*ghawāsiq*), he allowed to be cognizable by direct illuminational awareness, like pure body and pure quantity. Again, since animals possess cognition, at least of particulars, they must be taken, on his principles, to be endowed with Light; but since all cognition entails self-cognition, it follows that animals are pure intellects.[10]

Ṣadrā then proceeds to state his own view of knowledge:

> Knowledge is neither a privation like abstraction from matter, nor a relation but a being (*wujūd*). (It is) not every being but that which is an actual being, not potential. (It is) not even every actual being, but a pure being, unmixed with non-being. To the extent that it becomes free from an admixture of non-being, its intensity as knowledge increases.[11] Primary matter, which is pure indeterminacy and potentiality, is the furthest removed from possessing the status of knowledge. It becomes determinate by receiving a bodily form. But body itself cannot become knowledge, since it is not pure being: parts of a body, being mutually exclusive, are never present to each other and hence body can never attain a real unity which is requisite for true being and knowledge. None of the imagined parts of a continuous body can be predicated of the whole, nor can the whole be predicated of them, and yet the body as a whole attains its being through the continuity of these parts and its perfection lies in an increase in that continuity. Now how can something, whose perfection (*kamāl*) entails its non-being (*zawāl*), belong to itself (i.e., as a self-subsistent entity)? And a thing which cannot belong to itself, cannot attain or possess itself and when a thing cannot possess itself, how can it be possessed by something else? [12]

Now "attainment and possession (*al-nayl wa'l-dark*)" are of the essence of knowledge. Therefore, body and its physical relations can never be a proper object of knowledge, except through a form other than this bodily form. This other form is an altogether new form having a spiritual character, a form arising from within the soul. In the words of Coleridge:

> . . . We receive but what we give,
> And in ourselves alone does Nature live.[13]

Knowledge, then, *is pure existence, free from matter*.[14] Such existence is the soul when it has fully developed into an acquired intellect. The soul then does not need forms inhering in it as its accidents but creates forms from within itself or, rather, *is* these forms. This is the meaning of the identity of thought and being. This also explains the dictum referred to previously, viz., that all knowledge is related to the soul as the contingent world is related to God. For just as God is Pure and Simple Existence, the Absolute Mind and all other existents are related to Him, thanks to the "unfolding existence (*wujūd munbasiṭ*)," at different levels—which constitute a systematically ambiguous world of existence of identity-in-differences, at the same time generating a semi-real realm of essences—so the soul gives rise, thanks to the unfolding knowledge (which is a perfect analogue of the "unfolding existence" of God) to different levels of knowables—of perception, imagination, estimation, and intellection—as systematically ambiguous knowables which are, in a sense, different and in a sense identical.[15]

It is important to note clearly the sense in which the phrase "pure existence free from matter" has been used; otherwise, it is liable to be gravely misunderstood. Something which is free from matter is also called a form or pure and abstract form. Form, in this sense, can also mean essence. This is precisely what is *not* meant here, else we will revert to the doctrine of abstraction of forms whose relationship to the soul will again become one of accidental quality. On the contrary, when a form is free from matter, it becomes a pure existent, not an essence, and an existent cannot be known through a form but through an intuitive self-identity or direct knowledge. Without this existential dimension to the form and the consequent identity of knowledge and existence, it would, indeed, be possible to object that from the *concept* "form free from matter," it is not possible to deduce "knowledge," for the two are not the same. That is why even when we know that God, for example, is free from matter, we have still to *prove* His self-knowledge by a further argument. The answer is that we are not here talking of *an abstract concept* "form free from matter," but of the *fact* that existence cannot be known except through self-identity and direct intuition, and this is possible only in a being free from matter.[16]

A similar answer applies to the following objection reported by al-Ṭūsī to have been raised by al-Mas'ūdī: "If my self-knowledge is identical with my self, what about my knowledge of my self-knowledge . . . *ad infinitum?* If this latter is also identical with my self, then my self is no longer simple but composite. If not, then perhaps my primary self-intuition is also not identical with my self." The answer is that whereas my primary self-intuition is identical with my self, my higher-order statements are not about my self existentially but only indirectly or *as a concept*. Thus, whereas my primary intuition can be expressed by saying, "I know myself," my higher-order statement about my self-knowledge will take the form "I know *that* I know myself." This answer of Ṣadrā's does not appear to be sound, for it is obvious that even my primary self-intuition can be stated in the indirect form: "I know *that* I am." Al-Ṭūsī's answer, therefore, would seem to be more correct than Ṣadrā's, viz., that my primary self-knowledge is in an essential manner identical with my self, and therefore, direct, but it can also be stated in an indirect manner where it is not identical with my self but is *about* myself.[17] Elsewhere, Ṣadrā himself states that an indirect knowledge of the self is also possible, in which case it is not an intuition but is of a conceptual order.[18]

B. *The Problem of "Mental Existence (al-wujūd al-dhihnī)"*

Ṣadrā's statements that knowledge requires a new status of being for the known object, a "being-for-knowledge," raises the question of the nature of mental existence (*al-wujūd al-dhihnī*), and the relationship of this existence to the known object. The first task in this connection is to *prove* that there is such a thing as "mental existence" as distinguished from real existence; this Ṣadrā claims to have accomplished by showing that since, in sense-perception, the external material object in itself cannot be presented to the mind and hence known, the soul must create a corresponding form, of its own nature. This is much more true in the case of images which the soul creates from within itself. As for the intellective form, Ṣadrā's position is that these forms exist in their own right in a Platonic sense, and *as immaterial individuals* (*afrād*), and that when the soul fully knows them, it does so by an illuminationist direct knowledge whereby it becomes identical with them. However, since the ordinary soul cannot intellect them fully due to its preoccupations with the "affairs of the body and material things," it can see them only in a "blurred" manner as a weak sighted person might see a distant thing in the dark.[19]

Because of its "blurred vision" of the Form, the mind is then enabled to form "essences," which come to behave as "universals" applicable to different species. In doing so, the mind necessarily does violence to the nature of reality, since reality is not essence but a spectrum of existences. Essences are merely something "unreal" and "negative," being concomitants of partial existence and accompanying the latter at all of its levels. Nevertheless, the mind's operation with them is also a reality of its own order and it is true that in some sense they "exist in the mind."

Hence all forms, whether sensible, imaginative, or intellective, exist in the mind. But we must be very careful in trying to understand the meaning of the expression "in the mind." These forms do not *inhere* in the mind as the form of a horse inheres in a piece of wax, for example. They are rather attached to the mind as acts or creations are attached or present to their actor or creator.[20] The use of the particle "in" differs with different types of existents. Something may exist in a place as water exists "in" a pitcher or a pitcher "in" a room. But when things are said to be "in" space or time, this is a different use. A third, philosophic use of "in" is when things are said to be *"in* the external world." In this usage the "external world" does not mean a place "in" which things exist but merely denotes a status or level of existence, i.e., a level where things operate with their natural properties. When, again, something is said to be *"in* the mind," the mind cannot in this use be conceived of as a "container," but it simply means that the mind has a set of properties or essences which it is able to apply to the external reality and to classify things.[21] Of course, the mind, as an external existent and as a piece of the furniture of objective reality, is qualified (*muttaṣif*) by the known essences which can, in this sense, be said to qualify the mind (*kaif nafsāni*). However, intrinsically speaking, the mind looks upon the external world and operates upon it with notions, concepts, or essences (*ma'ānī, mafāhīm, māhīyāt*).

The question of the relationship of this mental form to the external reality has troubled most Muslim philosophers since Ibn Sīnā, and has produced elaborate discussions. At the root of these discussions is the consideration that if the mental form is to reflect the reality faithfully, then the former must preserve the latter's characteristics. From this arises the demand that if something is a substance in the external reality, the mental form must be a substance as well. But Ibn Sīnā and others have described the mental form as a quality or accident of the soul which, as we have said, is, in a sense, correct. But this description, from the point of view of knowledge, is extrinsic. Others have argued that the mental form retains the essential characteristics of the external reality with certain modifications. Just as for example, a piece of magnet, when outside the hand, attracts iron, but when held in the hand, does not attract it! This line of argument is absurd and commits the fallacy of confusing different orders of existence. For an idea or form in the mind does not move out of itself and exist externally so that when it is outside the mind, it has certain characteristics while, when in the mind, it has certain other characteristics.[22]

Others, in order to escape these difficulties, invoked the doctrine of abstraction and, as we have seen above, asserted that what the mind knows (and possesses) is not the outside reality itself but a picture or copy of it and that such a mental image need not possess what the outside reality possesses —it might not be a substance, for example. Some others define the mental form or image as *being such that if it exists outside the mind, it would be a substance*. This is the view, among others, of Jalāl al-Dīn al-Dawwānī. Shall we also conclude, then, that the mental form, say, of man, is such that if it exists outside the mind, it would have two hands, two feet, etc.? This abstraction doctrine is even more absurd and dangerous than the example of the magnet, for it has as its necessary consequences that we should not know reality. For, surely, the one thing that is certain about our mental act of knowledge is that we know about man, for example, that he is a substance, has a body with all its parts, has a straight or upright stature, etc.[23]

According to Ṣadrā, this problem has arisen from a confusion of the types of proposition of logically different orders. In an informative categorical proposition, the mental concept or idea is asserted of, and hence related to, something outside the mind, e.g., "such and such is a man." These propositions are "existential (*wujūdī*)," and such predications are called "ordinary informative predications (*al-ḥaml al-shā'i'*)." But in propositions where a concept or idea refers, not to reality, but to itself, the predication is called "primary or tautological (*al-ḥaml al-awwalī*)." In this case, the predicate only gives the meaning or definition of the subject, e.g., "man is a rational animal." The mental form is, therefore, only the meaning or the essence and does not go beyond itself whereas in the informative proposition the mental form is not contemplated *per se,* but is made only the "way of seeing through (*ḥikāya li'l-manẓūr ilaih*)" to reality.[24]

Indeed, even the talk about "mental forms" is not correct because it gives the impression of pictures, likenesses, etc. What the mind has are the notions or concepts or essences (*ma'ānī, mafāhim, māhiyāt*), as has been said before. In order to have these, the mind is not in need of "forms existing in the intellect." Philosophers have gone astray on this point because they have identified the mental act of knowledge with an accident or a picture in the mind and have not really believed in the identity of the knower and the known in the act of knowledge in a mental order of existence. There are other philosophers who do not concede the mental order of existence at all and think that the doctrine of mental existences, far from solving problems, creates certain formidable difficulties. We must now turn to the more serious of these objections to the thesis of mental existence, and its solution.

In the realm of concepts or notions, there are those which do not correspond to the outside reality; indeed, some cannot exist at all in reality since they are self-contradictory (like a square-circle). Now, these notions, as such, are genuine, since among other things, they are distinct from one another and have meanings. The belief in mental existence would, therefore, entail that these self-contradictions exist in the mind. Ṣadrā's reply is that although the mind can conceive impossibles, this does not make them genuine concepts. But their reality as notions must be admitted and there is no difficulty in this since we have argued that mental existence is disparate with real existence. We must, however, distinguish between a notion in this sense and a real essence. Some people, because they did not distinguish between the two, have asserted that when we say that, e.g., "a square-circle is impossible," a square-circle must exist in our minds to make such a proposition possible. Indeed, an impossible like "God's peer," must exist not only in the mind but also in reality, for if "God's peer" exists in the mind, then for it to be God's peer, it must also exist externally! By this argument, they seek to destroy the mental order of existence. According to Ṣadrā, the area of the conceivable is larger than that of the real and the possible. In other words, not all that is impossible—logically impossible—is absurd in the sense that it has no meaning at all. In this sense, a mind can even conceive itself to be non-existent—which is, of course, logically impossible. But to be a meaning—and hence exist in the mind—is one thing and to be a real essence is quite another. The impossible has no essence, for it can have no instances in reality. In general, Ṣadrā seems to distinguish between: (1) the real which has an essence and real instances; (2) the non-existent, e.g., the *'anqā',* which is not real and has no instances in reality but can logically have instances and since it is not impossible, also has an essence; and (3) the impossible, which logically *cannot* have real instances and consequently has no essence (*ḥaqīqa*), but is conceivable by the mind and therefore has meaning and is a genuine notion (*mafhūm*).[25]

In the realm of propositions, we predicate positive attributes of things that do not exist, e.g., in the proposition "every *'anqā'* (a mythical bird) can fly." Even in the case of a thing that really exists, we do not confine ourselves to its existent examples but also pass judgments on its potential members, as, for example, when we say, "the sum of the three angles of *all* triangles is equal to two right angles." The objection to the first example is that it does not really refer to anything non-existent or mental, but refers to external reality in a hypothetical mode. The proposition, therefore, actually states, "Something, if it were to exist and possess such-and-such attributes, would be an *'anqā'*." All existence is, therefore, real existence and no other order of existence is called for. In the case of the second example, the judgment must be true of an infinite number of particular instances of triangles, all of which must be simultaneously conceived in the mind, which is impossible. In his reply, Ṣadrā states that in the case of universal or general propositions, the judgment does not concern itself directly with individuals as such, as the latter-day philosophers appear to be "firmly of the view," but rather with the notion; and only through the notion does the judgment pass indirectly to the individuals and universality characterizes the meaning of the notion itself.[26]

Third, the antagonist argues on the basis of our propositions about the past, if we have seen a man A in the past, who is no longer there, but talk about him, surely we are talking about *him* and not about our present images of him. In reply, some people have suggested the identity of the object of this past experience and the mental image, which is absurd. Ṣadrā's answer is that we *use* our present mental images to refer to or to describe the object of our past experiences (just as, of course, we can use these images to describe subjectively or reflexively our own mental state now).[27]

NOTES

1. *Asfār,* I, 3, pp. 300–304. A fuller treatment of the identity of the knower and the known is in the context of intellective knowledge.

2. See Section B of the present Chapter.

3. *Asfār,* I, 3, p. 281, lines 5–6.

4. *Ibid.,* p. 282, lines 1 ff.

5. This is a consequence of Ṣadrā's view that the soul is God's analogue in simplicity and that a simple being *is* all the things and from it, therefore, flow all things.

6. *Asfār,* I, 3, p. 306, first para.; *Asfār,* IV, 2, p. 95, lines 6 ff.

7. *Ibid.,* p. 289, last para.

8. Knowledge as form is discussed in *ibid.,* p. 288, lines 8 ff.; knowledge as relation, p. 290, lines 3 ff.

9. *Ibid.,* pp. 305–8.

10. *Ibid.,* p. 291, line 16–p. 292, line 5.

11. I.e., until it becomes an absolutely simple form as intuitive intellect; see note 5 above.

12. *Ibid.,* p. 297, beginning–p. 298, line 4.

13. Coleridge in his poem *Ode to the Moon.* It is obvious that it is no part of this position as such that things do not exist in the external world, i.e., that it is not subjective idealism. Ṣadrā, however, does land himself in grave difficulties by saying that the direct object of the soul's knowledge are its native ideas *and the external objects are perceived indirectly or by second intention.* See the next Chapter for further elaboration.

14. *Ibid.,* p. 292, line 6; *ibid.,* p. 294, line 11; *Asfār,* I, 1, p. 290, line 6, etc.

15. See particularly al-Sabzawārī's n. 1, *Asfār,* I, 1, p. 290, and n. 1, *Asfār,* I, 3, p. 311. This also clarifies the meaning of Ṣadrā's oft-repeated dictum that knowledge is a form of existence, a higher form of existence than the material world.

16. *Asfār,* I, 3, p. 294, lines 5–14.

17. *Asfār,* I, p. 294, last line–p. 296, line 7.

18. *Asfār,* IV, 1, p. 47, lines 5 ff., where Ṣadrā describes both forms of self-knowledge, and al-Sabzawārī's important note, *ibid.,* p. 65, line 15; also al-Sabzawārī's note 7 on *Asfār,* I, 3, p. 295.

19. *Asfār,* I, 1, p. 289, line 1 ff.; *Asfār,* I, 2, p. 68, lines 15 ff.
20. *Asfār,* I, 1, p. 287, lines 9 ff.; see above, notes 5 and 15.
21. *Asfār,* I, 1, p. 311, last para.
22. *Ibid.,* p. 280, lines 9 ff.
23. *Ibid.,* p. 306, lines 3 ff.
24. *Ibid.,* p. 292, lines 11 ff.; p. 271, lines 17 ff.
25. *Ibid.,* p. 312, lines 3 ff.
26. *Ibid.,* p. 270, lines 4 ff
27. *Ibid.,* p. 271, lines 12 ff.

CHAPTER III

THEORY OF KNOWLEDGE—

II: PERCEPTION AND IMAGINATION

A. *External Sense*

According to Aristotle and the Muslim Peripatetics, sense perception consists in the fact that sense organs undergo a qualitative change under the impact of the external object of perception and receive its imprint. In this view, it is sometimes held that the object of immediate perception is this imprint which the soul then refers to the external object, sometimes that the imprint is a sensation while perception is directly of the external object. In either case, the occurrence in the sense organ is directly constitutive of the act of perception and the perceptible is a bodily form, either in the sense-organ or in the physical world. Plotinus holds that physical sensation, far from being constitutive of perception, is a mere outward reflection or image of the proper sensation of the soul, which has as its object of perception not the external object, but an internal form. Physical sensation is nothing but the "soul in sleep," as it were.[1] Plotinus nevertheless shows some hesitation about the nature of the imprint, as to whether it is in the bodily organ or only mediated by the bodily organ, although at all events it is received by the soul: "The soul receives the imprint which [either] is of the body [i.e. the physical organ] or comes via the body" (*Enneads,* II, 3, 26; see also *ibid.,* I, 1, 7).

Ṣadrā, who adopts a strongly neo-Platonic line of thought, argues, as we have seen in the preceding chapter, that nothing physical as such can become the proper object of knowledge, since knowledge involves an entirely new status of being with which the object of knowledge is invested (*nash'a 'ilmīya*). This is the result of the doctrine that (1) knowledge consists in a "presentation (*ḥuḍūr*)" of the object to the subject; (2) nothing physical can be "present" either to anything else or, indeed, to itself since its part are mutually "absent"; and (3) since both the external objects and the sense organs are physical, there is no question of the former being "present" t the latter. What is, then, sense perception, and how does it come about And how is this radically non-physical view of sense perception compatibl with Ṣadrā's view of the genesis of the soul, since unlike Plotinus (who hold that the soul is a transcendent substance pre-existing the body that subsequently enters it), and like Aristotle and Ibn Sīnā, he believes that the sou is "generated in and with the body?"

The answer to the second question is that, as indicated earlier, the soul although generated in and with the body, is, from its very inception, no *of* the body but something higher than it, for even the souls of plants ar not bodily but employ bodily functions. The emergence of the soul is, indeed, a spectacular case of substantive change. In the case of the anima soul, Ṣadrā's contention is that its faculty of imagination is separate fron matter. As for sense perception, its subject is also the soul and not the sense organ or the sense-faculty:

> You may say that the visual faculty which is in the eye is the orgar which perceives the perceptible object, then it transmits what it ha perceived through the connection which exists between it and yoursel and thus you gain an awareness of the thing which (actually) the visua faculty has already perceived. (In that case) we will ask: After the transmission to *you,* do you (again) perceive the visible object as the orgar had perceived, or not? If you say, "yes," then in that case your perception is one thing and your organ's perception is another. But if you sa that you do not perceive *after* the transmission, then *you* have not perceived or heard or felt your pleasure and pain. . . . For the knowledg that the *eye* sees, the *ear* hears, the *feet* walk, and the *hand* seizes i not identical with seeing, hearing, walking, and seizing, any more thar our knowledge that someone else is hungry or feels pleasure or pain i identical with our feeling hungry, pleasure, or pain.[2]

Physical organs are required for sense perception but only thanks to th accidental fact that we exist in a material world, not intrinsically. Pure soul when they are separated from the body can have all the perceptions whereir in ordinary life physical organs mediate. This is a psychic phenomenor which is a matter of experience and not a mere fantasy. Dreams alread point in that direction, since in dreams we see and hear and have all perceptual experiences.[3] Ṣadrā also holds that the heavenly souls are possesse of all perceptual experiences, and not merely imagination, even thoug their perceptions are not mediated by a potentiality and receptivity on th part of any perceptual organ; nor do they have localized organs of percep tion.[4] Since perceptual experience—like hearing pleasurable sounds and smelling and tasting pleasurable things—is in itself a perfection, it cannot be denied that the heavenly souls possess it. In fact, Pythagoras was able to perfect the art of music by ascending to the heaven by his pure soul, "hearing" melodious sounds there, and then translating them into physically audible tunes by the use of his physical faculties.[5]

The reason for this is that the external sensibles and the affections of the sense organ are merely preparatory and provide the "occasion" for the rise in the soul, or rather, the creation by it, of the perceptible form.[6] This is the very meaning of the famous statement—going back to Aristotle—that the actually sensible form and the actually sentient soul are identical, for how can the doctrine of the identity of the sentient and the sensible be upheld if we regard the sensible either as the external material form or the affection of the sense organ? Thus, when the tactible external form affects the tactual organ, the soul creates its own form or God creates that form in the soul. Similarly, in the case of audition, it is not the case that the external sound produces a movement in the air which is exactly transmitted through successive air-waves to the interior of the ear and thus hearing takes place. The movement of the air and its air-waves are preparatory conditions for the sound to be heard, but they do not transmit the sound.[7]

In the case of vision, again, three views have been held. Physicists (Aristotelians) have held that the form of the visual object is transmitted through the rays of light that impinge upon the retina of the eye. When the objection is raised against them that we see the object outside and not the form in the retina or the brain, they simply reply that what is perceived is the object itself and not its form, which is transmitted—as is the case with all external perceptibles. This reply, however, begs the very question. The second view, that of mathematicians (Platonists), is that vision takes place by the rays of light emanating from the eye and impinging upon the object. The third view was advocated by al-Suhrawardī. It says that vision is accomplished, when a luminous object is situated facing the visual organ, as a direct illuminationist event of awareness (*'ilm ishrāqī*). This view rejects the necessity of a transparent medium. "But the truth, according to us," says Ṣadrā, "is neither of these three views. The truth is that vision consists in the creation, by the power of God, of a form resembling it (i.e., the form of the external object) from within the domain of the soul, this form being separate from the external matter, present to the cognizant soul, and related to it as an act is related to its actor, not as something received is related to its recipient." [8]

It is to be noted that Ṣadrā's position on sense perception is a consequence of the doctrine of the identity of the subject and object in knowledge which was initiated by Aristotle but carried to its logical extremes by neo-Platonism and elaborated and rationally vindicated by Ṣadrā. For this is what Ṣadrā means by saying that *knowledge is being,* i.e., the status of being and the status of knowledge are the same. For knowledge to be possible, the being of the external material objects has to undergo a transformation, an actual metamorphosis, and this is the meaning of *nash'a 'ilmīya* or a being-for-knowledge. An important feature of the doctrine is the rejection of the "doctrine of abstraction" as expounded by classical philosophers. Ṣadrā says that the statement that perception "abstracts the form from matter" or that imagination "abstracts the form from material attachments" is not acceptable. In perception we know the *material* thing and not something that is "abstracted" from matter. The psychic nature of the act of perception, therefore, requires not abstraction but a *transformation* of the object of perception; and physical or physiological accounts, therefore, cannot explain it:

> Perception in general does not take place—as the well-known doctrine of the majority of the philosophers states—by the perceptual faculty's abstraction of the perceptible form itself from matter and encountering it along with its enveloping material attachments—since it has been established that forms imprinted in matter cannot move locally. . . . Perception occurs because the giver (of forms, i.e., the soul itself) bestows another psychic and luminous cognitive form, thanks to which perception or knowledge arises. This form is the actual sentient and the actual sensible at the same time. As for form-in-matter, it is neither sentient nor sensible, but is only a condition (or occasion) for the emanation of that (actually cognized) form [9]

An obvious question arising out of this account of perception is that if the proper object of our knowledge is the "forms within the soul," how do we know the external world? or how do we know, indeed, that there is an external world? Ṣadrā's own explicit answer to this question is extremely unsatisfactory: the external world is known accidentally, indirectly, and secondarily.[10] But he does not deny that what we know is the external object; nor does he hold that we know two things, the one outside us and the other inside us or in our sense organs.[11] Even though his commentator al-Sabzawārī holds, on this issue, a subjectivist point of view and adopts solipsism,[12] Ṣadrā himself gives no evidence of a solipsistic doctrine. Indeed, the suggestion of his anti-abstractionist account of perception is also clearly anti-subjectivist: what we know is not an abstraction or an arbitrary creation of our mind but the real world, and the real world in its totality, without loss or interpolation. The meaning of the dictum that as an object of knowledge the external world of matter has to be transformed into a new being or status of reality—the being-for-knowledge—does not mean that we know a different world, a duplicate, as it were, of the external world. Indeed, what we know is the external world, the full-blooded real world of sense perception, with all its relationships. That the soul creates its own forms is simply another way of asserting the identity of thought and being, of the truly existential and the mental. The world as we know it is exactly the world as it exists; but its status of being changes, and attains a mental quality for knowledge to become possible. In spite of his assertions that the external world is known "accidentally," Ṣadrā's overall position appears to be a kind of "idealist realism," which is the only position compatible with his critique of the abstractionist doctrines.

B. *Internal Sense: Imagination and* Wahm

Imagination is different from *sensus communis,* since sense perception, the function of *sensus communis,* is pure acquisition (*kasb*) without a skill (*malaka*), whereas imagination implies a skill or power on the part of the soul.[13] Since imagination creates its own objects *ab initio,* there is no need to postulate an ontological "active imagination" for the production of images, just as it is essential to postulate an "active sense" in the case of sensibles or an "active intelligence" in the case of intelligibles, since these latter two arise from potential sensibles and potential intelligibles, while images are always actual.

Ṣadrā believes, like al-Suhrawardī and subsequent thinkers such as Ibn 'Arabī, in the ontological "World of Images (*'Ālam al-Mithūl*)" with which the mind makes contact, but at the same time he regards the images as creations of the soul. There are thus subjective images as well as objective images. This is because the soul can and does create all kinds of grotesque and false images which cannot be attributed to the "World of Images," but to the activity of the soul itself.[14] As distinguished from the ontological realm which he calls the "Greater World of Images," he calls the soul "The Lesser World of Images." Indeed, the fact that the soul creates images is Ṣadrā's evidence *par excellence* that the soul creates all knowledge and that the soul is immaterial.

Ibn Sīnā, in his *K. al-Shifā'* and *K. al-Najāt,* gave an elaborate argument to show that all images are imprinted on and located in a bodily substance (although in some of his smaller works he tried to show that these images cannot be so located and at the same time noted the inconsistency of this doctrine with his general view of images, pointing out this difficulty in his thought).[15] Ibn Sīnā's first argument is that if we imagine two small but equal squares, each on one side of a big square, then the relative and distinct positions of these two small squares is due neither to the nature of squareness—since both are equal—nor to a dependency on the supposition of the person who imagines them, since it is not up to the imaginer to interchange their positions and, in any case, the imaginer cannot create distinctions between them unless they were already there in the image itself. Secondly, we can imagine a small and a big man; this difference in size must be due to the space the two images occupy, since it cannot be explained by the essence of manness, which is the same in both cases and is, in fact, universal. Thirdly, we cannot imagine both whiteness and blackness to occupy the same space in an image, although they can occupy different places in the same image. This shows that an image occupies a certain space and has extension; the organ of imagination must, therefore, be material.

Ṣadrā rejects this view. First, he says, it is impossible to relate the parts of the brain to images which differ infinitely both in number and in size; a one to one relationship between parts of the brain and images is impossible to establish. On the other hand, if all simultaneous images are related to exactly the *same* part of the brain, the putative part of the brain may just as well be taken to be superfluous, since it is indifferent to qualitative and quantitative differences in images.[16] The soul, indeed, says Ṣadrā, is not related to the images as their recipient, but as their creator; hence their character is radically different from the material forms in the outside world. In the case of a figure in the material world, say that of a square shaped out of wax, it is possible to change it because there is a receptive factor, the matter, and a received factor, viz the shape of a square; when the latter is removed, the former—the matter—still remains ready to receive another form. In the case of a mental image, there is only one factor, viz., the figure which is created by the soul itself. In other words, whereas in the case of a material figure, there is a "compound production (*ja'l murakkab*)," i.e., making of a material into a figure; in the case of a mental image, there is a "simple making (*ja'l basīṭ*)," i.e. making or creation of an image. Hence the unchangeability of the mental image. Ibn Sīnā's argument from the unchangeability of the mental image, therefore, far from proving the materiality of that image, proves its very opposite. Hence, contrary to what Ibn Sīnā asserted, viz that the character of a mental image does not depend on the imaginer's supposition, that character is the very creation of the imaginer's imagining; an image cannot, therefore, be changed, but only replaced by another image.[17]

The nature of an image is "pure extension," i.e., it does not occupy space. That is why we can imagine an image of the magnitude of the entire world and, indeed, entertain such images a number of times over without "intruding" into each other. It is also not true to say that these images are "in" the soul. The soul, indeed, creates them and becomes, therefore, identical with them, as in the case of all knowledge which is, nevertheless, not "in" the soul.

The images which the soul creates in this world are weak and unstable compared to the perceptual objects. This is because the soul in this life is immersed in matter. But when it leaves the material realm, it becomes capable of creating stable, "real" images. In fact, as we shall see in the discussion on eschatology, this image-life will be the fate of undeveloped human souls which have not perfected themselves with pure intellect. The images in the case of such souls will take the place of perception in this life and whatever the soul entertains in terms of images of physical pleasures and pains will be virtually true in the after-life. Therefore, although imagination in this world gives a hint of this second "emergent status (*nash'u*)" of the soul's being—a level of being which puts the soul outside the limits of natural, material existence—it is only in the afterlife that imagination will play its full role. Ṣadrā rejects the view adopted by al-Suhrawardī that after death undeveloped souls—whether good or bad—use some other body, like a heavenly body, for projecting their images. He says that in that case, such images cannot be the images of these souls but will be the images of the heavens. Moreover, these images do not need the help of a material body but are self-subsisting entities and will "appear" to the soul. Finally, since these images will be the representations of the deeds and acts of the agent himself, it is illogical to suppose that they could exist in a heavenly body. (The doctrine that undeveloped souls can contact a heavenly body or some other body for their imagination to function is reported by Ibn Sīnā in his *al-Risāla al-Aḍḥawīya* to be the view of "a certain serious scholar" identified by al-Ṭūsī as al-Fārābi.)[18] In any case, this will be experienced by the soul in its "second emergent level of being (*nash'a thāniya*)" in "After-Life" and not in this world as the accounts of al-Suhrawardī and Ibn Sīnā suggest.[19]

At that level of existence, since the images will take the place of perceptibles in this life, they will constitute sense perception and will be literally visibles, audibles, tactibles, etc. Indeed, sense perception in this life is nothing but an exteriorization and a shadow of imagination itself. Ṣadrā once again invokes his principle that "abstraction" in this context does not imply any removal or privation but simply means a higher level of existence which, far from excluding what exists at the lower level of existence, contains it in a unitary and more meaningful manner. Indeed, even the body is not excluded at this higher level; only it is not coarse material body but of a different nature, as will become clear in our account of eschatology.

Ibn Sīnā and his followers had posited a faculty among the internal senses called "*Wahm* (estimation)." The function of this faculty was to perceive non-material but particular ideas or meanings in particular sensible things, as, for example, a sheep perceives danger in this particular wolf or a mother perceives love in her particular young one. Ṣadrā rejects the existence of this faculty and says that *Wahm*, as such, has no being. The perception of harm or danger or love in a particular object is the function of *reason as attached to imagination*. Nor do the objects of perception attributed to *Wahm* have a being of their own, subsisting in the sensible image. The perception of these non-material ideas is not the work of pure reason because they are not universal, i.e., danger-in-general or affection-in-general. Nor can it be the work of imagination or *sensus communis* because they perceive only the exterior form and not the inner meanings. Nor, as we have just said, do these meanings actually exist or subsist in material objects because in that case they would have to be perceived by the external senses—like existence and unity.

How, then, are these meanings perceived and what does their nature consist in? They are perceived by a relationship of the rational faculty to a particular object or image. We perceive, not this particular dangerous figure, but danger *as attributable to* this particular figure. The relationship of a particular case of danger to the universal object of reason is analogous to the relationship of an instantiated universal or a case of a universal (*ḥiṣṣa*) to the universal. In a case or instance of a universal, the gaze is fixed on *the universal as so instantiated* and not on the particular object (*fard*) itself; for example, in the case of a human being A, the gaze falls not on A as this particular object (*fard*) as such, but *on this case or instance of humanness* or *humanness as attributed to this person*. The difference between an instance or a case, on the one hand, and a particular, on the other, is that, whereas the latter is not a universal—although a universal can be reached by a process of universalization from several particulars—the former already exemplifies a universal and the difference between a universal and its example is merely a difference of our own way of looking at them (*i'tibār maḥḍ*). Similarly an instance of danger already exemplifies danger-in-general and is, therefore, an object, if not of pure reason, of reason as attached to imagination.[20] Further, since nothing in terms of real existence corresponds to the findings of *Wahm* in an external sensible object, these findings are purely mental abstractions like 'cause' and 'effect' and are not like 'black' or 'white' which are universal mental reflections of the external reality.[21]

This highly 'unorthodox' doctrine of *Wahm* was severely criticized by Ṣadrā's commentators, notably al-Sabzawārī. How can a rational operation be attributed to animals which are by definition devoid of reason?[22] Besides such technical criticisms, it is, of course, equally obvious that the whole import of the perception of danger or love is *this particular danger or love* on the part of a percipient and not danger-in-general or love-in-general or as general ideas as instantiated cases. And if what is meaningful is *this dan-*

ger here and now, it is impossible to hold that nothing corresponds in the real structure of the perceived object to what we call danger or love and that these are purely mental abstractions. Whatever weaknesses there be in Ibn Sīnā's doctrine of *Wahm*—e.g., how can something be both non-material and particular on Ibn Sīnā's own principle?—it is evident that Ṣadrā's constructions upon *Wahm* as something quasi-universal hardly do justice to something whose whole meaning lies in the particularity of a certain situation. The only correct way to rescue Ṣadrā—and this may well be what he means when he says that *Wahm* is something between pure sense-perception and pure rationality, although his conceptual framework does not allow him to formulate this explicitly—would be to say that reactions like love, hate, and fear are certainly not perceptible by senses (as Ṣadrā does say) but while they are not technically rational either, they are not without reason. That is to say, they are instinctive and an instinct is not devoid of reason. So understood, Ṣadrā's doctrine would be perfectly sound and the objections raised against him would have no force at all.

NOTES

1. *Enneads,* III, 6, 6.

2. *Asfār,* IV, 1, p. 224, lines 12–21.

3. *Ibid.,* p. 39, lines 23–24; *ibid.,* IV, 2, p. 147, lines 5 ff.; p. 172, lines 5 ff

4. *Ibid.,* IV, 1, p. 17, lines 6 ff.; p. 177, line 2–p. 178, line 6.

5. *Ibid.,* IV, 1, p. 169, lines 7–9; p. 176, lines 17 ff. (cf. p. 17, lines 7 ff.).

6. *Asfār,* I, 3, p. 316, line 3–p. 317, line 7; p. 313, line 15.

7. *Ibid.,* IV, 1, p. 160, lines 1–10; p. 162, lines 3–4; p. 165, last line ff.; p. 172, lines 1–3.

8. *Ibid.,* p. 178, lines 15 ff.; quotation, p. 179, last line–p. 180, line 2; cf p. 181, lines 6–9.

9. *Ibid.,* p. 181, lines 3–9; *ibid.,* I, 3, p. 316, lines 6 ff.

10. *Ibid.,* I, 3, p. 299, lines 8 ff.

11. The meaning of Ṣadrā's statements can be only understood, as he himself insists, in the sense that the material form, when it becomes the object of knowledge, is transformed in its very nature, thanks to the substantive motion of existence. *Asfār,* IV, 1, p. 1758 ff.

12. *Asfār,* I, 3, p. 281, note 3, by al-Sabzawārī. The most explicit statement of Ṣadrā's is in *Asfār,* L, 3, p. 498, lines 9–12, where it is said that the perceptive faculty itself cannot know that its objects are in the external world; it is only through the rational power that perceptible forms are referred to the external world by a process Ṣadrā calls "experience (*tajriba*)." This presumably means that if a being had only one case of perception, it would be impossible to refer it to the external world; also *ibid.,* p. 499, lines 8 ff.

13. *Ibid.,* IV, p. 213, lines 9 ff.

14. *Ibid.,* p. 236, line 17–p. 237, line 8; *ibid.,* I, 1, p. 303, line 1, p. 264, line 10–p. 268, line 4.

15. See reference in Chapter I of this Part, note 26.

16. *Asfār,* IV, 1, p. 211, lines 3–11; p. 227, lines 3–12.

17. *Ibid.,* p. 236, lines 10 ff.

18. *Ibid.,* IV, 2, p. 151, lines 14–15.

19. *Ibid.,* p. 40, lines 2 ff.

20. *Ibid.*, p. 215, line 6-p. 218, line 12; *ibid.*, I, 3, p. 366, line 5–p. 362, line 2.

21. *Ibid.*, p. 218, lines 3 ff.

22. *Ibid.*, p. 216, al-Sabzawārī's lengthy note; also al-Ṭabāṭabā'ī's note on p. 217.

CHAPTER IV

THEORY OF KNOWLEDGE—III: THE INTELLECT

A. *Introduction*

The goal of Ṣadrā's doctrine of the intellect is to show that the human mind ultimately unites itself with the Active Intelligence or the Universal Intellect. Since, according to Ṣadrā, the end of all substantive movement is to achieve a new level of being, knowledge represents, for him, such substantive movement (*ḥarka jauharīya*) whose end is the union of the human intellect with the transcendent Intellect and hence the achievement of a new level of existence—that of pure, simple intellect. Further, since this evolutionary movement is cumulative, it represents something positive, inclusive of the lower levels of being and not excluding or negating them. The key term for his doctrine of the intellect is, therefore, "the simple." This term means that that which exists at the lower levels with separate or mutually exclusive parts, exists at the higher levels as mutually inclusive and unitary.

The Aristotelian–Ibn-Sīnāian theory of the intellect affirms that in intellective experience the potential intellect becomes actual, that it becomes identical with the "forms" of things and that this happens through the action of the Active Intelligence upon the human mind. It should be noted, however, that Aristotle's view is grounded in a purely philosophic theory of knowledge (particularly the idea of potentiality and its actualization) and has little by way of mystical tendencies. Ibn Sīnā's thought has been strongly influenced by neo-Platonism and definitely ends up in a kind of mysticism. Nevertheless, he keeps his theory of knowledge almost strictly philosophical in the sense that the end of knowledge remains cognition and is not the transformation of the soul into a new level or order of being. For Ṣadrā, on the other hand, *knowledge is a form of existence* (*al-ʿilm naḥw min al-*

wujūd), as he reiterates throughout his writing. From the other end, the doctrine of Illumination as propounded by al-Suhrawardī and his commentators and the Sufi gnosis, as it found its classic and monumental formulation at the hands of Ibn 'Arabī, taught a real and literal identity of the human intellect with Light or the Active Intellect. But this illuminationist-gnostic doctrine did not formulate the idea of a systematic substantive change as the fundamental process of nature. Ṣadrā's performance essentially consists in taking over this gnostic goal and grounding it philosophically in his doctrine of substantive change, supported in turn by his theory of the priority of existence over essence. This is carried out by an extensive and consistent critique of Ibn Sīnā's doctrine of the intellect at the following central points:

1. The doctrine of "abstraction"
2. Ibn Sīnā's account of the "simple intellect"
3. Ibn Sīnā's rejection of the identity of the mind and intelligibles in actual knowledge.

B. *The Problem of Abstraction*

From among the numerous passages where Ṣadrā has criticized the doctrine of abstraction, these two excerpts may be noted:

> These philosophers, when they read in the books of the ancient sages that the various types of knowledge—sense perception, imagination, *wahm*, and intellection—take place by a kind of abstraction, took this "abstraction" to mean that certain qualities or parts (of the known object) are removed while others are preserved. On the contrary, all knowledge comes through a sort of existence—one level of existence being replaced by another.[1]
>
> The meaning of their (i.e., the philosophers') statement that every type of knowledge involves a kind of abstraction and that difference in the ranks of knowledge corresponds to the difference in the levels of abstraction is—as we have already said—not that abstraction involves the removal of certain qualities and retention of certain others, but its meaning is that existence changes levels—from lower and baser to higher and nobler. Similarly, the "separation (*tajarrud*)" of man and his moving away from this world to the hereafter is nothing but the replacement of this level of existence by another. Thus, when the soul is perfected and becomes actual intellect, it is not the case that it loses

> some faculties, like the perceptive, and comes to have others, like the rational.[2]

According to Ṣadrā, the Aristotelian-Ibn Sīnāian theory of abstraction holds that, whereas the objects of knowledge change—from the sensibles, through the imaginables to the intelligibles—the cognizing subject, the soul, remains the same. The soul, that is to say, simply receives forms of different degrees of abstraction, without its own substance being affected. This is not the case. The soul itself undergoes an evolution and from its initial being of the material order, it becomes, at the intellectual plane, a being of the intelligible order.[3] This evolution of the soul itself—the successive levels of its existence (*nasha'āt*)—is an important proof, for Ṣadrā, of the law of substantive change to which the entire field of natural existence is subject, a law from whose operation only God and the transcendent intelligences (which are parts or attributes of God) are exempt. The soul, therefore, not merely "receives" forms but creates and *becomes* them, i.e., becomes literally identical with them. This doctrine of Ṣadrā obviously carries to its extreme conclusion, under the impact of the neo-Platonic way of thinking, the Aristotelian doctrine of cognition that the soul "becomes" its objects in the act of knowledge. For Ṣadrā, the soul "becoming" its objects is not a temporary affair lasting only during the act of knowledge, but denotes a new level of existence which the soul achieves; particularly at the level of "acquired" or absolute intellective power, the soul becomes "pure act (*al-fi'l al-ṣarf*)," i.e., pure knowledge without any trace of potentiality. Aristotle had applied the term "pure act (*kathara energeia*)" only to the transcendental Active Intellect which Alexander of Aphrodijias identified with God.

C. *Ibn Sīnā on the "Simple Intellect"*

Ṣadrā's substitution of the concept of evolution for abstraction in a process of cognition leads him to formulate his doctrine of the "simple (*basīṭ*)," where again Ibn Sīnā comes under criticism. Ṣadrā, however, gives credit to Ibn Sīnā for having at least formulated the concept of "simple knowledge" and defends this concept against the attacks of al-Rāzā and al-Suhrawardī. Ibn Sīnā had sought to establish the existence of a simple knowledge by saying that if a person is asked a question which he had not pondered before or is asked a series of related questions which he had not thought of in this manner before, he feels a sense of confidence in himself that he can answer the question or questions before he enters upon giving detailed answers. This sense of confidence and self-assurance shows that he has the knowledge in a simple form even though he attains detailed knowledge only when he answers the questions in detail. This detailed knowledge is, therefore, preceded by a simple knowledge; otherwise, the person would not have the confidence and self-assurance that he possesses. This simple knowledge is the creator of the detailed knowledge; in it the concepts lie united and undifferentiated while in the detailed knowledge they become multiple and differentiated; finally, simple knowledge is beyond time while detailed knowledge is in time, since concepts arise in it seriatim.[4]

This doctrine was rejected by al-Rāzī and al-Suhrawardī who held that knowledge is either potential or actual: when it is potential, it cannot be related to any given detailed form; when it is actual, it must be related to a *single* form. There is, therefore, no form of knowledge which is both actual and yet related to *all* forms at once. Al-Rāzī admitted that many forms may become present in the mind, but this does not prove a creative intellect which *is* all these forms at the same time.[5] In defending the reality of simple knowledge, Ṣadrā says that just as existents are of different degrees, the lower ones being characterized by mutual exclusiveness—like matter whose every given part excludes the rest and thereby generates physical extension—while the higher ones become more and more inclusive, so is the case with knowledge since knowledge is no more than a kind of existence—the higher forms of knowledge being all-inclusive and creative of all knowledge.[6]

But Ṣadrā is highly critical of Ibn Sīnā, who, while affirming simple intellect, at the same time affirmed abstraction in knowledge and denied the absolute identity of the intellect with the intelligibles. Because of his commitment to the idea of abstraction, Ibn Sīnā thought that higher forms of knowledge come about by elimination of certain things, particularly of matter and its concomitants—shape, color, etc. This led him to say that, e.g., man as an intellectual concept or the universal "man" has no body, since body makes a particular man. Hence Ibn Sīnā thought that the soul, at the apogee of its development as pure intellect, sheds everything about the body and the bodily faculties—like the affective, nutritive, perceptive, and imaginative. For Ṣadrā, on the other hand, the simple and the higher includes the lower and the detailed, and does not exclude any of the lower levels of existence. *Otherwise, it would not be simple but deprived and partial.* Hence, he says that the same soul is "intellective, perceptive, smelling, tasting, walking, growing, self-nourishing, appetitive, and angry." [7]

Ṣadrā draws support for this thesis by profuse quotations from the (pseudo) *Theologia Aristotelis* to the effect that the higher realm of the intellect contains everything below here in a higher and nobler manner; that the soul, when it comes into the body, fashions a man on the pattern of man in the higher realm; that, therefore, in that higher realm, man possesses all the faculties of life, perception, imagination and intellection, in a much superior manner to what is to be found in the "images" here down below since an image can never compare with the original; and finally, that "The First Man has strong and manifest perceptual faculties surpassing those of the image-man here." [8] The First Man "does not perceive perceptibles of the order of this lower existence. This is the reason why the perception of this lower man is in contact with and draws (strength) from the perception of the Higher Man just as fire down here contacts and draws from that High Fire." [9]

For Ṣadrā, the dictum that higher realms of existence *contain and do not negate* the low scales is the very meaning of continuous evolution where both the terms *continuous* and *evolution* are equally important. It is evolution because it involves a new emergent; it is continuous because it contains the previous stages "in a higher form." As we pointed out in our discussion of substantive movement (Chapter V of Part I), Ṣadrā gives there the analogy of the continuity of a body, the difference being that since one part of a body cannot contain other parts, extension results from this mutual exclusiveness of parts and thus a body is "extensively continuous." In the case of the higher scales of existence—the soul and the intellect—however, "intensive continuity (*jam'īya*)" is the result. This is the very meaning of "simple existence (*al-wujūd al-basīṭ*)," and of Ṣadrā's oft-repeated statement that "a simple nature contains or *is* all things."

As we shall see in our discussion of eschatology, Ṣadrā uses this doctrine to prove physical resurrection of some kind. But at this point we must take up the question of the identity of the intellect and the intelligible, without which, according to Ṣadrā, one cannot prove the simplicity of the intellect but which was strongly rejected by Ibn Sīnā.

D. *Identity of the Intellect and the Intelligible*

While subscribing to the general Peripatetic doctrine that the soul receives and becomes the forms of its objects of knowledge—in the sense that the knowing subject must be itself free from any particular form if it is to receive the forms of the cognizables—Ibn Sīnā had assailed the doctrine that the soul literally becomes its objects, a doctrine he attributed to Porphyry, who, in Ibn Sīnā's words, "was fond of figurative, poetic, and mystic diction." Ibn Sīnā describes the soul as a "place or receptacle (*makān, maḥall*) of forms," for all talk of the soul's literally becoming these forms is unintelligible.[10] Ṣadrā vigorously attacks Ibn Sīnā on this issue and accuses him both of inconsistency and failure to grasp the nature of knowledge, particularly intellective knowledge. As for Ibn Sīnā's inconsistency, this is because in the same breath he described God's knowledge as a unity where all concepts literally interpenetrate and do not leave any room for any duality or multiplicity as between them or as between them and God's mind; [11] and, on the other hand, as we have seen above, he affirms the existence of a simple, creative intellect in man. How can forms exist in this simple intellect unless they are a unity and how can the human soul receive these forms from the Creative Intellect unless the former unites with the latter, which Ibn Sīnā also denies since he holds that if the human soul were to unite with the Creative Intellect, then either the Creative Intellect will become divisible or all human souls will possess identical knowledge? [12]

Ṣadrā's refutation of Ibn Sīnā's arguments against the identity of the intellect and the intelligible is squarely based on his doctrine of the substantive change or evolution and the reality of existence to the exclusion of essence. The substance of Ibn Sīnā's argument was that if something becomes A, this means that it receives the form of A; but when subsequently it becomes B, it must abandon the form of A in order to receive the form of B, since it is absurd to say that something at the same time receives the forms of both A and of B. Therefore, when the soul becomes A, it receives the form of A and when it becomes B, it discards the form A, and receives the form B. Hence, in itself it can neither be A nor B but something receptive of them. Ṣadrā argues that this way of thinking likens the process of knowledge to accidental change, not substantive evolution. In the case of accidental or superficial change, it is true that when a thing becomes hot, it receives the form of heat and when it becomes cold, it can only receive the form of cold when it discards the form of heat. This is because accidental change cannot accommodate contradictories. In the case of substantive change, however, the case is very different, for substantive change is not just simple change but evolution. In evolutionary change, or development, previous forms are not discarded or simply replaced by new forms but are consummated and perfected. This demonstrates the absolute reality of existence over against essence, for whereas essences are multiple, static and mutually repellent, existence is unitary and inclusive: *conceptually,* growth, nourishment, locomotion, and knowledge may be all different, but they all come together in concrete human existence. Evolution consists in carrying over, not negating, the previous grades of perfection and yet transcending them.[13]

Since Ibn Sīnā did not concede the principle of evolutionary change and did not clearly affirm the unique reality of existence over against essence—which alone can supply the principle of identity-in-difference and difference-in-identity—he could not solve the riddle of knowledge, for knowledge and existence are the same. That knowledge represents evolutionary change is shown by the fact that when the soul knows A and then passes on to the knowledge of B, the knowledge of A is not thereby destroyed but consummated. New knowledge does not convert previous knowledge into ignorance, but puts it into the perspective of an ampler, more meaningful form of knowledge. Just like existence, the scale of knowledge moves from the rudimentary, the multiple, the mutually exclusive, to the higher, more complex, more inclusive and simpler forms.[14] This scale ends in a simple, intuitive kind of intellective cognition where the human soul becomes identical with the transcendent Active Intelligence.

It should be pointed out that there appears to exist a curious contradiction in Ṣadrā's account of the evolution of the intellect from the basic or elemental "necessary" propositions or truths to the higher forms of cognition. The contradiction exists in our philosopher's characterization of the value of the necessary truths like the law of contradiction, the proposition that the whole is greater than its parts, the general idea of being, etc. Following al-Fārābī and Ibn Sīnā, Ṣadrā regards the knowledge of these general concepts and propositions as the first stage of the actualization of the potential human intellect. But then Ṣadrā, in consistency with his doctrine of evolutionism in general and cognitive evolutionism in particular, goes on to say that a knowledge of these general truths has very little worth since these are only rudimentary and elementary and the general has less value compared to the concrete and the indefinite compared to the definite, just as a genus is lower in value than a concrete and definite species.[15] Ṣadrā even rebukes Ibn Sīnā for making the possibility of the survival of all human souls—including the relatively undeveloped ones—dependent on a knowledge of these primary truths with the sarcastic remark that a happiness that consists in a knowledge of such mere generalities and trivialities as these rudimentary truths is hardly worthy of an afterlife for a human soul. Yet Ṣadrā has consecrated a special chapter in his discussion of the doctrine of the intellect not only to a defense of these truths but also to proving that the law of contradiction is the source and highest principle of all knowledge and that this necessary principle is related to knowledge as God, the Necessary Being, is related to other existents.[16] The defense of the "primary truths" against intellectual skepticism is, of course, justified, but their description as the highest and most creative form of knowledge hardly squares with their characterization as vague generalities, indefinite truths, and pure tautologies.[17]

This last view is reiterated by Ṣadrā in his discussion of the two orders of knowledge—the one existing in the natural world, i.e., the human soul, and the other in the transcendent intelligence. Ṣadrā tells us (following al-Fārābī and Ibn Sīnā) that knowledge in the human soul starts with the more general and less valuable primary truths and advances to more concrete, definite, and existential knowledge whereas in the case of the separate Intelligences, this order is reversed. But this story is true of the human soul only insofar as the *genesis* of its knowledge is concerned. When the soul perfects its knowledge and becomes "acquired intellect" and achieves an existential status analogous to that of the Active Intelligence, its knowledge-order also becomes like that of the Active Intelligence.[18] In view of this, it becomes difficult to hold that primary and general truths, like the law of contradiction, have a status in the realm of knowledge analogous to the status of God in the realm of being.

In addition to refuting Ibn Sīnā's arguments against the absolute identity of the intellect and the intelligible, Ṣadrā seeks to establish this identity with a positive proof from an analysis of the term "intelligible" or "actually intelligible." Something which is actually intelligible, contends Ṣadrā, must be *ipso facto* both self-intelligent and self-intellected since an "intelligible" is unthinkable without an "intelligent." Now, if we suppose that the intelligible and the intelligent are two different entities and the relationship between them is, therefore, a contingent one, the intelligible will not, in that case, be intelligible when it is considered out of relation with that intelligent which has been supposed to be other than itself. The intelligible will not, therefore, be intelligible, which is a *contradictio in supposito*. It follows, therefore, that an intelligible must be self-intelligible, i.e., self-intelligent, whether or not there is something else which intellects it. Hence the identity of the intelligible and the intellect.[19]

Now, all pure forms free from matter, whether they are such by themselves or whether they are rendered such by a knowing mind, are self-intelligible in this sense. Therefore, they are self-intelligent whether any other agent thinks them or not. Ṣadrā once again draws an analogy between the intelligible and the sensible and asserts that just as the actually sensible and the actually sentient are identical—since neither of the two can be conceived without the other—so are the actually intelligible and the actually intelligent unthinkable without each other.[20]

It is obvious, however, that despite Ṣadrā's postulation of an Active Sense as an analogue to the Active Intelligence, this analogy will not hold in the present context. For the analogy to be perfect, Ṣadrā should be able to say that just as an actual intelligible is *ipso facto* self-intelligent, so must an actual sensible be self-sentient and that no other sentient is necessary for the actual sensible besides itself. This, however, he is unable to say on his own principles and in fact he does not make any such claim. The reason for the breakdown of the analogy is that the sensible form, even when it becomes actually sensible, is not free from its material nature, whereas the intelligible form is by definition totally free from matter. And, in fact, Ṣadrā recurrently defines intellective knowledge as "an existent free from matter" [21] or a "pure form free from matter" [22] or a being which is not veiled from, or divided against, itself, as is the case with a material being.[23] But a sensible or imaginative form is not free from its relationship to matter in this sense, for even though, as we have seen in the preceding two chapters, these forms are also created by the soul itself, they still bear some relationship to matter. The introduction of the analogy of sense in this context to prove the identity of the intellect and the intelligible, therefore, appears to be out of place.

From this account of the intellect and the intelligible it follows that forms or (Platonic) Ideas constitute a transcendental realm of pure knowledge where the entire range of Ideas is one unitary self-conscious being.[24] This realm is the transcendental Active Intelligence of which the Peripatetics speak.[25] It is this realm which creates the world of matter with material forms and it is with this realm that the human mind becomes united when it becomes the recipient of intellectual knowledge. The view of the Peripatetics that such a union is not possible because in the case of such union either the Active Intelligence will become divisible when several human souls unite with it or that every human soul will know the entire contents of the Active Intelligence and thus the knowledge of all human souls will be identical, is false. Indeed, for Ṣadrā, all intellectual knowledge comes about by a union of the human mind with the Active Intelligence.

To understand the nature of the union of the human soul with the Active Intelligence, it is necessary to keep two points firmly in mind. The first is, what has just been proved, viz., the identity of the intellect and the intelligible. The second important point, which has also been stated above, is the unitary character of a simple being like the Active Intelligence. We have seen that the progression of knowledge is from the multiple and the mutually exclusive to the simple and the mutually inclusive. Of this simplicity of intellective being, the Active Intelligence is the ideal. Such simplicity, let it be restated, is not, strictly speaking, the character of essences but of existence. What happens in the progression of being is that an ever-increasing number of essences is "taken in" and absorbed by a progressively higher scale of being and as existence becomes more and more strong and explicit, essences tend to become more and more implicit and recoil upon existence, losing their own being, as it were, until, when we reach pure Intelligences or God, all essences are "lost" and become "interiorized" in themselves, and Pure Existence takes over.

In this way one must conceive of the simplicity and unity of the content of the Active Intelligence. But this does not mean that by being united with a human soul the Active Intelligence will either become multiple and divisible or the knowledge of all human souls will become identical. To facilitate this understanding, we might give an illustration. The idea "animal" is a unity in itself, while at the same time containing several ideas under it, e.g., man, horse, bull, lion, etc. When we say "horse," we designate an animal, but we do not say that in "horse," "animal" has been partialized or made divisible: "animal" is not *partitioned* into these various species of animals. Nor would it be true to say that by being an animal, horse and bull become identical in content, for a horse is a horse and a bull is a bull. The unity of a concept like "animal" is, therefore, a different kind of unity from a numerical or a physical one. In a similar way, human souls can all participate in the Active Intelligence without partitioning it and without the contents of their knowledge becoming identical.[26] Ṣadrā also says that the Active Intelligence has two kinds of being, a being-in-Itself and a being-for-the-other, or a relational being (just as we saw in Chapter III of Part II in the discussion of Prophetic knowledge that the Angel has an absolute being and a relational being); it is in its latter aspect that it is contacted by the human mind.[27]

Fundamental though the idea of the union of the human minds with the Active Intelligence is for all knowledge, it was rejected, says Ṣadrā, by most Muslim philosophers because they wished to avoid any semblance with the doctrine of Incarnation. Incarnation, however, certainly does not follow from this. But the phenomenon of the Prophetic Intellect affirmed by Ibn Sīnā and others, i.e., the doctrine that special human souls receive from the Active Intelligence a creative power of knowledge, indicates that the human soul does come into some union or communion with the Active Intelligence.

In the case of the ordinary human minds, even after they have actualized their creative intellectual powers to the highest degree, they cannot become absolutely and totally identical with the intelligible realm so long as they are in flesh and blood. The highest point an ordinary accomplished philosophic mind can reach in its lifetime is to witness the intelligible realm from a distance and to identify itself with it partially. Thanks to this partial identification, it can possess a limited share of the creative simple intellect and is able to see what it would be like, when after death, it becomes totally identified with that simple intelligible realm. This creative power is, of course, not shared by everyone equally: humanity presents a whole spectrum ranging from cases of utter stolidity and uncreativity to those who are highly creative and original. There are, however, certain exceptional cases in whom a complete identification takes place and they are able to create all knowledge from within themselves without external instruction. These are Prophets.

Ṣadrā's account of the Prophetic Revelation differs materially from those of al-Fārābī and Ibn Sīnā, as we have seen in Chapter III of Part II of the present work, although it has certain general resemblances with them as well. His differences from these two philosophers result from his doctrine of knowledge and being. Whereas in al-Fārābī and Ibn Sīnā, the Prophet receives the Intellectual Truth as a totality which is then transformed by *his* power of imagination into a symbolic form and a verbal mode; according to Ṣadrā, the Prophet's mind becomes totally identified with the Active Intelligence *both at the intellectual level and the imaginative level*—that is to say, it is not the Prophet's mind which creates—although the Prophet has an inner psychological and unconscious compulsion—the symbolic or imaginative truth but his mind "perceives" or rather "becomes" that truth as well as the intellectual truth. This is because, Ṣadrā believes—following al-Suhrawardī and particularly Ibn 'Arabī—in an objective, ontological World of Symbols or Images or the "lower Angels." The difference between a prophet and a saint (or a sage) is that whereas the prophet is identified with both the inner spiritual (intellectual) and external (i.e., in terms of images, voice, visible figure, etc.) aspects of the Active Intelligence (the Angel), and, therefore, can identify the source of the Revelation, the saint is confined to the inner aspect and cannot identify the source of his knowledge, which, therefore, does not constitute Revelation but inspiration.[28]

Finally, this doctrine of the Simple Intellect—with its principle of identity—is used by Ṣadrā to explain God's knowledge of the particulars, a problem around which has centered a great deal of controversy between the philosophers and the orthodox for centuries. Although we have exhaustively discussed Ṣadrā's concept of divine knowledge in Chapter II of Part II, certain comments are called for in the present context of this problem of "simple knowledge" as related to particulars as possible objects of that knowledge and as related to existence. It was held, on strict Peripatetic grounds, that God cannot know particulars since such knowledge would involve change in God. To overcome this difficulty, Ibn Sīnā had devised the theory that "God knows all particulars but in a universal way." The substance of this theory is that God, being the ultimate cause of all things, knows the whole range of causes and effects and their relations and conglomerations and hence knows all particulars, not as particulars but as universals. For example, God knows from all eternity that a lunar eclipse will occur when the moon is at such and such a point and is in such and such a relation to the other planets and so much time after such and such previous eclipse. The totality of these descriptions identify that eclipse absolutely as a particular; nevertheless, these descriptions in themselves are universals—only their totality serves to identify a particular eclipse. This eternal knowledge in God is changeless, since it does not depend upon sense perception, which perceives a thing when it occurs but not before or after, and which is, therefore, liable to change. This doctrine of Ibn Sīnā's was severely criticized by al-Ghazālī and al-Rāzī from the orthodox Islamic standpoint, since it did not allow for God's perception of the particular. Al-Rāzī, in turn, defined knowledge as a relation so that when God's knowledge of the particulars changes, He Himself does not change. Ibn Sīnā's commentator al-Ṭūsī attempted to mediate between the positions of Ibn Sīnā and the Islamic orthodoxy. For al-Ṭūsī, God indeed perceives the particulars as al-Rāzī holds, but he rejects al-Rāzī's definition of knowledge as a relation. According to him, change affects only that percipient who is in space and time. To a percipient who stands beyond space and time—as does God—all particulars are the same, as objects of perception, vis-à-vis one another and also vis-à-vis their existence and non-existence. For a person who reads a book, word by word and line by line, the present moment is differentiated from the 'no more' of the past and 'not yet' of the future, since the lines he has perused belong to the past and the ones he has not yet come to belong to the future, while the present is where he has his gaze fixed. But for a person who has the whole book with him 'folded up' (i.e., in his mind), his relation to all the words and lines is the same, i.e., they are all 'present' to him. So is the divine knowledge in relation to all particulars since it does not require a succession of forms in God's mind.

As we have seen before, Ṣadrā rejects al-Rāzī's definition of knowledge as a relation. He is also strongly critical of al-Ṭūsī and asks: how can perception take place on the part of a being who is beyond space and time? And how can perception take place without sense-organs? How can spatio-temporal things, whose very nature consists in being mutually exclusive, come together in an undifferentiated manner to a percipient? Ṣadrā then concludes that if particulars are perceived as particulars, they must effect a change in knowledge. He is also highly critical of Ibn Sīnā, whom he accuses of not having properly understood the nature of 'simple knowledge.' The essence of Ṣadrā's criticism of Ibn Sīnā—as we have seen in Chapter II of Part II—is that Ibn Sīnā describes divine knowledge in purely conceptual terms: God is depicted as 'conceiving' one thing after another. It is true that Ibn Sīnā's aim is to establish (1) the changeless character of God's knowledge, (2) the fact that God's knowledge precedes the existence of things and does not follow them—contrary to what al-Suhrawardī and al-Ṭūsī believe—as is the case with mortal conceptual knowledge, and (3) the fact that God's knowledge is creative and not receptive as human knowledge is.

Yet Ibn Sīnā's description of divine knowledge in conceptual terms shows that he did not understand that simple knowledge is first and foremost a function of simple existence. And simple existence is an order of being, as we have repeatedly said, which envelops and contains all modes of existence in itself without being identical with them, since existence is systematically ambiguous. God, therefore, knows all things, particular as well as universal, because He envelops all of them as His modes and manifestations—without being predicated of them or they being predicated of Him—in different orders or gradations of existence. For if his knowledge were treated in conceptual terms, as Ibn Sīnā apparently treats it, it will have to be, as some kind of essence, additional to His existence. God's knowledge is, therefore, nothing but His simple existence, an order of being unique to Him.[29]

NOTES

1. *Asfār,* IV, 2, p. 95, lines 6–9.

2. *Ibid.,* p. 99, line 12-p. 100, line 4; *ibid.,* I, 3, p. 306, line 5–p. 307, line 11.

3. *Ibid.,* I, 3, p. 366, lines 2–9.

4. *Ibid.,* p. 369, last line–p. 372, line 5; see also the discussion of the simple intellect or simple knowledge in Chapter II of Part II where Ṣadrā's inconsistency has been pointed out.

5. *Ibid.,* p. 374, line 1–p. 377, line 7.

6. *Ibid.,* p. 373, lines 14 ff.; p. 377, lines 16 ff.

7. See reference 2 mentioned in note 2 above; *ibid.,* IV, 1, p. 65, lines 13–14.

8. *Ibid.,* IV, 2, p. 71, lines 12–13; *ibid.,* I, 3, p. 317, lines 8–15; p. 340, lines 3 ff.

9. *Ibid.,* IV, 2, p. 100, line 5–p. 103, end, particularly p. 103, lines 9 ff.

10. Quotations from Ibn Sīnā, *ibid.,* I, 3, p. 322, line 3–p. 324, line 9, and Ṣadrā's subsequent refutation of Ibn Sīnā.

11. *Ibid.,* I, 3, p. 437, lines 3 ff.; cf, also Chapter II of Part II above, where Ṣadrā accuses Ibn Sīnā of affirming the identity of the existence and knowledge of forms in God and at the same time denying this identity *per* quotations referred to in note 2 above.

12. *Ibid.,* I, 3, p. 213, lines 13 ff.

13. *Ibid.,* p. 324, lines 10 ff., p. 325, line 9–p. 326, line 122 *et seq.*

14. References in the previous note; also *ibid.,* IV, 2, p. 116, lines 11 ff.

15. *Ibid.,* IV, 2, p. 115, line 5 ff.; *ibid.,* I, 3, p. 420, lines 5 ff.

16. *Ibid.,* I, 3, p. 433, line 6–p. 444, line 10.

17. References in note 15 above.

18. *Ibid.,* I, 3, p. 464, lines 10 ff.

19. *Ibid.,* p. 313, line 13–p. 315, last line.

20. *Ibid.,* p. 316, line 3–p. 317, line 7.

21. For the Active Sentient, *ibid.,* p. 464, lines 1–3 and the discussion of the analogy between perception and intellection preceding these lines; for

knowledge as "an existent free from matter," see *ibid.*, p. 354, lines, 5 ff., and p. 345, line 8 ff.

22. For example, *ibid.*, p. 334, lines 16 ff.; p. 318, lines 13 ff.; also references in the preceding two notes.

23. See Chapter II of this part above; on how material forms differ from forms as known by the mind, see *ibid.*, I, 3, the whole chapter pp. 300–304.

24. *Asfār,* I, 3, p. 336, lines 20–21; p. 340, lines 3 ff. (quotation from the *Theologia Aristotelis*).

25. *Ibid.*, p. 335, lines 13 ff.; see also the discussion on the "Breath of the Merciful," Chapter IV of Part I.

26. *Ibid.*, I, 3, p. 337, last line–p. 340, line 2; *ibid.*, IV, 2, p. 143, lines 1 ff.

27. *Ibid.*, IV, 2, p. 140, lines 5 ff.

28. *Ibid.*, I, 3, p. 384, lines 11–13 and al-Sabzawārī's note on the same page; *Shawāhid,* p. 348, line 15–p. 349, line 4; see also Section B of Chapter III of Part II.

29. *Ibid.*, I, 3, p. 407, line 3–p. 417, end.

CHAPTER V

ESCHATOLOGY

A. *Impossibility of Transmigration*

With rare exceptions like Quṭb al-Dīn al-Shīrāzī, Muslim philosophers have discredited the doctrine of metempsychosis or transmigration of souls. Ṣadrā describes and supports the general anti-transmigrationist arguments of Peripetatics like Ibn Sīnā. According to these general considerations, the relationship of the soul with the body is an intimate relationship like the relationship of form and matter. In a form-matter complex, if the form or the matter is removed, its complement (matter or form) also goes out of existence, and it is absurd to say that either the form has transmigrated into another matter or a matter has transmigrated to another form: the whole disappears and, in its place, an entirely new whole is formed. In cases—such as the human soul—where the soul is an indestructable substance and, in particular, in the case of the actualized and developed human souls—which have become pure intellects—it would be still more absurd to talk of metempsychosis since such souls are no longer in need of a body at all.[1]

But, in addition, Ṣadrā gives his own "special" argument, based upon his conception of "substantive movement" to disprove metempsychosis. According to this doctrine, soul and body are both potential to start with. When these potentialities are gradually realized, both soul and body—as a complex whole—move upward by an evolutionary process: it is not the case that the soul alone moves while the body remains static or vice versa, but the whole moves through a gradual perfection to the new status of existence. When the embryo becomes a foetus, not only does life come into existence but there is a physical change as well, and this double-sided development continues through life. Since this movement of being is irreversible, it is absurd to suppose that a developed soul, after leaving its own body, can enter into a new undeveloped body and then start developing once again from scratch. In other words, devolution, which belief in transmigration assumes, is impossible.[2]

Denial of transmigration, however, entails certain serious problems, some of which arise from religious texts and others from certain philosophic views concerning the destiny of undeveloped humans, views held also by Ṣadrā. Among the religious difficulties are statements in the Qur'ān that a group of human beings, because of their evil deeds, were changed into monkeys and pigs by God.[3] There are similar statements in the Ḥadīth as well. And, on the whole, the popular doctrines of physical resurrection appear to imply transmigration insofar as they assume the reuniting of souls with bodies anew. So far as philosophic views of the hereafter are concerned, these posit that undeveloped souls, since they cannot be free from body and since the earthly body does not survive, have to be united with some other kind of body. Now transmigration just means this uniting of a soul with another body. Ṣadrā says that it is because of these difficulties that it has been said that all doctrines (about a physical afterlife) are ineradicably based on transmigration.[4]

Ṣadrā replies to all these difficulties on the basis of his doctrines of "substantive movement" and the World of Images (*'Ālam al-Mithāl*). All undeveloped souls or souls which have done evil deeds in this life, since they cannot be free from the body and since this material body cannot be resurrected once destroyed, will create a body of their own by exteriorizing their inner psychic habits and states—acquired in this life—in the form of a body in the World of Images, where all psychic states and dispositions are transformed into concrete images, as we shall learn in greater detail when we discuss the question of resurrection below. Thus, a soul which has been guilty of excessive greed will see itself as a real pig, for example, while an unduly stubborn soul will become an ass—i.e., by projecting its disposition outward as a veritable body. When the Qur'ān says that some people were turned into monkeys, it is not talking of an event that took place in this world but in the Realm of Images, where all the events of physical resurrection take place. In his work *al-Shawāhid al-Rubūbiya* Ṣadrā suggests that such people, even in this life, can come to resemble, in their appearance, such animals to which their inner characters have affinity (p. 233, line 9 ff).

This doctrine, according to Ṣadrā, differs from transmigration in two important ways which set the two clearly apart. First, the transmigrationist is not talking about an afterlife, i.e., in another world, but here, i.e., in this world. But life in this world, according to Ṣadrā, is lived only once and cannot be repeated. This is because the opportunity for work and attainment is the essence of this life and this is given only once. Although change and evolution may and do occur in the next life, this is not on the basis of realization of potentialities, works and attainment but through other causes.

Working and earning of good and evil is characteristic only of this life.[5] Secondly, the transmigrationist talks of change *in locus and person,* whereas our doctrine calls for evolutionary change or change in the status of being only while the person remains the same. Thus, whereas according to us, it is the same person who grows from an embryo into a man and then keeps his identity after death, according to the transmigrationists, at death the soul wanders into another body somewhere else and hence loses its identity.[6]

If the movement is evolutionary and is characterized by continuity, without ruptures—so that every single being keeps its identity and, further, if this process is unidirectional and irreversible—then all souls in the hereafter must be happy, by definition, as it were, and one should not speak of the unhappiness and torture of some souls. To this difficulty, Ṣadrā replies that the unhappiness of the evil and imperfect souls is itself due to their evolution. For such souls, while they do not feel pain in this life by doing evil, they will feel pain after death, which constitutes a step forward. Since the evil-doing souls come to have in themselves settled habits of carnal pleasure and since the material body will have been removed with death, these souls will have been deprived of the only source of pleasure they have known, viz., the body.[7]

Another difficulty is that all men are members of the same species and as such partake of the same essence; but in the afterlife they will come to possess essential differences insofar as some will be incorporeal intellects while others will have some kind of body and will be in the World of Images and not in the Realm of Pure Intellect. This is a contradiction. Ṣadrā once again meets this objection on the basis of his doctrine of the evolution of existence. All evolution of existence is characterized by moving from the less differentiated to the more differentiated—from the general and pure potentiality of the Prime Matter, through an ascending order of genuses, differentiae and species—until it reaches man. The species man, in turn, will, in the afterlife, behave as a genus which will become further differentiated in the measure of the acquisition of intellective forms.[8] At the end, we should reach a point where every human being will become a species in himself, like the transcendental intellects, each of which constitutes a species by itself.

Finally, the transmigrationist argues on the basis of the religious belief in the union of the soul with the body in the hereafter and asks whether this does not imply some kind of transmigration since, by the philosopher's own admission, it will not be the same body to which the soul was related in its earthly existence. Ṣadrā replies that that body, being a symbolic expression of the soul's inner states, has no potentialities like the earthly body and possesses no existence of its own. It is a mere symbol of the soul and is related to the soul as a reflection or a shadow is related to that of which it is a reflection or a shadow, or as a mere consequent is related to an antecedent; it has no independent status or nature of its own. The opponent then says that the statements of the Qur'ān apparently say that the body in the hereafter will be the same earthly body and not a merely symbolic one. Ṣadrā admits that this is so but adds that that body will have the same *form* as this earthly body and not *the matter of* the earthly body. Even in this earthly body, its identity is preserved by its form not by its matter, which is continuously changing. The body of a human at any given moment in this life is really its identical form plus an indeterminate (*mubham*) matter. In the hereafter, this body will be pure physical form without matter—but that physical form will preserve the identity of this body.[9]

Those philosophers like Ibn Sīnā, who believe that undeveloped and evil souls require a body after death—since according to them all human souls, including undeveloped ones, survive because they are indestructable—but who at the same time do not believe in transmigration, nor accept an intermediate World of Images (or Symbols), face grave difficulties. Ibn Sīnā attributed to "some scholars" (i.e., al-Fārābī) the view, apparently without committing himself to it, that such undeveloped or evil souls will, after death, attach themselves to some astral body. Ibn Sīnā himself seems to have believed that such souls will survive, along with their imaginative power which, after death, will take the place of sense-perception and these souls will, therefore, experience a kind of physical pleasure and pain.[10] It is clear that this kind of doctrine lent itself subsequently to being interpreted and elaborated into a doctrine of a full-fledged World of Images which, after al-Ghazālī's nebulous remarks, al-Suhrawardī was the first philosopher to affirm explicitly.[11] Yet al-Suhrawardī subscribed to the doctrine of the attachment of these souls to an astral body or heavenly sphere. As has been pointed out before in our treatment of the soul-body relationship, Ṣadrā strongly criticizes this view on the ground that it ignores the fact that between a soul and its body there exists a unique and intimate relationship which cannot obtain between a departed soul and an astral body. In any case, a heavenly body has its own proper soul and when other departed human souls get attached to it, this would involve several souls being in one body—an accusation laid by the philosophers at the door of the transmigrationists! [12] As has been hinted above and as shall be detailed in Section C of the present chapter, physical pains and pleasures will occur to the soul, by the soul's being attached to an image-body, not in this world, but in the Realm of Images or Symbols.

B. *Proofs of an Afterlife*

Before establishing an afterlife both for the soul and the body, it is necessary to give Ṣadrā's account of the various objections raised against an afterlife and of the views that have been held on this important matter. Some naturalists and medical men have denied the possibility of an afterlife by denying the existence of the soul as separate from matter, and then asserting that the body, once dissolved, cannot be recreated. It is reported about Galen that he hesitated about the afterlife of the soul because he was unsure of its separate existence. Our arguments so far, however, have clearly established that the human soul, while starting its career as a bodily form, can progress to a point of intellectual development where it is united with the Active Intelligence. This Active Intelligence exists, not by God's giving it existence but by God's own existence and hence is, in a definite sense, a part of God.[13]

Some philosophers like Alexander of Aphrodisias have held the view, shared by Ibn Sīnā in some of his smaller works like *al-Majālis al-Sab'a,* that whereas souls which have developed to the point of an acquired intellect survive without the body, non-developed souls perish with physical death and hence have no afterlife.[14] A refutation of this view will follow presently in this section. Again, some philosophers, among them Ibn Sīnā in most of his works, grant individual survival to all human souls since they regard every individual human soul as an indestructible substance, although they reject any afterlife for bodies on the principle that something that has been destroyed cannot recur in its identity.[15] This latter category of philosophers, in order to insure the survival of undeveloped souls, have, as indicated before, posited these departed souls' attachment to some astral or non-astral body above the earth. These views we have refuted before.[16]

The Ash'arites, who are materialists and deny the spiritual character of the soul, and other scholastic theologians of Islam, believe in a physical afterlife. In order to defend this belief, they sometimes resort to the proof that the recurrence of the destroyed body is not impossible and sometimes say that not the *whole* of the body is destroyed after death but certain "essential" parts of it survive. Those theologians who are atomists like the Ash'arites hold that a body has no other form except continuity and that this form survives even when the body has fallen apart into atoms so that God can again bring together those atoms and reconstitute the body. Other theologians say that even if the body has a form of its own, when God once again brings together its parts, a form *similar to* the original one may emerge even if not identically the original one. These theories are liable to several objections. First, they imply that life is not something substantive but something relational, and consist merely in relationships of bodily parts. Secondly, if those disintegrated bodily parts still retain the capacity to become that body once again and should come together once again by chance, the dead person would become alive while he is still dead! Thirdly, this doctrine leads to the acceptance of transmigration in essence. For if the capacity of the bodily parts to become that original body once again remains unabated, the dead person would become alive while he is dead, as we have just said. But if these bodily parts have lost that capacity which comes back through a new factor, then this new factor would call for a new soul and if we suppose that the old soul has also returned to it, then there will be simultaneously two souls in one body.[17] Fourthly, since even the memory will have perished, according to them, with the destruction of the body, how will the soul recognize its body? And even when we suppose that memory comes back, the existence of mere memory is not a sure criterion of actual identity, (just as loss of memory does not necessarily mean that actual identity has been lost). This is because for identity, the one to one relationship must exist not only from the side of the soul to *this body,* but also from the side of this body to *this soul.*[18]

Finally and most basically, the theologians are searching in the hereafter for an elemental carnal body, a body with potentialities to be perfected and hence subject to growth. But as we have said before and shall show again, this is not the case with the body of the hereafter since it is created instantaneously by the soul or by God through the soul, and it is not subject to change and growth. It is more like the body of the world taken as a whole.[19] Among the theologians, Fakhr al-Dīn al-Rāzī went to the greatest lengths to show that the body will be regathered from these elemental parts and he thought that this was required by the teaching of the Qur'ān. Nothing is further from the truth than this claim, for the Qur'ān repeatedly tells us that the afterlife is a "new creation, new level of existence (*khalq jadīd; nash'a jadīda*)." This clearly means that we cannot look for a reappearance of earthly elemental bodies there.[20]

Indeed, the banality of the theologians is that they try to locate afterlife at *a point of time and at a point of place,* whereas the Qur'ān, with its doctrine of a "new form of existence," is very clear that it is another kind of existence, radically different from the earthly existence; it is the "inwardness (*bāṭin*)" of this external existence and is beyond space and time. Rather than concoct these silly theories, it would be better for the theologians simply to accept belief in afterlife on authority, like old women! [21] As for the Qur'ān, it uses two types of argument to establish afterlife, both for the soul and the body, and these proofs possess complete demonstrative force in this field (as do mathematical proofs in their own),[22] but these proofs have not the slightest tendency toward a resurrection of the body in its elemental, earthly form. One of these two types of proof concentrates on the developmental and purposive side of human existence: it points out how man started as an embryo and then developed into a foetus, then a body, then a youth, and then a mature man. This shows that the Qur'ān wants to tell us that man even in this life passes constantly through new and emergent levels of existence, and that in the hereafter he will have an altogether new mode of life, away from the world of space and time, until finally some men may unite completely with the Active Intelligence or God. In the second line of argument, where the Qur'ān cites the examples of the creation of the heavens and the earth, the foremost idea is that God can create things, not necessarily out of preceding matter and its potentialities, but by a simple act of creation just as the heavens and this world as a whole have been created, not out of a pre-existing matter but all at once. So does the soul create its images, not out of a matter but by a simple act of creation, because the soul belongs to the Divine Realm in its substance. That is why the Qur'ān speaks of the creation of the other world all at once "like the twinkling of an eye." [23]

The theologians' conception of a physical afterlife is, in fact, the same as the popular conception according to which the events and experiences of afterlife are physical in terms of the material body. More refined than this is the conception of afterlife constructed on the model of a dream. Just as in dreams we experience things and even intense pleasure and pain—we see ourselves, e.g., burning in fire or enjoying pleasurable things—without there being any counterparts to our dream objects in the outside world, so is the case with afterlife. Indeed, in the afterlife such experiences will be much more intense, as they will be enduring. This is because, compared to the afterlife, this present life will appear as a dream, as a tradition from the Prophet has it. Another fundamental difference is that whereas dreams in this life are beyond our control, experiences in the next life will be consciously controlled by the agent. This view of afterlife was quoted by Ibn Sīnā (with possible tacit approval) from al-Fārābī, according to al-Ṭūsī, and was adopted by al-Ghazālī.

The third conception of afterlife is the philosophic one. According to this view, also described by al-Ghazālī, the subject will see either real intelligible forms—which are universal ideas—or he will experience psychic states *as though* he is perceiving real universals. This view is applicable to such souls as have attained full philosophic development and have reached the order of Intelligences. After narrating all these views, al-Ghazālī says: "Since all these views are possible, credence can be given to all of them (as a hierarchy). Thus each type of person will receive his share of the afterlife for which he is fit. Thus a person wedded to external form (will enjoy that form best), will be barred from perceiving true universal natures (of things)

. . . because the definition of Paradise is that it will yield to every person what he wants." [24]

Having described this three-graded view of the afterlife Ṣadrā now states his own. This is that all the forms which will be experienced by humans in the afterlife will be existential realities, although they will not be material. The mistake of the theologians who represent the popular view is that they posit *material* objects in the afterlife. The error of dreamists is that they fill the afterlife with images, not concrete realities; even the illuminationists like al-Suhrawardī believe in "suspended" images and symbols and not in actual existents. The World of Images and its contents are *real;* there will be a real body, a real paradise with its contents, a real hell with its fire, but none of these will be material. The intellectualist doctrine of the philosophers is also untrue. The intellectual paradise cannot be peopled with mere universals; its contents must be real existents. This last is a net result of Ṣadrā's doctrine that knowledge is a process of becoming or existence and that man, when he reaches the highest stage of pure intelligence, acquires a new, intelligible status of existence and *becomes* Intelligence or, in a sense, God. Knowledge, without transformation in existential terms, is unthinkable in Ṣadrā's teaching.[25]

Ṣadrā, then, erects his proof of afterlife basically on the principle of knowledge and its equation with being, particularly applied to rational or rather supra-rational knowledge, but he cites eleven other principles which he applies in particular to physical survival in the *'Ālam al-Mithāl,* the Realm of Images. The knowledge principle states in substance that real pleasure essentially belongs to knowledge. In this life we get real pleasure from sensation and pleasurables are equated by us with sensibles. The reason is that our intellectual and rational knowledge in this life is only indirectly related to real existence and is primarily concerned with essences which are, indeed, not real existents. When, through a continuous intellectual development in this life and particularly after death—when our contact with the material body and through it with the material world is ended—we perceive pure existence directly, i.e., become identical with it, we reach the apogee of pleasure. But it is false to think that the object of knowledge at that stage will be any general intellectual ideas. Rather, these ideas will be identical with actual existence and will, therefore, be concrete realities. It is in this life that we know that real existence through general ideas (i.e., "essences"), that is to say, indirectly and in a mediated manner. This is the reason why in this life even though we come to possess some sort of knowledge of the Rational Realm, we do not feel that pleasure which we feel through direct sensual experience and are consequently insufficiently motivated toward the Rational Realm, except in rare cases. In the afterlife, however, that Rational Realm will be converted into an object of living experience—ideas will become real existences—for the pure philosopher.[26] According to Ṣadrā, following neo-Platonism (i.e., *Theologia Aristotelis*), the body will also be there in the Rational Realm and it will accompany the Rational Soul; nevertheless it will be completely "interiorized" and consumed by the soul just as in this life the soul is, in a sense, "interiorized" and consumed by the body. This doctrine is Ṣadrā's compromise between the doctrines of Aristotle as interpreted by Alexander and Ibn Sīnā concerning the survival of the Intellect, on the one hand, and the clear injunctions of the Sharī'a concerning physical survival, on the other.[27] For Ṣadrā it is a necessary consequence of the principle that higher forms of existence do not exclude and negate but include and incorporate the lower forms; this is why he rejects the cognitive doctrine of abstraction, as we have seen in his theory of knowledge.

As for the ten points which constitute Ṣadrā's proof particularly for physical afterlife, these are essentially a recapitulation of the main principles of his philosophy and their consequences. Ṣadrā states them as follows:

1. The basic factor in reality is existence and not essence or abstract ideas.

2. The distinction of every thing from others, as an individual entity, is through its existence which constitutes its very being; as for what are called "individuating qualities and accidents," these are mere "signs" of particular existence and are subject to displacement (while the individual entity endures and develops).

3. Existence, which constitutes the simple substance of a thing, changes and develops by itself and this change is from the less intense to more intense, i.e., existence is "more or less" of existence. During this change and movement, the parts of the movement—its moments or "periods"—have no real but only potential existence (i.e., as mere essences, their existence is only in the mind). The movement *as a whole* has existence and this existence is the existence of the whole which constitutes the unitary "entity" of the thing.

4. and 5. Since what constitutes the entity of a thing is the totality of the movement and since the movement is developmental (i.e., from the less intense to the more intense), it follows that the entity is identical with the final form of a thing as *terminus ad quem,* and the previous terms of the movement, being potentiality and matter, do not constitute its identity. Thus, in those things which are composites of genera and differentiae, it is the final differentia, the concrete form which constitutes its real entity, as we saw in Chapter II of Part I on Essence. With regard to such things, the genera and differentiae will be mentioned when a logical definition is sought for; but from the point of view of the final simple emergent, no such definition can be given, but the thing can only be described by its necessary

attributes and consequences. Simple existents—i.e., transcendental beings—and, indeed, existence itself, have no definition composed of logical parts but can be described only in the second way.

6. The unitary entity of things is not of the same order. As the scale of existence progresses, new possibilities open up. For example, at the material level, parts are mutually exclusive so that, say, black and white cannot come together in a material thing. As existence progresses, its higher forms are increasingly capable of containing contradictions, and synthesizing them in a simple manner, until the human soul at the absolutely intellectual level, *becomes the entire range of reality: "a simple nature is everything."*

7. From the preceding account of the entity-in-movement, it is clear that the identity of the body is due to the soul which is its final form. The body, although in constant movement, nevertheless remains the same body in a sense. Even when the body turns into an image, as in a dream, it remains the same body. So also in the afterlife, the body keeps its identity, even though it has changed fundamentally, as, for example, it is no longer a material body. If the question is asked about A's body whether it is the same in A's youth and old age, then, from the point of view of the body as *matter,* it is obviously not the same, but from the point of view of body *taken as a genus,* it is definitely the same. But when the question is asked about A's *person* whether it is the same in infancy, youth, and old age, the answer is definitely "yes." Thus, the body and the person of A in the afterlife are identically the same as in this life—and throughout this life.

8. 9. and 10. The power of imagination, as has been proved in the theory of knowledge, is not a faculty inhering in any body, e.g., the brain. Indeed, it does not exist, any more than its objects, in this world of space. Therefore, as has been proved before, images—and, indeed, cognitive forms in general—do not inhere in the soul as their recipient; rather, they are creations of the soul. These images are created all at once by the soul, not gradually as in the case of material forms in the physical world. In the afterlife these images will be intense and enduring because the soul will be free from the material body. Hence heaven and hell will be enduring entities.[28]

In conclusion, Ṣadrā states that the body as it will be "resurrected" (i.e., created by the soul) will be identically the same as this body, except that it will not be material. Ṣadrā takes strong issue on this point with al-Ghazālī and denounces his view of the resurrection of the body as a variant of transmigration.[29] This denunciation does not appear to be quite fair and is one of the many examples in Ṣadrā's *Asfār* where he deliberately and with some manipulation carves targets out of his real or imagined opponents. Al-Ghazālī, as Ṣadrā himself quotes him, declares that since there is no constancy in the parts of the physical body in this life, it cannot be required that exactly the same body be resurrected in the afterlife, that this is not transmigration since in transmigration a new *person* is constituted but if someone chooses to call his (al-Ghazālī's) doctrine transmigration, let him do so, since there is no quarrel in mere names. Of course, al-Ghazālī goes on to say that philosophers have rejected the resurrection of the body in the name of avoiding transmigration and he himself proceeds to weaken the main argument against transmigration. Although al-Ghazālī rejects transmigration as false, he considers the rejection of physical resurrection as more false. To us it appears that fundamentally al-Ghazālī and Ṣadrā are very close on the question of a physical afterlife. And, indeed, in his *Shawāhid* (p. 232, line 4 ff.) Ṣadrā himself talks of afterlife as "the transportation (*intiqāl*) of the soul from this body into an eschatological body," just like al-Ghazālī whom he also quotes approvingly in that book (p. 286, line 10 ff.) on the nature of pleasures and pains after death. The only difference is—and it is undoubtedly a big one—that Ṣadrā rests his doctrine on the basis of his principle of substantive movement (*ḥaraka jauharīya*) and his theory of the World of Images. The World of Images, although explicitly a post-Ghazālian development, nevertheless has its roots in both al-Ghazālī and Ibn Sīnā, and Ṣadrā, with all his refinements, is basically indebted to them. The principle of substantive movement is, of course, Ṣadrā's own.

C. *The Nature of Afterlife*

"Afterlife," according to Ṣadrā, is a relative concept.[30] Intellect and soul have a transcendent existence before this world, but they are not human intellect and human soul. When a human soul comes into existence in this world, it is, therefore, genuinely an *originated* thing having its being in its initial career *in matter* and one cannot speak of its pre-existence, for what is pre-existent is not the human soul but the Universal Soul. Therefore, there is no such thing as "individuation" or "differentiation" of the Universal Soul into human individuals, although human souls have, in their origination, a metaphysical relationship to the transcendent principles, for although human souls are initially *in matter,* they are not *of matter,* as elucidated before in our discussion of the nature of the soul (Chapter I of this Part).

Since everything in this world moves and develops, including human souls, the orientation of everything being towards God, "afterlife" is a relative term: plant is the "afterlife" of inorganic matter, animal of plant, and man of animal. But there is a difference between man and lower beings: whereas lower beings, when they develop into higher modes of existence, have to change their species, i.e., individuals in lower species cannot develop into higher species but only the species as a whole can do so (an individual ape, e.g., cannot become man, but ape as species can, *Asfār,* IV, 2, p. 25, lines 1–3), it is man alone who, *in his individual existence,* passes once again (i.e., apart from change in species—from lower species into human) through and experiences all the levels of existence—from an embryo to a mature intellect. Individuals in lower species also move and develop, but each in his own species.[31] This is not quite true since just as man, at the embryonic stage, is like a plant, so must surely be the case with an animal embryo, although, of course, the end of man is to become Intelligence whereas an animal cannot transcend his species *as an individual.*

There is another basic feature characterizing this evolutionary process of life—and afterlife. Whereas in the lower rungs of existence, intra-species differences are not significant—all members of a species are about the same in value—as evolution proceeds upwards, these intra-species differences become greater and greater. This is particularly true with regard to man. The reason is that whereas, at the lower level the gap between potentialities and actualities is very little—at the lowest grades it is nil—this gap increases as we go higher. When we come to the human species, the gap becomes so large that you can literally speak of some men as being little of men and more of animals whereas other men are literally more of men, i.e., those who have actualized their intellects to the full. This view cannot be accused of violating the definition of man as "rational animal" wherein all members equally participate, since the definition refers only to potentialities, not to actualities.[32] At the beginning of a man's career, his soul is "in the body," as it were, but as the soul actualizes itself, the body gradually dwindles until at the purely intellectual level, the body is literally "in the soul."[33] This doctrine may shock a Muslim in view of the egalitarian nature of Islam; however, that egalitarianism does not refer to the inner worth of individuals. And, certainly, the Qur'ān and the Ḥadīth often speak of the infinite grades of inhabitants in Paradise and Hell and Ṣadrā exploits these materials to the full. Indeed, even in this life the Qur'ān speaks of most men who are obdurate to Truth as "animals—nay, worse than animals" (VII, 179). The Scriptures speak, of course, not so much of intellectual worth but moral worth, but for Ṣadrā moral worth and virtue ultimately depend upon intellectual value.[34]

The process of evolution, since it proceeds from the more general to the more concrete, from the more indeterminate and the undifferentiated to the more determinate and more differentiated—from less of existence to pure existence—must end up at a point where every human being—particularly those who have become actual intellects like the transcendental intelligences—will be a species unto himself. Nor does the process of evolution stop after death. For although there is no "becoming" there, no passage from potentialities to actualities (since "potentialities" as we know them here, exist only in matter), nevertheless there occur changes in afterlife (i.e., after bodily death), instantaneous changes. Undeveloped souls can still evolve there, thanks to the torture they will experience in the other world for not having developed here below.

Ṣadrā, therefore, strongly rejects the view according to which there is no individual survival.[35] For him, the differentiating factors are imagination and intellect, the latter even more so than the former. This is in complete contrast to all Greek doctrines—Platonic, Aristotelian, and neo-Platonic—according to which individuation is a function of matter and, with the disappearance of matter, no individuality can survive. For Ṣadrā, on the contrary, individuation is a function of the evolutionary process of existence itself. The highest point of evolution, the possession of pure being, *means* absolute individuality; hence God is the supreme individual.

The first stage after death is that of the "grave" i.e., the stage intermediate between bodily death and "resurrection." For Ṣadrā "grave" means the envelopment of the soul in the physical or rather imaginative faculties, since in the common run of mankind, the intellect is not fully actualized and hence imagination and even certain bodily dispositions will persist, even though the material body is gone. For those who have actualized their intellect, the stage of the "grave" will either be bypassed or will be passed through very quickly. The stage of the "resurrection" means the shedding, on the part of the soul, of all that is physical by way of dispositions or memory.[36]

Ṣadrā narrates various interpretations of a tradition according to which in a human "the root of the tail" (*'ajb al-dhanab*) will survive, from which God will recreate the whole human being. Some philosophers interpreted this expression to mean "soul." The theologians take this to mean the basic atom in the human body, while Ibn 'Arabī says it means the "essence of man." According to Ṣadrā, the expression means the power of imagination, because it is the "root of the tail" connecting man with the world of nature, i.e., matter.[37] It is this imagination which takes the place of matter in the next world. That is why in the afterlife there is no process of becoming or the passage from potentiality to actuality, but an instantaneous creation, since imagination creates its objects all at once.[38]

Those humans who achieve a pure intellectual being in this world—these actualized here but will become pure intellects soon after death, will share are rare beings like the Prophets—or those whose intellects are very nearly in Divine Life as members of absolute being. There will remain no difference between them—although as individuals they will be distinct—except insofar as pure existence is capable of "more or less." That is to say, in the realm of pure existence, the *what* or the quiddity of a thing and the *why* of it, i.e., formal and final causes, coalesce. This progressive hierarchy of pure beings is in itself a unity just as the continuous parts of an extended body form a unity.[39] The goal of this hierarchic progression is the Godhead who is infinite both in duration and intensity and number of actions; the rest will be infinite in duration but not in the intensity of their actions, since they are intermediate between the Necessary Being—God—and the contingent world. It is difficult to see, however, how these pure Intellects who differ, according to Ṣadrā, from God, and also within themselves in terms of "more or less of existence," can at the same time be described as "pure existences and absolute beings (*al-wujūd al-Ṣarf; al-annīya al-maḥḍa*)" —and Ṣadrā, indeed, often describes them as part of God—since it is clear that they must bear within themselves something of the contingent. Their position seems to be the same as that of the Attributes of God who are also said by Ṣadrā to be intermediate between the absolute being of God's Essence and the World of Contingency.[40] Ṣadrā expressly states that the admission of the intellect's continuity with God's being is necessary in order to avoid the acceptance of an infinite "bounded on both sides." That is to say, since any intellective being which is supposed to be next to God can always be supposed to be transcended by a still higher one which will then be next to God—and so on *ad infinitum*—this infinite regression can be cut at the upper end only by the concept of direct continuity. For God, being the top of a continuity, is Himself infinite.[41]

The intellects, being, as we have noted above, of the status of or identical with Divine Attributes, constitute a manifestation (*maẓhar*) of God. The "mirror" in which this manifestation or reflection takes place is no other than the being of God. God, therefore, contemplates Himself through this manifestation. Intellects are, therefore, forms or images of God, from this point of view. This proximity and presence of the intellects to God constitutes their "resurrection" and "afterlife." The same result is reached from the point of view of the theory of knowledge which requires the identity of the intellect and its objects—God in this case being the subject and the intellects the object of intellection. This, despite the principle that nothing higher contemplates the lower, but, then, these Intellects are parts of God Himself (taken as parts they are inferior, taken as being of God they are God Himself).[42] These intellects also contemplate God, but in a deficient manner—through their self-contemplation as effects of God—for otherwise they will have to become absolutely identical with God.[43]

Since Ṣadrā holds that imagination also survives, he believes that all higher animals whose imagination and memory are developed have individual survival. These animals will remain perpetually in the "grave" stage or *'Ālam al-Mithāl* (the Realm of Forms or Images), since they had no intellectual potentialities. As for ordinary humans, and these constitute the bulk of humanity (common folk, women, children, and Ṣadrā repeatedly asserts, people of ordinary professions and crafts, including medical men, and in this connection he lets loose a storm of bitter sarcasm against Ibn Sīnā who, while being [or trying to be?] a philosopher, thought fit to practice medicine!),[44] they will remain in the *'Ālam al-Mithāl* for a long time, depending on the amount of their immersion in the physical dispositions. All such souls will instantaneously create image-bodies, *real* bodies but non-material. These bodies, which will be related to the souls like shadows or reflections, since they are no longer instruments for the souls to perfect themselves with, as were earthly bodies, will mirror the souls' dispositions, whether good or evil, acquired on this earth. Since these bodies do not occupy space, they will no longer hinder each other and an infinity of them can co-exist.[45]

Ṣadrā is not very decisive about the causation of these projections of psychic dispositions into the image-bodies. He sometimes says that they will be caused by the soul thanks to the acquisition, on this earth, of certain dispositions, but sometimes declares that these images—good and bad—exist in the *'Ālam al-Mithāl* as such, will appear in the soul after death, will be reflected or projected by the soul into the body, and then the soul will experience pleasure or pain (as the case may be) "just as physical health and sickness in this world originate from the soul [into the body] and then the soul itself experiences either pleasure or comfort or pain and anguish." [46] The reason for this ambiguity seems to be that Ṣadrā believes in two kinds of *'Ālam al-Mithāl:* an absolute ontological one, independent of the soul, and a restricted one, created by the soul itself; he seems never to have been sure about the relation between the two. That body is itself infused with life and cognitive power, since it is a reflection of the soul, unlike this earthly body which in itself is dead and receives life and cognitive faculties only indirectly.[47]

The good ones among these souls will sooner or later join the intellectual realm, having been chastened by the fire of purgation, if they had had a taste of intellectual life at all in this world. Otherwise, they will simply enjoy the sensual-imaginative pleasures. So for the bad ones: their souls will project awesome and horrendous sensation-images. They will become pigs, tigers, or wolves, etc., according as they were greedy, pugnacious, licentious, etc. This does not mean that they will become real, material animals, since neither reversion nor transmigration is possible. What this means is that since the human species, as has been said before, displays in the range of its intra-specific differences, the whole spectrum of lower forms of existence, its bad specimens will, although they will have human bodies, *see themselves as real animals* of various kinds. These people, after burning a long time in the fire of animality, will generally be delivered, except for the few who were incurably evil. These latter ones may also perchance be transformed or lose the desire for intellection altogether.[48]

Lower animals and natures will also be "resurrected" not as particular or individual existents, but as species. They will be lifted up and will revert to what Plato called the World of Ideas and what the ancient Persian sages called the "Guardians" (or Masters, Lords) of dead images, i.e., material bodies (*arbāb al-aṣnām*).[49]

NOTES

1. *Asfār,* IV, 2, p. 2, line 10–p. 3, line 5; p. 3, line 22–p. 4, line 10.

2. On the irreversibility of the substantive movement, *ibid.,* p. 16, lines 12–23, and as applied particularly to the soul, *ibid.,* p. 21, lines 5–11. For the simultaneous development of soul and body, see the previous reference.

3. Qur'ān V, 60, II, 65; *Asfār,* IV, 2, p. 5, line 4.

4. *Asfār,* IV, 2, p. 6, line 1.

5. *Ibid.,* p. 153, lines 8–9; p. 7, lines 3–19; p. 26, line 12–p. 28, line 2; p. 33, line 8–p. 34, line 8, *et seq.* Ṣadrā's point here is that the earthly body is there to realize the soul's potentialities and its own. When these potentialities have been realized—whether for good or for evil, whether intellective or imaginative—this material body becomes or is replaced by a subtle body which no longer has potentialities to be realized; the soul also has attained its perfections and is no longer in need of movements and works. In this connection, Ṣadrā rejects the doctrine of medical men like Ibn Sīnā but which actually goes back to Aristotle (who said that in old age faculties decline, not of themselves, but because organs through which they work get fatigued and worn out, so that if an old man could obtain a young eye, his eyesight would be like that of a young person) that the separation of the soul from the body comes about because of the decay of the body, not of the soul. Ṣadrā contends that the separation of the soul from the material body comes about because the soul has attained whatever it could attain by way of perfection and does not need this body any longer (*Asfār,* I, 3, p. 50, lines 1 ff.; p. 55, line 19 ff.). According to Ṣadrā, the mind constantly grows *at the expense* of the material body (*ibid.,* p. 52, lines 1 ff.).

6. *Ibid.,* p. 165, lines 14–17; p. 4, lines 13 ff.; p. 11, lines 2 ff.; p. 12, lines 8–15, etc. For Ṣadrā, the most conspicuous example of substantive evolution is represented by the evolution of the human embryo into a mature human and particularly into the Perfect Man (*ibid.,* p. 53, lines 22–23).

7. *Ibid.,* p. 17, lines 14 ff.

8. *Ibid.,* p. 20, lines 16 ff.; p. 225, line 9 ff.; p. 235, lines 14 ff.

9. *Ibid.,* p. 31, lines 12 ff.; p. 43, lines 14 ff.

10. *Ibid.,* p. 150, line 17–p. 151, line 8.

11. See Section B, Chapter IV of this Part above.

12. *Asfār*, IV, 2, p. 40, line 2–p. 43, line 14; p. 180, lines 2–3; p. 148, line 10–p. 150 (in this passage, the attack is on Ibn Sīnā and al-Fārābī, and al-Ghāzālī as well. Ṣadrā also says that this doctrine is actually a case of transmigration, since a departed human soul is supposed to attach itself to a heavenly body, which is defined as an animal. Ṣadrā urges that even if a departed soul attaches itself to such a body, it cannot be *its* body [*ibid.*, p. 42, lines 20 ff.]).

13. *Ibid.*, p. 163, last line–p. 164, line 12; p. 140, line 5–p. 141, line 8.

14. *Ibid.*, p. 147, lines 5 ff.

15. *Ibid.*, p. 115, lines 5 ff.

16. See references in note 12 above.

17. Statement *ibid.*, p. 164, lines 12–16; p. 165, lines 4–6; p. 168, line 2–p. 169, line 2; p. 169, line 3–p. 170, line 18.

18. *Ibid.*, p. 171, lines 4–10.

19. *Ibid.*, p. 203, lines 1 ff.

20. *Ibid.*, p. 153, lines 4–16; p. 153, line 17–p. 163, line 8; p. 180, lines 7 ff.

21. *Ibid.*, p. 180, lines 21 ff.

22. *Ibid.*, p. 159, lines 3–7.

23. *Ibid.*, p. 159, line 1–p. 161, line 17; quotations from the Qur'ān, XVI, 77, LIV, 50.

24. *Ibid.*, p. 171, last line ff.; quotation, *ibid.*, p. 173, lines 5–9.

25. *Ibid.*, p. 174, last line–p. 175, line 19.

26. *Ibid.*, p. 121, line 6–p. 125, line 8, particularly p. 123, line 8–p. 124, line 5; also *ibid.*, p. 244, line 18–p. 247, line 7.

27. *Ibid.*, IV, 2, p. 97, line 1–p. 98, line 11; p. 99, line 8–p. 100, line 4; p. 197, last line ff.; p. 47, line 9.

28. The eleventh principle is relatively unimportant and states that reality is basically three-tiered—Physical Nature, Imagination, and Intellect. *Ibid.*, p. 185, line 7–p. 197, line 2.

29. *Ibid.*, p. 197, lines 8 ff.; p. 207, lines 4 ff.

30. *Ibid.*, p. 22, lines 1 ff.; p. 162, lines 12 ff.; p. 159, lines 12 ff., and the various quotations from the Qur'ān referred to in the preceding notes about second or new creation (*nash'a thāniya, khalq jadīd, nayh'a jadīda*) as contrasted with *khalq awwal* or first creation, etc.

31. *Ibid.*, p. 24, lines 1 ff.

32. See references above in note 8; also the whole important passage, *ibid.*, p. 19, line 10–p. 20, line 15.

33. See references in note 27 above and in the preceding note.

34. This intellectual perfection is the sole basis of Ṣadrā's—and Ibn Sīnā's—doctrine that in the hereafter, the intellectual elite will have a purely intellective life to which virtuous and pious non-intellectuals cannot

aspire and will have, therefore, to be content with an imaginative paradise.

35. *Asfār,* IV, 2, p. 250, lines 12 ff.

36. *Ibid.,* p. 218, lines 13 ff.; p. 224, lines 13 ff.

37. *Ibid.,* p. 221, lines 3 ff.

38. References in note 9 above.

39. *Asfār,* IV, 2, p. 245, lines 1 ff.; *ibid.,* III, 1, p. 261, lines 11 ff.

40. See Part I, Chapter IV on the multiplicity of God's Attributes and their status as Intelligences; also discussion of God's knowledge in Section B, Chapter II of Part II.

41. *Asfār,* IV, 2, p. 245, lines 6–13.

42. *Ibid.,* p. 245, last line–p. 247, line 7; cf. the First Effulgence of God in Chapter IV of Part I.

43. *Asfār,* IV, 2, p. 245, last line–p. 246, line 1.

44. *Ibid.,* p. 248, lines 11 ff.; however, there is some difference in the hereafter between these developed animals and undeveloped humans—see *ibid.,* p. 249, lines 3 ff.; *ibid.,* p. 181, lines 2-6; on Ibn Sīnā, see *ibid.,* p. 119, lines 1–6.

45. *Ibid.,* p. 200, lines 13–18; cf. references in note 9 above.

46. *Ibid.,* p. 43, line 14–p. 44, line 4; *ibid.,* p. 191, line 13–p. 194, line 11.

47. *Ibid.,* p. 99, lines 2 ff.

48. *Ibid.,* p. 4, line 11–p. 6, line 4; p. 247, line 8–p. 248, line 10.

49. *Ibid.,* p. 248, lines 11 ff.

EPILOGUE

Looking back at this highly complex and original system which is nevertheless characterized by several inconsistencies and some basic contradictions, one may say that the idea of existence is its very foundation. Existence is, indeed, so fundamental that it is the only reality: even essence, in so far as it has any reality at all, is seen to be only existential substance with which it becomes identical, thanks to the differentia. Existence is the unique and irreducible fact which cannot be captured by the logical or conceptual mind; it can only be intuited by higher reason. At the conceptual level, there is, to be sure, a *concept* of existence which, however, does not reveal the unique nature of real existence. But even as a concept, existence is not like other concepts since it implies real existence which is not the case with other concepts.

Beginning with prime matter, existence incessantly evolves through successive stages, thanks to substantive movement wherein the very substance—not just the qualities—of everything evolves and is never the same any two moments. The entire phenomenal world or physical nature (including celestial and human souls which are also part of the phenomenal world since they are, in this life, attached to bodies) is subject to this evolutionary change. At each level of evolution, existence includes and transcends the earlier, lower forms or modes. In the phenomenal world, the movement of "modal" existence reaches its highest stage in man; man, therefore, is the highest mode of existence. But since "modal" existence is not absolute existence, and is, therefore, imperfect, implying some sort of duality between existence and essence, man must strive to attain as absolute and concrete existence as possible where he becomes a member of the Divine Realm, or simply Godhead which, as absolute and most concrete existence, is the final *raison d'être* of all "modal" existence. At this apex of evolution, stands the Perfect Man, the most concrete differentia of all phenomenal existence. Yet, Ṣadrā, inconsistently as we have seen, speaks of God as possessing attributes and he has devoted a very lengthy discussion to prove that God has knowledge, not just as concrete existence but as "substantive forms." This inconsistency is due to Ṣadrā's effort to reconcile various currents of Islamic religio-philosophical thought, particularly the Peripatetic tradition with Ibn 'Arabī.

It would be tempting, on the part of some students of Ṣadrā, to draw parallels between our philosopher's doctrines of existence and its organic evolution and certain modern western philosophical doctrines, for example, existentialism, a Bergsonian type of evolution and certain basic aspects of Hegelianism. That there may be certain similarities between products of human thought, however remote they be in terms of place and time, need not be denied and is, in fact, no matter for surprise since the human mind all over the world has raised similar questions about the nature of reality and the various answers given may also reveal certain thought-affinities. It may also be conceded that such affinities between Ṣadrā's thought and certain modern doctrines sometimes appear peculiarly striking. It would, however, be a grave error to push similarities too far and read into Ṣadrā doctrines of twentieth century western existentialism and Bergsonian evolutionism, etc. Every thought-product has a historical context and is born of a certain "thought-climate"; Ṣadrā's context is given by the religio-philosophical thought-currents of the Islamic tradition, which is obviously very different from the background in which modern existentialism and evolutionism grew (we are not saying that the context *determines* a thought-product but that it *conditions* it).

As for modern existentialism, it differs radically in both its attitude and in its thought content from Ṣadrā's philosophy. Basic to modern western existentialism generally are concepts like "anxiety," "dread," "fateful choice," "leap in the dark" and "choice" or "freedom of will"—all foreign to Ṣadrā's thought. Existentialism is basically concerned with moral phenomena and contrasts an irrational will with intellectual rationality. Ṣadrā, on the other hand, is a rational metaphysician through and through and his morality is just this metaphysical endeavor, provided metaphysical truths are not just intellectually believed but actually experienced. Far from recognizing any unique act called "will," Ṣadrā reduces it—as we have seen in Chapter III, Part II, of this work—to a cognition-conation process and concludes that a voluntary being is "he who *knows* what he is doing and likes it." Modern existentialism, at the hands of its most representative exponents, is a thoroughly pessimistic doctrine, spurning rationality; Ṣadrā, in both his attitude and philosophy, is both optimistic and rational, and even though his rationality is primarily intuitive rather than discursive, he regards discursive thought as extremely valuable, at least as far as communication of intuitive thought is concerned.

Nevertheless, Ṣadrā has one basic tenet in common with existentialism. This is the reality of existence and the unreality of essences or general notions. These general notions cloud reality rather than reveal it, since reality is not something general but something existential, particular, concrete and determinate. Further, for him, will and knowledge are co-terminous with existence and are as specific as existence itself. There is no such thing as will-in-general or knowledge-in-general which are merely general notions abstracted from concrete existence. But here Ṣadrā parts company with modern existentialism. While existentialists technically reserve the term "existence" for human beings only, for Ṣadrā, all actual reality exists. He believes, of course, that a human being has more of existence than an animal—thanks to the systematic ambiguity of existence, nevertheless, all reality does *exist*. Hence, Ṣadrā's believes that even inorganic material objects have knowledge-cum-will *at their own level of existence.*

Similarly, certain striking points of affinity may be pointed out between Ṣadrā's thought and Bergson's conception of evolutionary dynamism: both emphasize intuition over against conceptual thought which falsifies reality through stratified concepts, while the nature of reality is dynamic. But, beyond this, there are fundamental differences between the two as well. For Ṣadrā, God, although all-pervasive, is not immanent but transcendent; indeed, for him, the ubiquity of change in the world is also a sign of its imperfection and this very imperfection implies the transcendent reality of God. Also, while for Bergson, intuition is more of the order of feeling, Ṣadrā's concept of intuition, in line with the mainstream of Greco-Muslim philosophic thought, is that of a higher, creative form of reason itself. A purely vitalistic conception of evolution is foreign to Ṣadrā, for whom, as we have seen, *intellect* is the essence of all being, shared also in some nebulous way by inorganic matter.

Similarly, again, Ṣadrā's thought presents certain interesting features resembling Hegelianism, notably, the explicitly stated idea that contradictions at a lower level are systematically synthesized at a higher level which is, therefore, more concrete and real. This idea patently belongs to all thought-systems that recognize grades of reality *plus* intrinsic movement. In Islamic philosophy, while the idea of grades of reality was explicitly present since al-Subrawardi and Ibn 'Arabī, Ṣadrā contributed the essential element of substantive movement. Indeed, the doctrine of the grades of reality is endemic to neo-Platonism whence it came both to Islamic and modern Western philosophy. In the West, the element of movement was systematically worked out by Hegel. In Ṣadrā, however, while the *existence* of opposites is recognized at all contingent levels, which are synthesized at higher levels (that is why, for Ṣadrā, the law of contradiction is applicable within the perimeters of opposites at a given level only and does not extend beyond that level so far as those opposites are concerned), there is no trace of any explicit formulation of the characteristically Hegelian doctrine of the generation of its opposite or anti-thesis by a thesis.

While, therefore, it is legitimate and even interesting to draw analogies between thinkers belonging to traditions of different intellectual and spiritual provenance, the primary key to a proper understanding of a given thinker is to study him within his own context, which elucidates his thought and renders it meaningful. Analyses of Ṣadrā from this historical point of view are almost non-existent, and, indeed, the study of the development of Islamic philosophical thought in the East after al-Ghazālī still remains almost virgin soil.

SUBJECT INDEX

Philosophy and philosophers, Islamic, and specific theologians
Theosophy, 2, 4-5, 22; see also under Ibn 'Arabī
Timaeus (Plato), 113
Time, theory of, 62, 108-13;
relativity of, 109
Transcendental existence, 53-5, 257;
reality, 49, 54;
unity, 86;
beings, 256; see also Existence
Transmigration of souls, 206, 247-50

Universals, 48-9, 126, 215, 253-4

Voluntary assent (*riḍā*), 76-7

Will, 59-62, 167-71;
God's, 167-79, 180-1;
Mu'tazilite view of God's, 174-5;
man's, 174-9; see also Free will
Uṣūl al-Kāfī, Ṣadrā's commentary on, 16-17
al-Wujūd al-munbasiṭ, see Self-unfolding Being
World, 13, 17; reality of, 49, 77; non-eternity of, 59-60, 65-6, 111-12, 127; relation to God, 82-91; see also Soul, World
World of Images (*'ālam al-mithāl*), 8, 11-12, 107, 184-5, 200-2, 225, 248, 250, 254, 257, 260-1

Yearning (*'ishq*), see Love

INDEX OF PROPER NAMES

37810030R00160

Printed in Great Britain
by Amazon